BEYOND RACIAL DIVIDES

Already published in this series, in association with CEDR
(Series Editor *Robin Lovelock*)

Changing Patterns of Mental Health Care A case study in the development of local services *Jackie Powell and Robin Lovelock*

Partnership in Practice The Children Act 1989 *ed. Ann Buchanan*

Disability: Britain in Europe An evaluation of UK participation in the HELIOS programme (1988-1991) *Robin Lovelock and Jackie Powell*

The Probation Service and Information Technology *David Colombi*

Visual Impairment; Social Support Recent research in context *Robin Lovelock*

Workloads: Measurement and Management *Joan Orme*

Living with Disfigurement Psychosocial implications of being born with a cleft lip and palate *Poppy Nash*

Educating for Social Work: Arguments for Optimism *eds Peter Ford and Patrick Hayes*

Dementia Care: Keeping Intact and in Touch A search for occupational therapy interventions *M. Catherine Conroy*

Suicidal Behaviour in Adolescents and Adults Research, taxonomy and prevention *Christopher Bagley and Richard Ramsay*

Narrative Identity and Dementia A study of autobiographical memories and emotions *Marie A. Mills*

Child Sexual Abuse and Adult Offenders: New Theory and Research *eds Christopher Bagley and Kanka Mallick*

Community Approaches to Child Welfare International perspectives *ed. Lena Dominelli*

Social Work in Higher Education Demise or development? *Karen Lyons*

Valuing the Field Child welfare in an international context *eds Marilyn Callahan and Sven Hessle, with Susan Strega*

Beyond Racial Divides

Ethnicities in social work practice

Edited by

LENA DOMINELLI
University of Southampton and President, IASSW

WALTER LORENZ
University College, Cork

HALUK SOYDAN
The National Board of Health and Welfare, Sweden

ASHGATE

Published by
Ashgate Publishing Limited
Gower House
Croft Road
Aldershot
Hampshire GU11 3HR
England

Ashgate Publishing Company
Suite 420
101 Cherry Street
Burlington, VT 05401-4405
USA

1003020944

Ashgate website: http://www.ashgate.com

British Library Cataloguing in Publication Data
Beyond racial divides : ethnicities in social work practice
    1. Social work with minorities - Congresses 2. Social service
    - Congresses 3. Race discrimination - Prevention -
    Congresses 4. Pluralism (Social sciences) - Congresses
    I. Dominelli, Lena II. Lorenz, Walter, 1947- III. Soydan,
    Haluk, 1946-
    362.8'4

Library of Congress Control Number: 00-109610

ISBN 0 7546 1437 9

Reprinted 2002

Printed in Great Britain by Biddles Limited,
Guildford and King's Lynn.

Contents

List of Contributors   *vii*
Acknowledgements   *xi*
Preface   *xii*

INTRODUCTION   1
Lena Dominelli, Walter Lorenz, Haluk Soydan

**PART I: EXPLORING THEORETICAL FRAMEWORKS
      FOR SOCIAL WORK**

1   Emerging Ethnicities as a Theoretical Framework
    for Social Work   9
    Janis Fook

2   Ethnic Sensitivity: A Theoretical Framework
    for Social Work Practice   23
    Wynetta Devore

3   Multicultural Organizational Development   43
    Lorraine Gutiérrez

4   Inclusive Thinking and Acting   59
    Edwin Hoffman

PART II: COMMUNITY-ORIENTED MODELS OF PRACTICE

5   The Social Pedagogical Model in the Multicultural Society
    of Germany   89
    Franz Hamburger

6   Social Development as a Model of Social Work Practice:
    The Experience of Zimbabwe   105
    Edwin Kaseke

7   Social Work Education with Migrants and Refugees
    in France   117
    Tasse Abye

**PART III: MAINSTREAMING SOCIAL WORK PRACTICE
            WITH DIVERSE CLIENT GROUPS**

8   Linking Our Circles   137
    Richard P. Barth

9   Minority Ethnic Elderly: Ageing with Care   147
    Naina Patel

10 Lost in Public Care: The Ethnic Rights of
    Ethnic Minority Children   171
    Darja Zaviršek

11 Mental Health Services to Ethnic Minorities:
    A Global Perspective   189
    Barbara Solomon

**PART IV: RECLAIMING HERITAGES THROUGH
           SOCIAL WORK PRACTICE**

12 Making Circles: Renewing First Nations Ways of Helping   213
    Gord Bruyere

13 A Maori Social Work Construct   229
    Waereti Tait-Rolleston, Sharon Pehi-Barlow

14 Appropriateness of Social Work Practice
    with Communities of African Origin   257
    Asher John-Baptiste

FINAL OBSERVATIONS   281
Lena Dominelli, Walter Lorenz, Haluk Soydan

Index   291

List of Contributors

EDITORS

Lena Dominelli is Director of the Centre for International Social and Community Development at the University of Southampton, and President of the International Association of Schools of Social Work (IASSW). She is an experienced social work educator and has worked as a practitioner and has done research in social work and related areas. She is also the author of 17 books and numerous other publications.

Walter Lorenz holds a Jean Monet Chair in European Integration Studies at University College, Cork, and is co-editor of the *European Journal of Social Work*. He co-ordinates several European networks concerned with a critical approach to European dimensions in the training of the social professions.

Haluk Soydan is a Research Director at the Centre for Evaluation of Social Services, Swedish National Board of Health and Welfare. He is also a Professor of Social Work and Migration Research at Gothenburg University. He has long experience of teaching and research in social work and is a visiting professor at the Columbia University School of Social Work in New York City.

CONTRIBUTORS

Tasse Abye has been serving as Deputy Director of the Institute for Social Worker's Education of Echirolles, France since 1999. Before that, he was the Director of and a lecturer at the International Institute for Social Development, Rouen, France from 1991 to 1999. His research is concerned with the issues of migration and refugees and their integration. He is currently serving on the board of the International Association of Schools of Social Work.

Richard P. Barth is the Frank A. Daniels Professor of Human Services at the University of North Carolina at Chapel Hill. He was the 1998 recipient of the Presidential Award for Excellence in Research from the National Association of Social Workers. He is currently co-principal investigator of the National Survey of Child and Adolescent Well-Being, a large national study of child welfare services.

Gord Bruyere is an independent First Nations scholar, writer and researcher. Formerly an Assistant Professor at the School of Social Work, University of Victoria, Canada, he has worked in First Nations communities and resource-based towns as a child protection worker, a probation and parole officer and a university counsellor.

Wynetta Devore is Professor Emeritus at Syracuse University School of Social Work, Syracuse, New York. She was the 1998 Social Work Educator of the Year in New York State. One of her main contributions to social work education and practice is a model for ethnic-sensitive practice, which she developed together with Elfriede G. Schlesinger.

Janis Fook is currently Professor of Social Work at Deakin University, Australia, where she is engaged in establishing a new social work course programme. She is probably most well known for her work on critical and reflective practice. She has written a number of books on various aspects of social work theory and practice.

Lorraine Gutiérrez is Associate Professor with a joint appointment at the School of Social Work and the Department of Psychology at the University of Michigan. Her research focuses on multicultural social work practice with large and small systems. She has published on various topics including empowerment, the multicultural community and organisational practice, and women of colour.

Franz Hamburger is Professor of Social Work at the Department of Education at the University of Mainz in Germany. He has research experience in the fields of migration and minorities and has conducted international comparative studies in social work. He is also founder and Director of the ISM, Institute for Social Research, Mainz.

Edwin Hoffman works in the Department of Social Work at the Fontys Hogeschool Sociaal Werk Eindhoven, the Netherlands, as a trainer consultant in Intercultural Communication and Management of Diversity. In addition to his training activities, one of his responsibilities is to work for increased cultural awareness in his department.

Asher John-Baptiste is a practising social worker specialising in community social work. She is currently employed by Bradford Social Services and works with communities of African origin. She is also currently doing research for a Doctorate degree at Southampton University, focusing on the importance of African-centred perspectives in social work.

Edwin Kaseke is the Head of the School of Social Work, University of Zimbabwe. Prior to joining the school of social work, he worked as a social worker in the government, Department of Social Welfare. He was also the Director of Urban Community Development. He has written extensively on social policy issues. He is currently President of the Association of Schools of Social Work for Eastern and Southern Africa, and sits on the board of the International Association of Schools of Social Work.

Naina Patel is the Director and founder of PRIAE, Policy Research Institute on Ageing and Ethnicity, a UK independent charitable organisation. Before PRIAE, she was the Head of the UK 'Race' Programme at CCETSW, Central Council for Education and Training in Social Work. She has developed various 'first-of-its-kind' initiatives and has managed the orchestrated campaign against anti-racist social work (1992–1995).

Sharon Pehi-Barlow is a staff member of the Regional Community Polytechnic Social Work Programme in Whanganui, New Zealand. Her research interest is the collection and documentation of tribal songs, stories and forms of social intervention in connection with tribal groups.

Barbara Solomon has been a faculty member at the University of Southern California since 1966 where she has also served as Vice Provost for Faculty and Minority Affairs. Her teaching and research have focused on social service delivery systems in health and mental health settings as well as empowerment and family preservation in ethnic minority communities. She is currently Stein/Sachs Professor of Mental Health in the School of Social

Work and principal investigator for an outcome study of family preservation programs in Los Angeles County.

Waereti Tait-Rolleston is seconded to Waiariki Polytechnic, Rotoruea, New Zealand to participate in the joint delivery of the Victoria University MA Diploma Social Work programme in the Central North Island. She is also Wahine Maori Lecturer at Central North, Wellington and Top of South Island.

Darja Zaviršek is a lecturer at the School for Social Work at the University of Ljubljana, Slovenia. She is also a visiting professor at the M.A studies at the Central European University, Budapest. She is a Director of the Open Society Institute project, 'Re-calling Experiences and Visions of Disability in Slovenia', and is a member of various women's organisations. She also serves on the executive committee of the European Association of Schools of Social Work (EASSW).

Acknowledgements

The editors would like to express their gratitude and thanks to all who have contributed to the advancement of the text during the conference 'Beyond Ethnic Divides: Ethnicities in Social Work Practice'. The conference was organised by the Center for Evaluation of Social Services, Stockholm, and supported by the Swedish Council on Social Research and the Swedish Association for Social Work Research. Special thanks go to Mari Forslund for co-ordinating the editorial work, to Noella Bickham for preparing the camera-ready-copy and to Eva Franzén for her work as conference secretary.

Lena Dominelli   Walter Lorenz   Haluk Soydan
Southampton   Cork   Stockholm

Preface

'Race', racism and anti-racism feature prominently in discourses aimed at challenging the myriad forms of racial oppression that exist across the globe. However, the attempt to talk 'across racial divides' has proved extremely difficult, for even definitions of the terms shift and move, depending on who has been involved in the discussions. Moreover, many of these definitions have proved to be controversial and exclusionary, for they have reproduced in their substance the very oppressive relations that were set for eradication.

The complexity of the issues prompted the three of us to look for ways of going 'beyond racial divides', to try and carve out a space in which peoples of different 'races', ethnicities, and nationalities could come together to talk to each other about their different starting points for action aimed at eliminating racism and discrimination, the particularities of their models for action and analyses, and the commonalities that might link different struggles together. This objective prompted us to set up a conference, hosted by the Centre for Evaluation of Social Services, Stockholm, the Swedish Council for Social Research, and the Swedish Association for Social Work Research, entitled *Beyond Racial Divides: Ethnicities in Social Work Practice*.

Here, we brought together academics, practitioners and activists who have a wealth of experience of working in this area and knowledge from which to contribute to the discussions. In setting up the conference, we aspired to create an environment where peoples of diverse origins could share with each other their experiences without getting into competitive relationships aimed at proving the superiority of one position or model over another. This was to allow dialogue and exchanges to occur within, between and across the 'differences' articulated in the different models so as to strengthen evaluation research and practice in social work to the benefit of clients and practitioners.

The products of these discussions form the basis of this book that shares its name. In it, we have tried to maintain the integrity of each chapter by allowing each author to speak for himself or herself. Thus, the words in each one reflect the views of the author(s) and not necessarily those of either the editors or the publishers. We hope that you will read these words and engage with them with an open mind to allow plenty of scope for them to inform your understandings of the issues that are presented for your consideration and to ultimately enable you to intervene more effectively in your own struggles for establishing a world free from racial oppression.

Lena Dominelli, Walter Lorenz, Haluk Soydan
November, 2000

Introduction

LENA DOMINELLI, WALTER LORENZ, HALUK SOYDAN

Ethnicity and 'race' are contested and troubling categories because they have become sites in which and through which relations of oppression are constituted. Of course, ethnicity and 'race' form only one of the dimensions of identity which can become the basis for oppression. There are others – gender, class, age, disability and sexual orientation amongst them. However, in this book, we will focus primarily on 'race' and ethnicity, although we acknowledge that these interact and intersect with the other bases of oppression. Ideally, all forms of oppression would have to be understood within their complex totality as they occur within any social work intervention (Dominelli, forthcoming).

However, we would argue that there is merit in placing each of these aspects under separate scrutiny to examine the specificities that operate in each of them. Thus, our prime focus here is on 'race' and ethnicity in relation to social work theories and practice. Whilst the two words are often taken together, and sometimes used interchangeably, we would want to caution against their being elided into one category. They are interdependent, yet distinct (Ratcliffe, 1996). The interrelatedness between them will become evident in the handling of these terms at both the theoretical and practice levels within the different chapters of this book.

We have conceptualised the book as a way of providing readers with the opportunity to explore the need for social work academics and practitioners to respond to 'race' and ethnicity in dynamic terms. We acknowledge the ability of people to exercise agency in the formation of racialised categories and ethnicity as a constantly changing and interactive aspect of their social and cultural identity. We propose that the notion of agency with regard to identity is a characteristic that needs to be taken on board as a central feature of any social work intervention. For us, the phrase 'going beyond racial divides' encapsulates this aim. It challenges practitioners and academics to develop forms of theory and practice that begin with the idea that ethnicity is a construct that remains firmly embedded yet largely unacknowledged within their theoretical frameworks and working practices and move on to consider its ramifications as an integral part of their work.

We have chosen a method of analysis that examines each model considered within the pages of this book in terms of three interactive elements:

- a theoretical framework;
- the embeddedness of that theoretical framework within mainstream practice; and
- the articulation of different approaches within specific examples of practice that stand as models that have worked within a particular socio-economic, political and historical context.

We distinguish between a theoretical framework and a model of practice on the following basis. A model of practice is a description of the analysis, processes and methods within a particular perspective on how social work intervention is carried out. A theoretical framework, on the other hand, is based on the conceptual understandings that go into the creation of a model of practice. Our overall aim for the book is not one of providing one prescriptive model that holds good for all circumstances, all places and all time. Instead, we want to encourage the creation of context-specific approaches that reflect and respond to particular sets of social and historical conditions.

Grounding theoretical and practice developments in this manner should facilitate comparative analyses of the different solutions that different ethnic groups have developed to engage with the complexities of their own situations. Furthermore, it should enable us to examine whether there are more universal principles of theory formation that can be pulled out to inform us in working together across racial divides.

We take the view that the issue of ethnicity in social work has been poorly articulated to this point. Many of the debates in anti-racist social work consider ethnicity in simplistic dichotomous terms that have ignored the complex range of ethnicities and hybridities within them (Modood, Beishon and Virdee, 1994). Consequently, the demand for 'ethnically sensitive' services by people from minority ethnic groups been has met with an uneven and inadequate response at the levels of theory and practice. The complexities of coming to grips with issues around definitions of ethnicities and their relevance for practice are especially evident in two of the chapters: one is by Janis Fook, who considers the issue of hybridity in an Australian context; and the other is by Wynetta Devore, who examines the relevance of the concept ethnically sensitive social work for practice in the United States. Both authors demonstrate that there are no easily formulated, neutral concepts that can be drawn upon to facilitate discourses in the realities of experience, whether at the level of personal feelings (Fook) or in multi-cultural practice (Devore).

The failure of social work to engage with issues of diversity in an appropriate manner has been a common theme throughout the history of social work and can be linked closely to the profession's location within the nation-state (Lorenz, 1994), a point also made in the chapter by Barbara Solomon. On a broader level, the initial professional and academic response to this weakness was to recognise that there was an issue, but to address it in ways that polarised the ensuing discourses. Of particular relevance here were discourses that universalised the issues and those that essentialised them. These debates do not provide fixed points of reference for they have changed over time in response to critiques lodged against them and to their demonstrated failure to achieve their purpose of eliminating racism.

Those rooted in universalism ignore the ethnicised and racialised nature of social relations and the importance of diversity amongst the clients they work with, and between the practitioner and the client. This came to be called the colour-blind approach (Dominelli, 1988; Williams, Soydan and Johnson, 1998). Social work's position within state structures has given it the mandate of treating 'clients' as a homogeneous category in which the very existence of difference has been implicitly denied as part of a uni-versalistic discourse that treats everyone as equal (see Dominelli, 1988). Those subscribing to a universalistic approach have refused to acknowledge the importance of racial and ethnic identities in social work by 'treating people as people', that is, as part of a homogeneous (national) whole. Tasse Abye's chapter demonstrates how this problem has been expressed and addressed within the French context.

By contrast, there is an essentialising discourse, represented by some multicultural and anti-racist approaches, in which ethnicity has been treated as fixed and determined for any particular group. These approaches have become rooted in static positions that have ossified culture and failed to consider the fluid and changing nature of identity as cultures and peoples interact with one another. The chapters by Gord Bruyere, Sharon Pehi-Barlow and Waereti Tait-Rolleston, and Asher John-Baptiste indicate the importance of seeing ethnicity and culture in their specific contexts, but also as entities that peoples construct in ways that ensure their continuity over time and space in the face of extreme racialised oppression. In reclaiming their heritages, these authors demonstrate that social work has been deeply implicated in denying their well-being in ethnically and racially appropriate terms in the countries that they cover – New Zealand/Aotearoa (Pehi-Barlow and Tait-Rolleston), Canada (Bruyere) and Britain (John-Baptiste). Moreover, these authors highlight the resilience of their own indigenous cultures as they interact with others to create social work responses that meet their needs.

Drawing boundaries that constitute 'communities' and the people they include or exclude has been an integral part of the modernist project advanced by nation-states. The construction of communities as artifacts within which particular actions are allowed or disallowed has been part of the social work repertoire. Although these boundaries are usually contested and created through particular types of interactions between people, communities can form locations in which and through which people seek to establish their claims to egalitarian racial relations. Though based on the experiences of different ethnic groups in Holland, Edwin Hoffman's chapter shows how language establishes linguistic communities and terms that can either enhance or limit diversity. Edwin Kaseke's work demonstrates how action at the level of community can be used to facilitate social development that both challenges hegemonic social relations whereby African people in Zimbabwe are reduced to living in conditions of poverty and aspires to create the conditions under which people can lead more fulfilling lives. Hamburger's contribution reveals how cultural encounters in Germany can be facilitated in more progressive directions if they are locality-based and rooted in community-based interventions that address people's consciousness of their particular situation. Gutiérrez's writings reveal the importance of working on organisational issues and seeing these as sites for change when working in multicultural communities in the United States.

Some of the authors seek to demonstrate the importance of working with and across 'racialised ethnicities' in relation to specific client groups. Naina Patel's chapter focuses on anti-ageist approaches to work with ethnic elders in Britain; Darja Zaviršek considers how children's rights can be advanced through ethnically sensitive social work despite ethnic tensions in the former Yugoslavia; Richard P. Barth does likewise for American children; and Barbara Solomon highlights the importance of issues of 'race' and ethnicity with regard to people who experience mental ill health in the United States.

All in all, the contributions to this book provide considerable expertise, which has been harnessed to the task of allowing us to explore the relevance of racialised ethnicities in each person's life, thereby helping us proceed on the personal journey to growth in this area that each person has to make. On another level, their concepts and understandings are also there for each social work scholar and practitioner to begin to develop more appropriate responses in an area that has been fraught with ambiguity, denial and resistance on the part of those who have been in a privileged position vis-a-vis their power to impose their particular views of ethnic and racial superiority on peoples from cultures and ethnicities other than their own. We hope that readers will engage with the insights that each chapter contributes to the complex project of creating new and egalitarian forms of social work theory and practice in which each of us may find our own ethnicity and culture validated as we engage in validating and celebrating those that are different.

References

Dominelli, L. (1988), *Anti-Racist Social Work*. London, Macmillan. Second edition published in 1997.

Dominelli, L. (forthcoming), *Anti-Oppressive Practice*. London, Macmillan.

Lorenz, W (1994), *Social Work in a Changing Europe*. New York, Routledge.

Modood, T., Beishon S. and Virdee, S. (1994), *Changing Ethnic Identities*. London, Policy Studies Institute.

Ratcliffe, P. (ed.) (1996), *'Race', Ethnicity and Nation: International Perspectives on Social Work*. London, UCL Press.

Williams, C, Soydan, H. and Johnson, M. (1998), *Social Work with Ethnic Minorities*. London, Routledge.

PART I:

EXPLORING THEORETICAL FRAMEWORKS FOR SOCIAL WORK

1 Emerging Ethnicities as a Theoretical Framework for Social Work

JANIS FOOK

Introduction

The concept of ethnicity is highly controversial in both popular and academic circles, yet is relatively underdeveloped in academic literature. This is unfortunate in a time when increased mobility and globalisation are forcing questions of ethnic identity into international and community arenas. In the last century, wars of global scale and national disputes that have attracted international involvement have resulted in mass migrations and re-workings of national and cultural boundaries. In this context, traditional ways of viewing ethnicity are either troublesome or inadequate. What are new ways of conceptualising ethnicity that are relevant to our practice, in the context of the international changes we witness daily? Because I examine vexed questions, and because I am trying to chart new ways of understanding, I have chosen to take a non-traditional path in discussing the idea of ethnicity. I have developed this chapter on reflective lines. The reflective approach is particularly useful in making connections between personal lives and structural conditions, between concrete experience and more generalised theorising. It is beneficial because it deliberately eschews traditional academic splits between the individual person and social structure, between practice and theory, and allows a more holistic appreciation of situations. In this way a reflective approach provides a way of understanding and developing practice that is more contextually relevant (Fook, 1996, 1999).

Ethnic identities and the idea of ethnicity are highly uncertain in the current context of global changes. The reflective approach may prove effective in trying to connect our more abstract time-honoured explanations with everyday changing experiences. I have therefore chosen to illustrate concepts of ethnicity with reference to my own personal experience as someone with a mixed and uncertain ethnic identity. For me, many of the

9

current complexities about ethnicity are mirrored in the microcosm of my own life. By drawing out the broader questions from my personal experience, I hope to illustrate, and argue effectively for, more complex and dynamic notions of ethnicity.

*   *   *

Who am I? In answer to this question, I have been called a 'banana'. (I do not expect you to understand this term unless you are one, too.) This term has a special significance for Australian-born Chinese, or perhaps American-born Chinese. It means I am yellow on the outside but white on the inside. I look Chinese, but have been raised as a white Australian. One of my first memories of my awareness of this occurred when I was in my early teens. I was window-shopping one day and was shocked to see a Chinese-looking person reflected in the glass. It took me a few seconds to realise it was me.

I had not really thought of myself as Chinese until this time. Obviously I had looked in the mirror before – I can only think I must have seen a fair-haired fair-skinned person. It was only when I saw myself, in a public place, in an objectified way, as I imagined that other people who saw me anonymously and disconnected from my personal identity might see me, that I realised I was not a white Australian.

Unless you think I am particularly unaware, or strangely at pains to deny my Chinese heritage, let me explain the context and circumstances of my growing up. I was raised in the 1950s in rural Australia, when it was a time of unquestioned assimilation. I was born into the third generation of my family to be born in Australia. My family, of Cantonese origin from near Shanghai, had migrated to Australia late in the last century. I was raised to think of myself as Australian. We wanted to fit in. We did not want to cause trouble. My parents understood some Cantonese, but spoke only English, so consequently they could teach me only English, which is the only language I can speak. All my friends were White Australians, and all the people we mixed with on a daily basis were White Australians, except for the so-called 'New Australians', our term for post-World War II European migrants. It was a time when there were no allowable uncertainties about ethnicity. You either fit in, or you did not. In Australia of the 1950s, one simply did not recognise a Chinese ethnicity.

For me, the idea of 'bananahood' encapsulates many of the driving questions about the way we understand ethnicity in the contemporary world. It bespeaks the possibilities of ethnic identification and acculturation which are not automatically tied with racial appearance. It bespeaks an allowance for a much wider range of differences. It potentially questions the idea of fixed ethnicities based on static categories of race, religion, language, lineage, shared histories and customs.

My quest for my own ethnic identity has thus become one of conceptualising ethnicity in a way that incorporates the changing complexities of a world in which short- and long-term migration, global residence and affiliations, mixed lineage and political competition shape the way we are seen and present ourselves.

In pursuing this quest, let me return briefly to the concept of 'bananahood'. When I first heard the term, it held a certain appeal for me. It did recognise my sort of 'white' self-image, at the same time not denying my physical appearance. It did seem to label my ethnic identity quite well. It did not force me into oppositional thinking (Sands and Nuccio, 1992: 492), to choose between either a Chinese or a white Australian identity. However, on reflection, I also noted the context in which I acquired the identity of 'banana'. I was called this by a relatively recently migrated Chinese psychiatrist, a member of an Asian research group I had joined. He had called me this good-naturedly, but his label clearly served to 'other' and distance me from those of his kind. He was saying that *he* was *really* Chinese. *I* was *not*. I felt a bit of a fraud, as if I had somehow been caught out at claiming to be Chinese, but was really Australian. The contextual meaning of the use of the 'banana' categorisation cast me into more uncertainty about my ethnic identity.

I felt that although raised to see myself as no different from Anglo-Australians, I knew I could never be the same as them, partly because of my physical appearance. I recognised, in a matter of fact way, that socially I would always be seen and related to as 'non-Anglo'. Not that this bothered me, but I wondered whether the difference *was* only skin deep. Perhaps it was not enough to see myself as a 'banana'. I felt that there must be some vestige of Chinese heritage, some quaint customs or family values that were Chinese, even if not named as such. I became keen to identify these, hoping I could put a more definite label on myself, and answer the question 'who are you?' in a more personally, socially and intellectually credible way.

This tension between personally perceived identity and social ascription became the basis of my earliest attempts to understand the complex nature of ethnicity from an academic standpoint. To what extent is ethnicity determined by inherited features, and to what extent is it constructed through social definition and conditions?

Bentley (1987) argues that these questions began to be debated in the 1950s and 1960s by anthropologists such as Leach (1954) and Barth (1969). The ascendant position became that of a recognition of the importance of subjective processes – which do not necessarily bear a relationship to the observations of observers – in the identification of ethnicity (Bentley, 1987: 25–26). Ethnicity, then, in this view, is a product of self *and* other definition, but it is necessary to focus primarily on how ethnic group identities are formed, and how people use these identities (Marger and Obermiller, 1983: 230) in gaining a full understanding of ethnicity.

How then, was my own ethnic identity formed? I began a type of professional search for the ethnic group to which I belonged. I spent time attending various groups with whom I thought I might share a common heritage or experiences. They were all groups formed to lobby, profile or gain support for some aspect of Asian life in Australia. I took up with a group of Asian social science academics for a short time. I enjoyed their company, but this was the group that quickly picked me as a 'banana'. Whilst I felt accepted, I did not feel fully at home. I attended a couple of functions of the Chinese Association in my local state, only to find that they were much too politically right-wing for me, and that my politics was more important to me than I had thought. I became a member of a management committee of a Chinese community welfare group, only to find that it felt like much of the group's purpose was to bolster the ego and community standing of the male businessman-president. I supported a group of Asian social workers for a good while, but was unsettled by the fact that it seemed culturally inappropriate to talk about, or be angry about, the racism we had experienced in professional circles. Maybe I was just simply realising that my ethnic identity could not be 'found' in groups whose identity was particularly Chinese. I learnt, however, that whilst I desired to find a group who shared, as closely as possible, my history and social characteristics, there were also groups who for their own reason wished to claim me, whether or not I shared their objective cultural characteristics or experience.

In a sense this realisation is mirrored in the debate between primordial and instrumentalist views of ethnicity. More recent theorising around ethnicity now recognises that dominant, primordial conceptions of ethnicity, defined by static and essentialist features of race, culture, language and history are now becoming outdated (Bentley, 1987; McCoy, 1992; Gross, 1996). Alternatively, an instrumentalist view characterises ethnic groups as interest groups, occurring because of the need to pursue collective advantage (Bentley, 1987: 25). Ethnicity in this sense is functional, and ethnic groups can be seen as voluntary organisations (Gross, 1996) formed to allow the group to better press its claims in a competitive political environment.

In my own case, I found that although I did not feel enough shared identity with the groups I had associated with, we all gained some form of enrichment from our mutual association. They could claim the prestige of my membership, and I could claim the privilege of difference, or marginal status. There is certainly an instrumental aspect to my ethnicity, as used by me and perceived by others. I am often the only person (in a roomful of white Australians) who can acknowledge, and critically examine, the issue of racism within non-white communities towards white Australians. I recall vividly, when discussing racism in a postgraduate class, how I introduced some 'insider' knowledge about Chinese stereotypes of white Australians as 'lazy' and 'rude', only to be met with silence and dismay. It is politically acceptable for me to tackle the hard, difficult and complex issues, because I am not seen as coming from a mainstream privileged position. From the perspective of mainstream Anglo-Australians, I, apparently, cannot racially discriminate, since I come from a group that normally has it done to them! Because I come from a marginal group, I can be 'othered' but cannot 'other'.

My own difference also gives me a privileged voice to speak up for other marginal people, and often other marginal people derive comfort from my presence. Italian-Australian clients love me as a social worker. Other Asian-Australians are happy to be in the room with me. They believe that if this is a situation in which I am accepted, they will be too. They do not expect me to discriminate against them, and I am privileged by their trust. We do not even need to speak about our 'Asian-ness' – our racial appearance gives us a common bond.

Yet whilst I enjoy the privilege, this is not enough to give me an ethnic identity. The instrumental view of ethnicity might in part explain the formation of ethnic groups and some aspects of ethnic identification, but still does not plumb, for me, other complexities about my own ethnicity that I experience. For instance, I am engaged in an ongoing process of discovering and constructing my ethnic affiliations. Recently, I watched a TV documentary made by a third generation Australian-born Chinese woman, exactly my own age. Despite our class differences (her father was a wealthy businessman and prominent member of the Melbourne community, whereas my parents were struggling small business owners), we shared much in common, even down to our mothers having the same kind of Australian-born Chinese English-speaking accent. Yet there were lots of differences, too. She had returned to China, married her first husband from there and learnt Mandarin. I have only ever made cursory efforts to learn Cantonese (because I am not really committed), have never been to China and am not rushing to go (I am a self-confessed Anglophile and love travelling to Europe too much), and my partner is an Irish-Australian-Japanese person. Whilst I recognise that ethnicity is not defined by these objective characteristics, my own need for ethnic identification is thwarted because of such differences. I clearly do not feel about my 'Chinese-ness' the way she does, even though, ostensibly, we share about as common an ethnic heritage as it is possible to find.

What this highlights for me is the way ethnic groupings can accommodate differences and many different constructions, and the ways in which ethnicity might be constructed differently, in different circumstances and situations. She had returned to China and learnt Mandarin as part of an economic imperative, to participate more effectively in her father's importing business. In my case, it was important that I 'pass' as English-speaking and as white Australian as much as possible if I was to succeed in professional middle class circles. The instrumental imperatives are different, and so is the self-definition of ethnicity.

Obviously, ethnicity does not define me nor, I imagine, many other persons' total identity, and that to cast me primarily, or even initially, in 'ethnic difference' terms I find dismissive and patronising. For instance, I find that the gender dimensions of interactions with Chinese professionals often frustrate me, as it is often men who run the show (regardless of qualifications) and expect women to take subordinate positions.

Also, I well remember my frustration and annoyance when attending a workshop on cross-cultural counselling run by a prominent white North American trainer. He began the training by informing us that many people in traditional cultures have particular meanings attached to their names, so it is a good idea to begin an interview by asking the meaning of a person's name. We then conducted role-played interviews, starting with this question. I remember thinking I didn't have a clue what my name, 'Janis', meant (unless my parents had deliberately named me after Janis Joplin the rock singer, whose first name is spelt the same as mine), and what's more, I couldn't care less. Not that I thought I was typical of the different cultural groups with whom practising professionals interact, but I was pretty sure I wasn't *atypical* either. In fact, nearly 20% of the Australian population are second or third generation migrants (Jayasuriya, 1997: 11). What offended me about the example of asking the meaning of a name was its almost innocent assumption of difference, a clear route to 'othering' and distancing a person. I felt I had somehow been assigned an inferior status, constructed as different to, and perhaps patronised by, my interviewer. Without waiting to find out who I was, in my own terms, the interviewer had assumed my difference and related to me in those terms. He was not concerned about finding out *who I thought I was*, only initially relating in terms of *what he thought he saw*.

Critics of the primordial view of ethnicity argue that such a view can perpetuate uncritically elitist assumptions about cultural differences, in that ethnicity is assumed to be characterised by observable characteristics that are defined by the very nature of their difference from the 'mainstream'. For instance, Gelfand and Fandetti (1986: 542–543) in particular make the pertinent point that much of the social work literature on ethnicity assumes a traditional view of culture, one that has been brought to a new country. This can lead to reductionism and unwanted generalisations about other cultures. It can also lead to the unexamined assumption that the process of migration will either ultimately end in assimilation, or a culturally pluralist position, that emphasises the importance of cultural persistence (Yancey, Ericksen, and Juliani, 1976: 391). Neither view may necessarily indicate relevant directions in the current cultural global mix.

It is argued by a number of theorists that more dynamic notions of ethnicity are appropriate (Staiano, 1980), particularly in understanding the ethnicity of migrants. The ethnicity of migrant groups, particularly that of later generation migrants has been termed 'emergent' (Yancey, et al., 1976; Gelfand and Fandetti, 1986; McCoy, 1992), denoting a process whereby ethnicity and ethnic identity are undergoing construction through a dynamic interaction with structural and cultural conditions (Yancey et al., 1976: 392; McCoy, 1992: 249). For instance, it can be argued that certain ethnic groups, particularly long-term and later-generation migrants, develop a new culture from that of the original migrating generation, partly through the influence of intermarriage and economic mobility (Jayasuriya, 1997: 11). It may be a culture that can become quite disparate with that of the homeland. As the culture of their homeland changes, as it must, long-term migrants tend to preserve an outdated version of it, and are often shocked to discover changes when they revisit their original countries after long periods of absence. On the other hand, the culture that they have supposedly preserved from the old country in the new country has itself undergone modifications, due to conditions in the new country. As Gelfand and Fandetti observe (1986: 543), it is erroneous to assume that the present culture of immigrant groups is the same as that which was brought by migrating generations a century earlier.

The idea of emergent ethnicity became attractive to me because it recognised that one's ethnic identity did not have to fit into preconceived classifications, defined through centuries of history and shared nationhood. Rather, ethnicity is constantly changing and developing as it takes account of new conditions. It also provides a label for my own ethnicity, one that is not fully conceived, but is in a process of construction as I discover, discount and reconceptualise new and old experiences. It is acceptable for me to be uncertain about my ethnic identity, to not have to claim that I am either Chinese, or Australian, or even Chinese-Australian. Sometimes I may be all, or any one of them, or none, depending on the context and situation of the time. It almost sounds like common sense to acknowledge that identities are numerous and defined by context, yet it is this view of ethnicity that is only recently developing. Furthermore, it is this view of ethnicity that I would argue is more relevant to understanding the many types of recent and long-term migrants, the people of mixed heritage and birth, of multiple ethnic identifications, and of numerous other cultural identities related to class, gender, religion and age: people whom any social worker encounters in the course of a normal day's activity.

Gross (1996) makes a series of sophisticated points in building up a concept similar to that of emergent ethnicity, which he terms a critical paradigm. He bases his argument on a critique of both primordial (or organic) and instrumental (or organisational) paradigms of ethnicity. Primordial paradigms are outdated in their inability to recognise the transitory, changing and often functional nature of ethnicity, and therefore are an erroneous base on which to build notions of health and subsequent policy. Organisational paradigms are much more robust in the contemporary context, providing a framework for understanding how and why different ethnic groups rise and fall, relative to their political success (p. 53). However, they run the risk of enhancing individualism, as I indeed found through some of my own experiences, and therefore alienating their constituencies.

Alternatively, Gross posits the idea that in a postmodern world, ethnic groups need to 'recreate an ethnic identity without resorting to essential models of group affiliation' (1996: 53). The critical paradigm, as he terms it, is a transformative paradigm, one that emphasises 'the makeshift nature of contemporary ethnicity' (p. 54). Gross describes the critical paradigm as endorsing the view that 'popular identities, whether racial or non-racial, are constructed as people define their social and political objectives' (p. 54).

The critical paradigm argues that ethnicity is invented to maintain meaning-ful goals, not solely because they are based on 'natural', real or eternal units, and that ethnic groups can be reconstituted, if political or social conditions change.

This emergent view of ethnicity, this critical paradigm, is more flexible than either purely primordial or instrumental views as it allows a reflexive element. Ethnic identity is made by an interaction between personal and social elements. It is dynamic in that it is constantly remade according to changing conditions or personal perspectives. Gross argues that the critical paradigm is more inclusive because it takes into account the possibility of differing perspectives from those of the same cultural groupings, potentially disaffiliated members such as ethnically-mixed families, alternative house-hold groups, converts to new religious affiliations. In recognising these non-traditional ethnic differences, however, comes the recognition that ethnic communities are fragmented, but that differences must be recognised if the affiliation of non-traditional sub-groups is to be fostered. In this broad sense, then, a critical view of ethnicity is transformative – ethnicity evolves and develops to take account of the social, demographic and economic context.

*   *   *

What are the implications of this type of understanding of ethnicity as a theoretical framework for social work? The critical paradigm potentially provides a quite different way of understanding issues of multiculturalism, the situation of indigenous peoples, community health and welfare policies, approaches to research (Gross, 1996), education and training in social work (Jayasuriya, 1997) and cross cultural practice. Whilst I do not have the space to fill out the details of all these here, I will attempt to draw out some more general principles from the foregoing discussion and apply to them to a selection of these examples.

With regard to the situation of indigenous peoples in Australia, for instance, there is a substantial literature criticising the essentialist view of Aboriginal culture (Lewin, 1991; Patton, 1995), particularly as one con-structed by anthropologists (Finlayson and Anderson, 1996). It is possible to view the history of aboriginal ethnicity as constructed through harsh state policies of segregation and assimilation in which Aborigines were institu-tionalised (put on missions or reserves), their children removed and their rights to marriage and movement curtailed. While not to deny the injustice of such practices, there is also, however, an argument that none of these policies could be all-pervasive in the construction of Aboriginal identity –

many Aboriginals learned to both accommodate and contravene these practices (Finlayson and Anderson, 1996: 53–54).

In discussing the political dimensions of a dynamic view of ethnicity in relation to Aboriginality, Lewin (1991) notes that Aborigines are increasingly taking responsibility for defining Aboriginality, which is not a homogeneous category. Not recognising this has political consequences, in that

> ... ideological commitment to the existence of a homogenous culture and its independence from social context prevents recognition of key structural factors, such as Aborigines' and migrants' recognition of their disadvantaged position and their use of those perceptions to mobilise to help redress that disadvantage (Lewin, 1991: 175).

In other words, an essentialist view of Aboriginality can easily function as a victim-blaming political stance in which a homogenous and fixed Aboriginal culture is seen as the cause of the structural disadvantage of Aboriginal peoples. Lewin finishes by arguing that universalist and essentialist ideas of Aboriginality also function to legitimate governmental control over the definition and solution of problems in the Aboriginal community.

The key point for us as social workers and policy makers from this type of analysis is that the politics of ethnic identity construction become integral in resisting and challenging domination. Identity construction plays an important role in the empowerment of disadvantaged groups. For example, Karen Crinall (1999) points out that, although feminist analysis is perceived at one level to be helpful to young homeless women, at another level it is disempowering because it is based on the necessary assumption that young homeless women are powerless victims. And with Aboriginal peoples, as argued above, it is the control over the construction of Aboriginality that is also important. There are therefore two key issues that have a direct bearing on social work practice in relation to identity politics: the elements of the ethnic identity and the control over its construction are vital in ensuring a critical social work practice with multiple differing ethnic groups. Young (1990) notes the politicising effects of a process of control in the construction of identity:

> Assumptions of the universality of the perspective and experience of the privileged are dislodged when the oppressed themselves expose those assumptions by expressing positive images of their experience. By creating

their own cultural images they shake up received stereotypes about them (Young, 1990: 155).

Another important policy direction pinpointed by the more dynamic conception of ethnicity is the notion of community and of ethnic group 'health'. For instance, rather than fostering or pursuing assimilationist or pluralistic notions of a healthy community, perhaps communities need to aspire to notions of group living that focus on accepting differences within shared broad parameters. Healthy ethnic communities may best be conceptualised as those that provide meaning and security of self-definition, but not at the expense of recognising important and emerging differences, and not at the expense of participating effectively and interacting co-operatively within a broader social structure. Strong ethnic communities may in fact be those whose boundaries are open, who can tolerate fluctuating and changing membership. This strength may only be able to be developed in conjunction with the recognition being two-way, when the broader community also recognises, accepts and celebrates differences. As Young (1990) says when speaking about the problem of oppressed groups defining themselves in terms of the culturally dominant groups, a solution may be to encourage all members to see themselves as 'plural, shifting and heterogeneous' (p. 148).

This issue of how to recognise and celebrate differences and at the same time create structures and processes that are inclusive is a question that lies at the heart of these more dynamic conceptions of ethnicity. In part, I believe an answer lies in the reflexive nature of these notions of ethnicity. If we recognise that ethnicity is an identity that is reflexively created through an interaction between personal and environmental factors, then this gives us some indication of the kinds of processes we might need to engage in to create ethnic identities that are both personally meaningful and socially responsive. Identities are created through a process of self-definition and perception, often in response to social ascription and changing social conditions.

Let me illustrate this by referring back to my own story. I am in the process of creating my own ethnic identity through reflecting on my own experience in interaction with other people, groups, changing reactions and perceptions of me, as well as changing social attitudes towards me and people of similar ethnic heritage. I interact within changing contexts, and in reflecting on these interactions I construct an identity which I choose to present to my social world, and which I think fits and benefits me in some way. I recognise that this identity might change (I might choose to change it, or other people with whom I am interacting might not share my perceptions of my own identity) in different contexts and times. This does not mean that I do not necessarily have an ongoing and continuous notion of who I am. What is continuous for me is that I am in control of defining myself and that I can recognise, and not feel compelled to take on board, other peoples' perceptions of me when they are different from mine. This view of ethnicity locates the site of ethnic identity-making squarely in the interactive (and changeable) realm. No one perspective is therefore necessarily dominant at any point in time – the identity is recreated in each particular context.

What therefore becomes important with this reflexive notion of ethnicity is the process of dialogue and negotiation about who controls the identity construction, the elements of the identity that are involved and how this view of identity functions to challenge domination. The process of communication is therefore vital with a reflexive view of ethnicity. This is a key point in that it indicates that the dual concerns to celebrate difference and at the same time be inclusive may in fact not be mutually exclusive endeavours. It may be that the mutual process of open and non-privileged dialogue is the necessary ingredient in both recognising difference and discovering commonality. The process of celebrating commonality cannot be begun unless it includes the mutual celebration of difference.

There is another dimension of this reflexivity that is also important. This is the willingness and ability to reflect upon and recognise elements of prejudicial thinking and acting which may (often unconsciously) construct ethnic identities in ways that serve to distance and 'other' different ethnic groups. Earlier in this chapter I referred to the example of how I felt the North American cross-cultural trainer had distanced and patronised me by assuming that my name had a special meaning. He was assuming that all cultural groups with which professional social workers would practice were somehow 'traditional' cultures in which first names had a special meaning, and that this was, therefore, a good general starting point for cross-cultural interviews.

While it is easy for me to point the finger at him as a white North American male, an unaware member of a mainstream and culturally imperialist group, a preparedness for reflexivity also shows me how to point the finger inwards. As a member of a white Australian society, albeit a yellow-coloured member, I am not somehow miraculously free from prejudice or unexamined thinking. I take on received assumptions all the time, and I am also responsible for creating my own wisdoms which serve to distance other groups in ways that serve my own interests. For example, I have been quite successful in years subsequent to my encounter with this man to construct his approach as completely oppositional to mine, in ways that may have glossed over some of the important complexities involved. I have taken a certain delight in creating my view of cross-cultural practice as one developed by an 'outsider', a member of a marginal cultural group, with the implication being that my perspective is superior. On reflection now, I am sure it is not quite so simple as this. My own knowledge and identity creation is not somehow 'innocent' of the structural, cultural and personal conditions in which it exists. The best I can hope to do, as a participating citizen and as a responsible social worker, is to be prepared to examine my own assumptions so that I am as open as possible to negotiated dialogue with others, whether they appear different from me or not.

It is this reflective disposition that forms an integral part of any negotiative process for change, whether it be at an interpersonal, group, community or structural level. In terms of cross-cultural practice that is non-discriminating, I now recognise that a reflexive understanding of the way identities, all identities, are made in relation to political, social and structural conditions should reduce our capacity to 'other' and distance those whom we might perceive as 'objectively' different. This understanding lies in our realisation that first and foremost the ascription of difference lies in all our assumptions and prejudgements about it. We all participate in helping to construct our own and other people's ethnic identities. Difference is relational and contextual. We are all different, or all the same, depending on with whom or what we compare ourselves. Only a mutual acceptance of difference or commonality, arrived at through dialogue, will ensure some justice and relevance in developing new ways of acting. I now try to be aware and critical of my own assumptions, preferring instead to explore differences or commonalities through a joint process with whatever groups or individuals I am interacting.

The challenge facing social workers in a changing global context is to develop the ability to interact effectively in the particular context at hand. This does not involve trying to gain a notion of which features of a culture differentiate it from others and from the mainstream; rather it involves a notion of ethnicity that is inclusive, reflexive and reflective – that allows the worker to locate herself or himself within an interactive context of multiple levels. The structural and the personal meet at the site at which ethnic identity is created. We need to be able to be at that site, to participate in that process, if we are to be able to engage effectively with all types of people who may be different from, or the same as, ourselves.

Acknowledgements

My thanks to Christine Morley for assistance in the preparation of this chapter.

References

Barth, F. (1969), *Ethnic Groups and Boundaries*. Boston, Little Brown.

Bentley, G.C. (1987), 'Ethnicity and Practice', *Society for the Comparative Study of Society and History*, pp. 24–55.

Crinall, K. (1999), 'Challenging Victimisation in Practice with Young Women', in B. Pease and J. Fook (eds.), *Transforming Social Work Practice: Postmodern Critical Perspectives*. London, Routledge and Sydney, Allen and Unwin, pp. 70–83.

Finlayson, J. and Anderson, I. (1996), 'The Aboriginal Self', in A. Kellehear (ed.), *Social Self, Global Culture*. Melbourne, Oxford University Press, pp. 45–56.

Fook, J. (ed.) (1996), *The Reflective Researcher: Social Workers' Theories of Practice Research*. Sydney, Allen and Unwin.

Fook, J. (1999), 'Critical Reflectivity in Education and Practice', in B. Pease and J. Fook, (eds.), *Transforming Social Work Practice: Postmodern Critical Perspectives*. London, Routledge, and Sydney, Allen and Unwin, pp. 195–208.

Gelfand, D.E. and Fandetti, D.V. (1986), 'The Emergent Nature of Ethnicity: Dilemmas of Assessment', *Social Casework*, vol. 67 (9), pp. 542– 550.

Gross, M.L. (1996), 'Restructuring Ethnic Paradigms: from Premodern to Postmodern Perspectives', *Canadian Review of Studies in Nationalism*, vol. XXIII (1/2), pp. 51–65.

Jayasuriya, L. (1997), 'Understanding Diversity and Pluralism for Education and Training', in L. Jayasuriya, *Immigration and Multiculturalism in Australia*. Perth, School of Social Work and Social Administration, University of Western Australia, pp. 1–19.

Leach, E. (1954), *Political Systems of Highland Burma*. London, G. Bell and Sons.

Lewin, F. (1991), 'Theoretical and Political Implications of the Dynamic Approach to Aboriginality', *The Australian Journal of Anthropology*, vol. 2 (2), pp. 171–178.

McCoy, D. (1992), The Influence of Structural Factors on the Emergent Ethnicity of Immigrant Groups', *Ethnic Groups*, vol. 9, pp. 247–265.

Marger, M. and Obermiller, P. (1983), 'Urban Appalachians and Canadian Maritime Migrants: A Comparative Study of Emergent Ethnicity', *International Journal of Comparative Sociology*, vol. XXIV (3/4), pp. 229–243.

Patton, P. (1995), 'Mabo and Australian Society: Towards a Postmodern Republic', *The Australian Journal of Anthropology*, vol. 6 (1/2), pp. 83–94.

Sands, R.G. and Nuccio, K. (1992), 'Postmodern Feminist Theory and Social Work', *Social Work*, vol. 37 (6), pp. 489–94.

Staiano, K.V. (1980), Ethnicity As Process: The Creation of an Afro-American Identity, *Ethnicity*, vol. 7, pp. 27–33.

Yancey, W.L., Ericksen, E.P. and Juliani, R.N. (1976), 'Emergent Ethnicity: A Review and Reformulation', *American Sociological Review*, June, pp. 391–403.

Young, I.M. (1990), *Justice and the Politics of Difference*. Princeton, Princeton University Press.

2 Ethnic Sensitivity: A Theoretical Framework for Social Work Practice

WYNETTA DEVORE

Introduction

This chapter begins with a discussion of the persistence of ethnicity with reference to the work of Milton Gordon (1964). His concept of ethclass is the sociological foundation for ethnic-sensitive practice which calls attention to the activity that occurs at the meeting of social class and ethnic group membership. The influence of ethnicity in the United States and Europe will be examined. In the United Sates, Census 2000 reconsiders ethnic group membership of mixed race parentage. Ethnic wars continue in Europe and the media provides a continuing narrative of destruction. Even though we have considerable knowledge about ethnicity, there is a paucity in the social work literature addressing this essential human characteristic. This omission has led many to examine the power ethnicity has on the lives of developing persons. This environment provides the impetus for the development of ethnic-sensitive social work practice. The primary components of ethnic-sensitive social work practice, the ethnic reality, and the layers of under-standing are introduced and related to practice in the United States. It is to be understood that this model for practice is not to be limited to the United States.

The strains related to membership in certain ethnic groups continue to be current news items. The media relays pictures and sounds of ethnic violence related to racial discrimination, physical attacks on individuals, long held animosity for another ethnic group. Television provides moving pictures of the violence; newspapers print similar images, but these are still pictures and may remain with us longer. The radio in news broadcasts provides the sound of conflict. These are not the limits of ethnic group membership. Rituals and traditions of a group carry with them a sense of joy that flows from the sense of belonging. Celebrations at marriage, birth, first communion, particular Holy Days, call for families to come together to be reminded of the comforts that may be found in the sense of peoplehood. It is incumbent upon social work educators and practitioners to understand that ethnicity has the ability to provide comfort as well as stress (Devore and Schlesinger, 1999). The model for ethnic-sensitive social work practice transcends practice in the United States. Social Workers in the United Kingdom and South Africa particularly, have found the model useful.

This chapter begins with the general theme of ethnic-sensitive practice that responds to the persistence of ethnicity. The United States Census 2000 incorporates queries related to ethnicity that are much more detailed than in the past. This action calls for social workers to pay attention to changing demographics in their immediate environment and in the larger society as well.

A review of social work literature in the United States from 1900 to 1948 will provide a history of the social work response to ethnicity in that era. It was more inclusive then than we are in the present. Perhaps the waves of immigrants from many European countries demanded this response, but services to Negroes were documented as well. Reviews of more current literature indicate that little attention has been paid to white ethnic groups whereas considerable attention is paid to oppressed ethnic groups.

As this chapter ends there will be guidelines for ethnic-sensitive practice and an assessment of practice needs for the future as demographics change and the number of interethnic, or inter-religious, marriages increase.

The Persistence of Ethnicity

In 1964 the American sociologist Milton Gordon presented his thesis on ethnicity and its realities:

> ... the sense of ethnicity has proved to be hardy. As though with a wily cunning of it's own, as though there were some essential element in man's nature that demanded it – something has compelled him to merge his lonely individual identity in some ancestral group of fellows smaller by far than the whole human race, smaller often than the nation – the sense of ethnicity has survived (p. 24–25).

This thesis became the foundation for how we (Devore and Schlesinger) have since worked to develop ethnic-sensitive practice. Our life experiences have been in two distinct ethnic groups: African-American (Devore) and Jewish (Schlesinger). We understood oppression through personal experience of racism and anti-Semitism. Despite our experiences during childhood and as adults, we expect that our ethnic heritage will attempt to survive. Younger members of our families, as well as the families of our friends and colleagues, have experiences that provide very clear evidence that they will extend the ethnic experiences of our families. We look forward to what our families may become, yet we will retain pride in our own ethnic experiences.

Richard Alba (1985) posits that European Americans are at the twilight of ethnicity as the young enter into alliances unheard of or unacceptable in the past. As American ethnic groups join together, frequently honored rituals and traditions will be revisited and revised to accommodate new configurations. No matter what the combinations may be, ethnicity will remain an essential part of an individual's development. The joining together of several ethnic groups may serve us well as families are offered opportunities for enriched ethnic experiences.

Demographic predictions in the United States suggest that mixed marriages will continue to occur. Presently there are 1.3 million married couples in the United States in which the race/ethnicity of the husband is different from that of the wife. As Census 2000 approaches, these parents have pressed for a reconsideration of categories for the collection of racial and ethnic data. Their school-age children have not been permitted to claim more than one group as they identified themselves. Parents believe that these limitations may be harmful to their children's sense of shared ethnic group membership (O'Hare, 1998).

The United Sates Office of Management and Budget, which establishes census policy, has determined that establishing new categories will generate more details about who we are in relation to race and ethnicity (Cloety, 1998). Census 2000 has included a new question that conforms to the revised standards for racial identification. These will offer greater detail and the opportunity for individuals to make choices in relation to race. The instructions say: 'Mark one or more ...' followed by a range of ethnic groups including Black, African-American or Negro, Asian, Indian, Chinese, American Indian or Alaskan Native and other. Parents of mixed-race children will be pleased with the change in policy for Census 2000. However, there are oppressed ethnic groups who will be dissatisfied. Asian-Americans particularly note that the result of this new policy will have a significant impact on the count of Asian-Americans. An undercount would jeopardize the amount of state and federal assistance allocated to minority organizations. There are indications that Asian-Americans are more likely to intermarry than any other group, thus the concern expressed may be well founded.

The Census 2000 'white' category denies choice to this large group of Americans. Many would be able to identify themselves as Irish-Italian, English-Hungarian, or Polish-Irish Americans. An increasing number of families are much more than a generalized 'white,' and so the ethnicity struggle persists in the United States.

Early Social Work Responses to Ethnicity

Social Diagnosis, the premier work of Mary Richmond (1917), was among the earliest social work publications. The foundation for this work was the notes she had taken during her professional career. The wide range of practice concerns that claimed her attention included neglected children, single mothers, persons with disabilities, the homeless, and immigrant families. Immigration was at a peak early in the 20th century; many of these families needed a variety of helping services. Richmond developed social study guides that provided directions for practitioners as they attempted to understand ethnicity as an important variable in the lives of European immigrant families. Richmond's guideline are still relevant, for knowledge about ethnicity is as important now as it was in 1917.

Mary Richmond warned that caseworkers would be liable to surprises if they assumed that each of these unfamiliar ethnic groups were 'members of a colony or of a nationality having such and such fixed characteristics' (Richmond, 1917: 382). If caseworkers were to ignore national and racial characteristics and try to apply to the immigrant the same standards of measure that would apply to colleagues, family, or friends who were American born, additional surprises could be expected. She believed that in time caseworkers would learn that national characteristics could not be ignored. With experience they could learn to be discriminating in ascribing ethnic characteristics (Richmond, 1917: 382).

A well-planned social study developed by Richmond (1917) provided directions for the collection of data related to individuals and families. New inquiries that were suggested related to education, culture, religion, family life, the position of women, community customs, and the history of the immigration experience. A more extensive study required information about family experiences in their country of origin, marriage and family life, employment and social adjustment, needs, and available resources (pp. 387–

394). These well-conceived studies were the forerunner of what we have come to call ethnic-sensitive practice.

There have been recent literature searches of the social work literature in response to concerns about the profession's commitment to inclusiveness in practice (Lum, 1992; Schlesinger and Devore, 1995). A cursory search of social work journals published from 1901 to 1942 uncovered interesting trends.

The 1910 issues of *Charities Review*, a journal of philanthropy, called attention to services and agencies funded by philanthropic groups. Among the recipients were The Cuban Orphan Society that cared for and educated orphan and destitute children of Cuba (February 2, 1901, p.84).

The January 26, 1901 issue reported that the Colored Home and Hospital in New York City 'provides a home for the support and comfort of aged and infirm, and destitute colored persons of both sexes, a home for incurables, a hospital for surgical cases...'. Training for colored nurses had been introduced in 1898 in the belief that colored women were especially suited for the profession (*Charities Review*, 1901: 55). These efforts were not an indication of ethnic-sensitivity, rather we are provided with data about the conditions of two oppressed ethnic groups early in the 20th century. Cuban children, who were orphans received support from the State Board of Charities. Adults in the Colored Home and Hospital were referred by the Superintendent of Outdoor Poverty. These adult men and women were experiencing poverty, poor housing, and poor health, consumption in particular, as consequences of their social class and race.

Charities Review for March 2, 1901 provided an account of the first Jewish Conference of Jewish Charities, which was held in Chicago. The prevalence of consumption among Jewish people in America was of great concern. The disease was widespread, long in duration and accumulated excessive medical costs. At greatest risk were new immigrants who were a large portion of the Jewish poor. These consumptives filled hospitals, their families were added to the pension lists, their children crowded in orphan asylums. The Jewish community had organized to assist needy families and found that Jewish immigrants from other countries were at risk of poverty and poor health.

Richmond (1917) would later alert caseworkers of the need to be aware that ethnic dispositions would vary from group to group. If they responded appropriately they would become more aware and more sensitive to ethnic difference. Colored men, women and children, and Jewish immigrants, two distinctly different ethnic groups, shared poverty and poor health. The reports in *Charities Review* gave no direction for practice, but they did provide insights into the living conditions of poor, oppressed ethnic groups as well as an inadequate social work response with which to begin the 20th century.

Charities Review changed its format in 1910. Longer articles addressed current social issues of concern to social workers. This limited search determined that attention was paid to two ethnic groups, the first being Negroes and the second European immigrants including Poles, Russians, Italians, Finnish, Bohemians and an assortment of other European ethnic groups. Teaching foreigners to read and compelling them to speak English as well as 'Americanizing Eighty Thousand Poles' were goals held by Americans for aliens and the foreign-born (Daniels, 1910; Moore, 1910).

Mary White Ovington (1910) provided a report in *The Survey* from the Second Annual National Negro Congress. Among those in attendance were Ida Wells-Barnett and Mary Church Terrell, who would become noted for their social reform activities. Novelist Charles Chestnutt and Dr. W.B. Dubois, identified as a scholar and prose poet attended as well. The conference identified 'complete disfranchisement of the colored man' as its most pressing issue. Without the vote, Negro power was 'nil,' leaving him without the ability to influence the conduct of the government in any way.

In a racist diatribe, Hoke Smith, the then governor of Georgia, declared 'you must stop Negro education and to do this you must put into the schools Negro teachers who are not able to do the work. Do not offer increments to highly trained teachers' (*The Survey*, May 28, 1910, p. 345). Ovington implied that the readers of *The Survey* would be interested in an educational policy that denied Negro children an education, 'believing as they must that all our children should have the opportunity of training in good public schools.' In this manner, the position of social workers in relation to the distribution of funds for education was challenged. State funds for education were distributed unequally – white children received a larger share than did Black children. Social workers were called to action, but the response was inadequate. In many districts underfunded segregated schools continued to exist well into the 1960s. The profession did not invest any reasonable effort that would call for the desegregation of schools or equal funding for all schools. Clear evidence of racism did not seem to stir the conscience of many social workers. Still, workers in St. Louis, Negroes and whites, joined together for general and inclusive cooperation in dealing with social problems common to both races (*The Survey*, May 28, 1910).

Slowly, an understanding of the power of ethnic group membership developed. An editorial in the May 25, 1910 edition of *The Survey* called for ethnic sensitivity in relationships with children of immigrants who, because they were born in this country, were citizens; but it also called for efforts 'towards encouraging the children of the foreign born to appreciate the culture of their parents' native land' (p. 213). Culture was seen as a possession that would grow if its 'life roots' were passed from one generation to the other. Children cut loose from the past of their parents and starting their lives in 'our country' were thought to be at risk without nourishment from this part of their lives.

The editorial writer presented a rationale for learning English with the claim that without English men were at a disadvantage in the workplace if they could not understand the directions of the American boss. Children who learned English more rapidly than their parents became important family members. It was possible for them to develop a sense of superiority in relationships with their foreign-born parents. This respect for ethnic identity and the understanding of child development moved the profession closer to ethnic sensitivity.

Alexander Whitehead (1918) of The Committee of Foreign Birth and Descent, provides evidence of developing ethnic sensitivity. Part of the work of 'Americanization' of the foreign-born was accomplished through a committee that encouraged the purchase of Liberty Bonds. Members of the committee included Albanian, Czech, Danish, Italian, Jewish, Polish, Russian, and other European ethnic groups. Differences in ethnic traditions caused some conflict, but in the end the campaign was successful.

Whitehead acknowledged that immigrants had not been welcomed and little effort had been expended to help them to understand that they were an important part of life in America. This omission was such that he felt we had missed 'a wonderful chance to weld the twenty-five or thirty races that compose our population into a strong, virile, and intelligent people.' He understood that this welding together could only be done by setting aside racial distinctions and joining together in a common cause for the good of the United States (pp. 311–312).

Readings in Social Case Work 1920–1938: Selected Reprints for the Case Work Practitioner, edited by Lowry (1939), and the *Social Work Year Book 1949* edited by Hodges, give evidence that there was some movement toward an ethnic-sensitive perspective. Stumbling would be a more concise description. Yet, by 1949 social work publications began to provide some guidelines for a practice that was more sensitive to ethnic group membership as a factor in the planning for intervention. In 'The Case Worker's Need for Orientation to the Culture of the Client', Boie (1937) supports Richmond's (1917) caution about the need for knowledge about the ethnicity of immigrant families. Boie suggested that works of literature and case vignettes in which social class was significant could be useful. The study of various ethnic groups would increase understanding of society at large. Casework relationships could become a greater outlet for expression and a more informed acceptance of feelings related to cultural conflict.

The *Social Work Year Book 1949* as described by the editor M. Hodges is a description of organized activities in social work and related fields. The two anthologies published in 1939 and 1949, respectively, contribute significantly more to the development of ethnic-sensitive practice than publications reviewed earlier. Contributors provided detailed descriptions of work with ethnic groups that included Negroes, Indians, Mexicans and Puerto Ricans, Japanese-Americans, Jews, and the foreign-born.

Current Social Work Responses to Ethnicity

In 1992, Doman Lum published the results of his search of social work texts and journals. Although his interest is limited to oppressed ethnic groups, it is important in this discussion for it provides a perspective on social work's interest in these groups. Twenty-three practice texts published between 1970 and 1990 were reviewed seeking to identify the ethnic minority content. The assumption was that, given the thrust of interest and energy given to minority content, the profession would respond with content in texts and professional publications. The results were disappointing with content ranging from practice texts with no specific minority chapters, texts with some chapters, texts with some minority chapters or articles, to texts with subject index pages related to ethnicity, culture, and minorities. Final tabulations revealed that only 3% of the pages in practice texts included some content about ethnic minorities.

A search focused on content in social work journals from 1970 to 1990 found that only 7% of the journal items contained content related to minority groups (Lum, 1992/1996). Included in the search were *Families in Society* (Social Casework), *Social Service Review*, and *Social Work*. Given the cursory search of publications from 1910 to 1948, there is little evidence of interest in minority groups.

The Schlesinger and Devore (1995) ten-year search concurred with Lum's findings; in addition, they discovered that minimal attention was given to other American ethnic groups. The mention of white ethnic groups was related to a comparison with selected oppressed groups such as Jews, Italians, Greeks, the Irish and individuals from various African countries. No articles were found that mentioned Japanese, Middle Eastern people, or people from Eastern and Western Europe.

These searches conducted in the 1980s and 1990s revealed that social work scholars appeared to consider only two very general ethnic groups – there were white people and people who were not white. Non-white persons were a numerical minority, marginalized by the larger society and subject to the humiliation of racism as a consequence of their ethnic identity. Color continued to be a barrier that immediately announced difference. Persons with a dark complexion commanded little respect, and in some encounters, no respect at all. Fair complexions signal superior status. Given this differential response to color, the profession made attempts to respond. Egalitarian motives had led the profession to believe that an understanding of human needs and the dynamics of behavior could serve as a foundation for efforts toward equality in the delivery of services. A revaluation of this perspective was necessary (Devore and Schlesinger, 1981).

The revaluation was limited and not mindful of the wide range of white persons. The assumption was that all white persons had similar experiences, a notion that negated membership in distinct ethnic groups. The emerging militancy of young African-American university students propelled the matter of race into the forefront. The Council on Social Work Education, the accrediting body for social work education, was among the organizations that responded to the charges leveled by African-American students. The Council decreed that for programs (undergraduate and graduate) to receive accreditation, they must include instruction related to the diverse ethnic and minority groups as an integral part of social work education. Subsequent Council on Social Work Education Curriculum Policy Statements (1984, 1992, 1996) affirmed and expanded on this position.

In response to the mandates from the Council on Social Work Education scholars have made contributions that deliberately focus on ethnic issues and the development of practice-related principals (Devore and Schlesinger, 1981/1999; Lum, 1986/1996; Julia, 1996; Rivera and Erlich, 1992/1995/1998). Each author and editor has diminished, to a slight degree, the paucity identified by Lum (1992, 1999) and Schlesinger and Devore (1995). Each of the authors mentioned here has multiple publications. The dates refer to those works. Each author is listed in the references.

In the United States the response to the call for inclusion of ethnic-sensitive perspectives has been uneven. Professional literature contributed very little to encouraging inquiries into the meaning of ethnicity and race by students or faculty. It took organized political action led by students to catch the attention of the nation and social work education. Educators came to understand that social work had not been as egalitarian as it claimed to be. With this new understanding, the Council began to develop a series of policy statements, mentioned earlier, that would require content on ethnicity, race, and culture to be included throughout the curriculum.

The mandate, once given, called for a reconsideration of prevailing practice models and theories used in education and practice. This environment encouraged the development of ethnic-sensitive social work practice.

Ethnic-Sensitive Social Work Practice: Model, Framework, or Theory

The preface to the first edition of *Ethnic-Sensitive Social Work Practice* (Devore and Schlesinger, 1981) presents two basic themes:

- Ethnicity and social class play a large part in the shaping of life's problems as well as giving perspectives on problem resolutions.

- Social work is a problem-solving endeavor that must pay simultaneous attention to micro and macro problems if it is to respond effectively to problems within its domain (p. vi).

The model for ethnic-sensitive practice was developed from these perspectives. With each edition there have been revisions, deletions, and additions. Perspectives are continually refined as ethnicity commands more attention in social relationships, employment, and sports. Census 2000 will tell us more about who we are in relation to ethnic group membership. Will the census assist the social work profession when white is offered as an ethnic group? 'Which "white" are you?' may become a reasonable question.

From the first edition of *Ethnic-Sensitive Social Work Practice* (1981) to the fifth edition (1999), attention has been paid to evolving trends in ethnicity. The 1981 edition had four paragraphs and a vignette devoted to dual ethnic backgrounds. In 1999 there are more comprehensive discussions presented, including responses to immigration and attention to AIDS in the African-American community. In relation to the impact of interracial marriage, Chapter One contains an entry called 'Intermarriage and the New

Ethnicity' (pp. 16–18). During an eighteen-year span the authors have come to understand more clearly and take more seriously the notion that ethnicity is indeed fluid, ever changing. We may wonder how this fluidity will influence ethnic identity and lead us to add to or revise the model for ethnic-sensitive practice.

Immigration policy in the United States is often lacking in sensitivity to ethnic group membership. As policy changes it often favors individuals and families from European countries. Immigration policy in place during World War II denied European Jews a safe haven in the United States. Welfare reform policies in the late 1990s placed aging members of some immigrants at risk in relation to the amount of income that they would receive to meet their most basic needs.

The Ethnic Reality

While the profession was making attempts to become more inclusive by adding practice with ethnic minorities to the curriculum, there was scant attention paid to social class. Income, education, and occupation are significant indicators of social class. The question that presented itself was, does ethnic group membership influence the ability to earn a living, determine a family's place of residence, or the amount of education that children might receive?

Milton Gordon (1964) introduced the concept of *ethclass*, defined as the point at which ethnicity and social class meet and generate identifiable dispositions and behaviors. Ethnic-sensitive practice pays attention to the activity that occurs at this juncture and characterizes them as the ethnic reality or ethclass in action. Chestang (1982) suggests that the ethnic reality makes the notions contained in earlier perspectives of the 'ethnic experience' or 'ethnic condition' more concrete, suggesting that there is a place to look to gain a better understanding of a particular individual or family's ethnic experience. He wonders if ethnic-sensitive practice is indeed a model, or does it provide guidelines that may be applied to any number of approaches to practice.

The Layers of Understanding

With this perspective that ethnic-sensitive practice offers, when the knowledge, values, and skills needed for practice merge, they form layers of understanding. These layers include

- an awareness of and positive response to social work values,
- a basic understanding of human behavior,
- knowledge and skills related to social welfare policy and services,
- insight into one's own ethnicity and how it might influence practice,
- an understanding of the impact of the ethnic reality on daily life,
- a knowledge of the various routes that may be taken to the social worker, and
- the adaptation of strategies, skills and procedures for ethnic-sensitive practice.

This chapter focuses on the first layer related to social work values; the second layer is related to basic knowledge of human behavior, but poses a question about the 'rightness' of any theoretical theory about behavior. Self-awareness is required to accomplish the tasks of the third layer. This layer may present the social worker with a series of question that ask:

- Who am I in the ethnic sense?
- What do I know about my own ethnic group, about other groups?
- Do I really want to know? and,
- Will membership in my own ethnic group influence my practice with other groups?

The fifth layer asks how does the meeting of ethnicity and social class actually influence the daily lives of individuals, families, or communities?

The National Association of Social Workers Code of Ethics was ratified in 1996 by the NASW Delegate Assembly. This code identifies the core values that form the foundation for the mission of social work. These values include: service, social justice, dignity and worth of the person, the importance of human relationships, integrity, and competence. The code is explicit as it sets forth standards for social work practice. Competent ethnic-sensitive social workers will be expected to have:

... a knowledge base of their clients' cultures and be able to demonstrate competence in the provision of services that are sensitive to the client's culture and to differences among people and cultural groups (1.05b).

The second layer of understanding for ethnic-sensitive social work practice expects workers to have knowledge of human behavior exhibited by individuals, families, groups, or communities (Devore and Schlesinger, 1999: 95). Padilla (1990) and de Anda (1997) suggest that behavioral theory, taken for granted in the past, be reconsidered particularly in relation to its usefulness with oppressed ethnic groups. Padilla's work addresses the Mexican-American experience and cautions that theories developed by social scientists related to human behavior may not be applicable to all ethnic groups. Much that has been accepted as truth is more likely to be myths about individuals and their behaviors. Extended Mexican-American families may be accused of attempting to hold their members in the immediate family to the detriment of all. To the ethnic-sensitive worker this behavior may be an adaptive function that helps the family to meet the demands of urban life successfully.

Social science theorists have posited that ethnic minority groups will face similar barriers in the dominant society. However, there are groups, similar to Mexican-Americans, who will encounter situations that are related to the migration experience and the inability to find a significant place in the labor force. Social science theory is not to be entirely discarded but needs to be considered with caution in relation to the ethnic reality.

De Anda (1997) on the other hand, questions the availability of theories that are sufficiently 'culture free' and useful in work with multicultural clients. She considers 'culture free' to mean that theoretical principles may be applied to the dynamics of human behavior in an accurate and culturally syntonic manner (pp.142–143). Familiar theories about behavior are contextual. In order for them to become operationalized, one must use constructs according to definitions provided by the individuals to whom the principles are being applied. Identifying the principle of reinforcement as contextual, de Anda suggests that reinforcers will vary among cultural groups, as they reflect unique differences in contingencies within any given group (p. 152).

Varying theories related to human development and the life course continue to generate discussion, particularly as social work education responds to the Council on Social Work Education curriculum's policy. Social work faculty will need to look beyond familiar theories and support students as they examine theoretical perspectives. In this process each will need to pay attention to the relationship of theory to the ethnic reality. The ethnic reality, social class and ethnicity will influence individual development in ways that are not congruent with accepted theory. Competent ethnic-sensitive workers will pay attention to universal theories explaining behavior with the understanding that these may not always explain the behavior of all individuals from childhood to adulthood.

To accomplish the goals of the fourth layer of understanding social workers must be willing to search for insights contained within their own ethnicity. Self-awareness cannot be taught, but an inventory may be helpful. Karla Miley and her colleagues (1998) suggest four themes to be explored: personal identity, spiritual beliefs, knowledge of others and cross-cultural skills (p. 39). An inventory such as this requires a personal examination of areas that may have been avoided in the past. Suggested inquiries include:

- Have I been a racist or the recipient of racist attacks?
- What privileges do I accrue because of my ethnicity or gender?
- Am I religious?
- What ethnic dispositions influence my identity?

A summary question might be: What am I doing to increase my knowledge about people in other ethnic groups? The search for answers can be a continuing process, but it is in this process that workers learn about themselves as members of an ethnic group or groups. At the same time they gain knowledge about other groups that they may meet during the helping relationship.

The story of the Novacs, a Polish-American family, provides an opportunity to examine the fifth layer of understanding, an awareness of the impact of the ethnic reality on the daily life of clients. The incident in this family that has been referred to the social worker is 'trouble' at school.

Each morning the Novac family awakens in a little house 'across the tracks.' No matter how they try, the house continues to look shabby. The landlord makes few investments in the property.

John Novac finds work occasionally as a helper with a landscaping business. There is no health insurance for him or his family. His Polish relatives cannot understand why he does not have a steady job with a sure income. His mother decries his laziness; this is not what she expected from her son. The children are out of control, unwilling to take on any responsibilities at home. They defy both parents and are disruptive at school. The

Novacs are a low-income family residing in a Polish community (Devore and Schlesinger, 1999: 163).

To be ethnic-sensitive the school social worker must understand the impact that unemployment has on this family. It directs the family to substandard living conditions and an uncooperative landlord. John is a disappointment to his mother who expected much of him. Ethnicity and social class have converged, the children act out in school, and the social worker is called upon for assistance. He or she must not limit the intervention to the school setting; as a competent ethnic-sensitive worker, his/her inquiries will include other members of the family. The recognition of the impact of the ethnic reality on this family will provide a good foundation.

These three layers of understanding – social work values, knowledge of human behavior, and recognition of the impact of the ethnic reality on daily life – are an integral part of the model for ethnic-sensitive practice. They support the problem-solving process, as social workers attend to such a process by paying attention to both micro and macro issues. This simultaneous activity provides greater assurance of problem resolution.

Evaluation of Ethnic-Sensitive Social Work Practice

To date, there has been no systematic empirical evaluation of ethnic-sensitive practice as a model for practice. However, this practice model has led others to reconsider previously accepted modes of practice with various ethnic groups, particularly ethnic minority groups which Devore and Schlesinger (1999) have come to term oppressed ethnic groups. Ethnic-sensitive practice challenges myths and stereotypes that diminish certain ethnic groups. It suggests a way to think about practice built upon the ethnic reality and the different layers of understanding. The ethnic reality provides strength to the model as it affirms social class as a significant variable influencing life chances.

The poor in any ethnic group are marginalized, particularly those who claim membership in oppressed ethnic groups including African-Americans, Native Americans, Puerto Ricans, and Asians. Children and adults of these groups are more likely to experience racism in school, the workplace, or within the justice system. The layers of understanding provide guideposts for practice that ask ethnic-sensitive social workers to examine their values, their sense of own ethnicity, and to make adaptations to practice that respond to clients' ethnic reality.

Available social work literature related to the impact of race, ethnicity, and social class has helped fill some of the gaps mentioned at the beginning of the chapter. We believe that Leon Chestang's (1982) comment in a review following the first edition still holds even as the work evolves over time: '... they have clearly demonstrated the ethnic issues and clearly demonstrated how attention to these issues can enhance social work practice' (p. 177). He concluded:

> Social work teachers, students, and practitioners will do well to take seriously what they have to say. Indeed the model has been taken seriously and ethnic-sensitive social work practice has become a valued model for practice in several countries in addition to the United States (Chestang, 1982: 177).

The Future of Ethnic-Sensitive Practice

A Nation of Immigrants – A Nation of Strangers

As suggested earlier, the United States has had a fickle immigration policy even though we characterize our country as a nation of immigrants. A general knowledge of immigration history will provide ethnic-sensitive social workers with a sense of who is here, where they came from, and when. The 'where' and 'when' will provide some clues to what the immigrant experience may have been. Individuals and families who are 'people of color' who arrived during the 20th century will be less welcomed than Europeans whose ancestors arrived during the 18th or 19th century. Immigration will continue to be a political and a personal problem. It is a personal issue in that it includes the process of individuals and families leaving home and arriving in a new place where understanding a new language is required. Grief may accompany the need to relinquish a comfortable ethnic lifestyle for unfamiliar customs, traditions, rituals. These personal challenges may create a threat which the ethnic-sensitive social worker could help to identify and resolve.

The United States is a nation of immigrants; indeed, this coming together of so many people is the substance of our uniqueness. Still, we remain in so many ways a nation of strangers. This has been our past and it appears that this will be our future. Immigration policy will continue to change as it has done ever since the arrival of the first English settlers.

The wise social worker will understand that Germans, Irish, Italians, Russians, Poles, and other European groups have not always been welcomed despite their considerable contributions to the development of the country.

Africans, who were stolen from Africa and forced to be immigrants, still made significant contributions to the development of this country.

The mixed message of welcome and rejection continues. It is incumbent upon social workers to hold to the principles of practice that evolve from our values. The practice principles include: acceptance, individualization, non-judgmentalism, objectivity, self-determination, access to services, confidentiality and accountability (Miley, O'Melia and DuBois, 1998).

Crossing the Color Line

The ethnic reality has implied that at the ethclass juncture social class will meet with one ethnic group. The increasing number of inter-racial and inter-religious relationships calls for some reconsideration of the meaning of ethnicity. People in such relationships have been ostracized by family and friends, their parents are concerned that the grandchildren will be 'mixed,' colleagues wonder what race they are, and public displays of affection may be criticized. In public places persons of mixed race may be 'objects' of curiosity and a public display of affection may receive stares and questioning glances.

Ethnic-Sensitive Social Work Practice (1999) addresses the impact of the ethnic reality on a biracial adolescent (pp. 254–257). Social workers are provided with suggestions for intervention. It is clear that ethnic-sensitive practice and its ethnic reality foundation must move beyond this single vignette. Census 2000 has listened to parents who are concerned about affirming their children's dual identities.

What Kind of White Are You?

Social work education has, through various curriculum policy statements, mandated that the curriculum will respond to the need students have to develop knowledge and skills that prepare them for competent ethnic-sensitive social work practice. A body of literature is developing to respond to this policy established by the Council on Social Work Education. There is, however, a paucity of literature that lends attention to the experiences of white ethnic groups. The available literature views 'white' Americans as a culturally monolithic group. Little credence is given to the variations in their experiences. While we have focused attention on oppressed ethnic groups – people of color – we have paid scant attention to the lifestyles, religious beliefs, child-rearing practices, appropriate roles for men, women, children, or the elderly. We deprive social work students, whatever their ethnic identity might be, of knowledge about the wide range of ethnic groups in this country, many of whom they will meet during the helping process.

It is suggested here that there are at least three areas of concern that deserve greater attention in ethnic-sensitive practice perspectives:

- the impact of the immigration process on immigrants and immigrant families,
- although biracial relationships may have greater acceptance in some portions of society, a residual disdain in other quarters that generates anger and stress,
- omission of 'white' ethnic groups from the curriculum.

While all students are required to learn about ethnic minority groups, there is no expectation that they will have knowledge about 'white' groups. We seldom ask, 'What kind of white are you?' The question assists white ethnic students to gain a greater understanding of their position as an ethnic person, one among the many ethnic groups in the United States. The dichotomy between 'them,' oppressed ethnic groups, and 'us,' white Americans, will begin to lose its power when we understand that ethnic includes all of us who are residents of the United States.

It is essential that the model for ethnic-sensitive social work practice continues to adhere to practice principal that expects workers to 'pay simultaneous attention to individual and systemic concerns as they emerge out of client need and professional assessment' (Richmond, 1917: 153). An evolving model must revisit this principle and call for more sensitive responses to the concerns that arise in the lives of white ethnic groups along an understanding that institutional discrimination is a barrier that extends beyond the experiences of oppressed ethnic groups. Perhaps we will begin to please Mary Richmond (1917) as we adhere to her caution that we 'understand that we cannot ignore "national and racial characteristics"' – if we are to be competent ethnic-sensitive practitioners (Richmond, 1917: 382).

References

Alba, R. (1985), *Italian-Americans: Into the Twilight of Ethnicity.* Englewood Cliffs, NJ, Prentice Hall.

Boie, M. (1937), 'The Case Worker's Need for Orientation to the Culture of the Client,' in F. Lowry (ed.), *Readings in Social Case Work 1920–1938.* New York, Columbia University Press, pp.798–804.

Chestang, L. (1982), Book review: 'Ethnic-sensitive social work practice,' *Social Work*, p. 177.

Cloety, M. (1998), 'Census 2000: Asian or Pacific Islander: New census seeks specifics,' *Northwest Asian Weekly*, vol. 17 (9), p. 5.

Council on Social Work Education (1984, 1992, 1996, 1998), *Curriculum Policy statement for Undergraduate and Graduate Programs*. Alexandra, VA.

Daniels, J. (1910), 'Americanizing eighty thousand Poles,' *The Survey*, vol. 28, pp. 373–385.

de Anda, D. (1997), 'Are there theories that are sufficiently "culture free" to be appropriate and useful for practice with multicultural clients?' in D. de Anda (ed.), *Controversial Issues in Multiculturalism*. Boston, Allyn and Bacon, pp. 142–152).

Devore, W. and Schlesinger, E.G. (1981), *Ethnic Sensitive Social Work Practice*. St. Louis, The C.V. Mosby Company. (Also subsequent editions).

Devore, W. and Schlesinger, E.G. (1999), *Ethnic-Sensitive Social Work Practice* (5th ed.). Boston, Allyn and Bacon.

Editor (1918), 'Making the foreign-born one of us,' *The Survey*, vol. 40, pp. 213–215.

Gordon, M.M. (1964), *Assimilation in American Life: The Role of Race, Religion and National Origins*. New York, Oxford University Press.

Hodges, M.B. (1949), *Social Work Year Book 1949*. New York, Russell Sage Foundation.

Julia, M.C. (1996), *Multicultural Awareness in the Health Care Professions*. Pacific Grove, Brooks/Cole.

Lowry, F. (1939), *Readings in Social Case Work 1920–1938*. New York, Columbia University Press.

Lum, D. (1992), *Social Work Practice & People of Color: A Process-Stage Approach* (2nd ed.). Pacific Grove: Brooks/Cole. (Several editions.)

Lum, D. (1999), *Culturally Competent Practice: A Framework for Growth and Action*. Pacific Grove, Ca, Brooks/Cole Publishing Company. (Several editions.)

Miley, K.K., O'Melia, M., and DuBois, B.L. (1998), *Instructors' Manual and Test Bank for Generalist Social Work Practice – An Empowering Approach*. Boston, Allyn and Bacon.

Moore, S.W. (1910), 'The teaching of foreigners,' *The Survey*, pp. 386–392.

O'Hare, W. (1998), 'Managing multiple-race data,' *American Demographics*, pp. 42–44.

Ovington, M.W. (1910), 'Closing the little red school house,' *The Survey*, pp. 343–345.

Padilla, Y.C. (1990), 'Social science theory on the Mexican-American experience,' *Social Service Review*, vol. 64, pp. 261–275.

'Proceedings of the first Jewish conference,' (1910), *Charities Review*, vol. IV, pp. 163–165.

'Racial programs in social work,' (1949), in M.B. Hodges (ed.), *Social Work Year Book*. New York, Russell Sage Foundation. (pp. 414–423).

Richmond, M. (1917), *Social Diagnosis*. New York, Russell Sage Foundation.

Rivera, F. and Erlich, J. (1992/1995/1998), *Community Organizing in a Diverse Society* (1st, 2nd, and 3rd ed.). Boston, Allyn and Bacon.

Schlesinger, E.G. and Devore, W. (1995), 'Ethnic-sensitive social work practice. The state of the art,' *Journal of Sociology and Social Welfare*, vol. II, pp. 29–58.

'Social work for St. Louis Negroes,' (1910), *The Survey*, May 10, pp. 55–56.

'The colored home and hospital,' (1910), *Charities Review*, vol. 1, pp. 55–56.

'The Cuban orphan society,' (1901), *Charities Review*, vol. 6, pp. 84–85.

Whitehead, A. (1918), 'Our new Americans and war activities,' *The Survey*, June 15, pp. 310–314.

3 Multicultural Organizational Development

LORRAINE GUTIÉRREZ

Introduction

Over the past decade, issues of multiculturalism have entered popular discourse and public debate within the United States (Banks, 1992; Gould, 1995; Schoem, Frankel, Zuniga and Lewis, 1994). Although the more formal elements of this debate originated in academic settings, the challenges of living in an increasingly diverse and multicultural society have been addressed by social workers since the inception of our profession (Iglehart and Becerra, 1995; Daly, 1998). As the United States and other nations increase in cultural and racial/ethnic diversity, social workers will need to pay increasing attention to how diversity can transform our policy, practice, and service delivery systems.

Within the United States, immigration and fertility patterns have led to an increasingly multi-racial, multicultural, and multi-ethnic society (Gould, 1995). At the same time, conditions of economic inequality and economic stratification by gender and race have not abated (Dressel, 1994; Simon 1994). These demographic projections have led to concerns that we could become a nation of poor children and youth of color and older people of European-American descent, with neither group capable of producing the economic resources necessary to support existing social services or other social goods (Ozawa, 1986; Williams, 1990). These trends in the substance and structure of society challenge our profession to evaluate how it can best address these demographic shifts (Gutiérrez, 1992). To what degree will our focus be on social control or social justice in an increasingly multicultural world?

The business world has responded to the challenges of increasing workplace diversity and of a workforce which may not have the necessary education or skills (Cox, 1995). For example, some large corporations have developed remedial education and literacy programs while others are engaging in partnership programs with local school districts. In contrast, there has been little discussion within the social services regarding the implications of these demographic trends for program development and service delivery.

43

The focus of multicultural and culturally competent practice in social work has primarily involved developing interventions with individuals, families and groups. This area of practice has paid closer attention to the cultural dimensions of this work than to issues of poverty, racism, and oppression. In order to increase our effectiveness in meeting these emerging challenges, social work must reconsider its approach to cultural diversity and social inequality within human services organizations. I propose that a multicultural approach to organizational practice is a critical element of developing practice for the 21st century.

Multicultural Practice in Social Work

Multicultural practice is an emerging concept that refers to methods that work toward the development of disenfranchised groups while creating mechanisms for greater inter-group interaction and change (Gutiérrez, Rosegrant, Alvarez, Nemon, and Lewis, 1996). It is work that attempts to address the central challenge of living in a diverse society – how do we respect diversity and reduce inequality while working toward a common good? This practice is built upon a pluralistic foundation, yet goes beyond pluralism to recognize and work to eliminate social injustices and oppression based on group membership (Gutiérrez and Nagda, 1996; Jackson and Holvino, 1988; Sue, 1995).

Table 3.1. Social Work Approaches to Social Diversity and Oppression.

Perspective	Feelings	Goal of Practice
Ethno-centric	repulsion, pity	To change the individual, family, or group to reject their identity and adopt dominant values, beliefs, and behaviors.
Ethnic-sensitive	tolerance, acceptance, and support	To have individuals, families and groups experience a sense of pride in their identity. To develop social work practice, this takes into account the unique needs, values, and choices of diverse groups.
Ethno-conscious	admiration, appreciation, nurturance and advocacy	To create social structures that are affirming of all people. To create social work methods that remove social barriers to the full development of all individuals, families, and groups.

Source: Gutiérrez, L. and Lewis, E. (1999), *Empowering Women of Color*. New York, Columbia University Press, p. 12.

Multicultural practice in social work was developed in response to conflicts and to challenges by communities of color[1]. These challenges questioned the role of social work in a society where people of color continue to be over-represented in agencies with social control functions, such as the criminal justice and child welfare systems, and under-represented in agencies of a more voluntary and preventive nature, such as mental health clinics or counseling centers (Flaskerud, 1984; Rogler, 1982; Sarri, 1986; Sue, 1995). Research on this trend has found that client typification and tracking, barriers to services, and the organization of social services contribute to these conditions (Gutiérrez, 1992). These practices are symptomatic of the *ethnocentric perspective* that has traditionally dominated the social services system. This perspective reflects the social control function of social work and social welfare policies within our market economy (Wenocur and Reisch, 1989). Subsequent changes in our orientation toward culture and race reflect conflicts and struggles regarding our profession's role in relation to social inequality.

Ethnocentrism is in our roots and in our history. It was reflected in the development of the social services by predominantly upper class men and women who created programs that often reflected classist, racist, and nativist social mores (Wenocur and Reisch, 1989). The focus and purpose of these programs and services was to contain and control the threats to social homogeneity posed by those who were culturally different. The ethnocentric perspective considers, either explicitly or implicitly, the norms, values, and needs of European-American culture to be the most desirable (Banks, 1992; Dunn, 1998). It places little or no value on the unique experiences of people of color and may approach their cultures as the basis of many of the problems faced by these groups. In response to this perspective, immigrant, Native American and African-American communities developed their own systems of self-help and mutual aid (Iglehart and Becerra, 1995; Mankiller, 1993; Wenocur and Reisch, 1989).

Ethnocentrism is manifest in social service organizations as the provision of segregated services (Stehno, 1982), in the deportation of "aliens" (Sanchez, 1994), or in "Americanization" programs that resulted in the loss of culture and community (Iglehart and Becerra, 1995; Sanchez, 1994). For example, social service organizations have been instrumental in removing Native American children from their families into boarding schools or white foster families, which resulted in the break up of families, communities, and the loss of language and cultural heritage (Cross, 1986). Similarly, during the depression of the 1930s, social service agencies in the Southwest spearheaded efforts to "repatriate" people of Mexican descent in order to reduce public assistance costs. This resulted in over 400,000 people of Mexican descent, a large percentage of them American citizens, being sent to Mexico and separated from their homes, families, and employment (Sanchez, 1994).

The impact of less direct, more insidious forms of ethnocentrism has been damaging as well. The presence of some ethnic groups, such as Asian-Americans, has been ignored by service planners and providers (Lee, 1986). Some ethnic groups and their needs have been overlooked based on the notion that they "take care of their own" or may not respond well to the treatments offered at agencies (Land, Nishimoto, and Chau, 1988; Lee, 1986; Starret, Mindel, and Wright, 1983). Rather than evaluating ways in which existing agency procedures, structures, or treatments can be altered to better respond to the needs of ethnic minorities, the ethnocentric approach assumes that the "problem" in accessing and using services exists in the client group and that it is their responsibility to change.

The ethnic-sensitive perspective. The development of the ethnic-sensitive approach to social service organizations and programs was developed by communities of color in reaction to ethnocentric approaches (Chau, 1990; Devore and Schlesinger, 1987; Gallegos, 1982; Scott and Delgado, 1979). The goal of the ethnic-sensitive approach is to create or recreate programs and organizations that will be more responsive and responsible to the culture of minority groups. It is based on the notion that the nature of our society is multicultural and that positive gains can result from learning about different cultural groups and incorporating culture into agency procedures, structures, and services (Devore and Schlesinger, 1987; Gallegos, 1982). Many of these programs were initiated by community-based organizations or by social workers of color working within larger organizations.

The ethnic-sensitive approach has contributed to different thinking by some service providers regarding communities of color. Ethnic-sensitive programs and services can take the form of separate programs, specialized programs, or specific social work methods tailored to the cultural values and experiences of cultural groups (Gutiérrez, 1992; Rogler, Malgady, Constantino, and Blumental, 1987). Working from an ethnic-sensitive perspective requires the capacity to work effectively with different ethnic, racial, social class and other groups. Developing this capacity as a social worker requires that one develop the knowledge, values, and skills to work across social boundaries (Devore and Schlesinger, 1987; Green, 1995). This includes the ability to understand the importance of culture in the everyday life of the worker and program participants; self-knowledge regarding one's own values and social position; skills in cross-cultural communication and non-judgmental listening; and the ability to be open and learn from others, comfort with the discomfort of ambiguity, being the outsider, speaking a different language, or being confronted with biases. Also essential is the ability to deal with internal and external conflict, to sit back and facilitate rather than direct processes, and to form and facilitate groups. The development of ethnic sensitivity and cultural competence is an ongoing developmental process that can engage social workers throughout their professional careers (Green, 1995).

The ethnoconscious approach: The ethnic-sensitive and culturally competent approaches to practice are now viewed as legitimate and important aspects of social work practice. For example, accreditation standards for schools of social work in the United States and the code of ethics of the National Association of Social Workers both identify cultural competence as necessary for social workers. However, although the development of the ethnic-sensitive approach to social services has led to changes in the training and thinking of service providers and the creation of new programs, it is not an adequate response to the challenges related to the low status and power of communities of color (Gutiérrez, 1990; Iglehardt and Becerra, 1995; McMahon and Allen-Meares, 1992; Solomon, 1976; Washington, 1982). It ignores the role of power in the social order and social work practice (McMahon and Allen-Meares, 1992); is more concerned with individual change at the expense of maintaining an institutional status quo (McMahon and Allen-Meares, 1992); equates ethnicity to culture with the danger of stereotyping and typifying clients (Green, 1995; Jayasuriya, 1992; Longres, 1991); is more suited for working with refugees than with ethnic minorities who have been in the United States for generations (Longres, 1991); and lacks a social development agenda (Midgley, 1991). If we are to work to improve the overall social status of disenfranchised groups, we must think of ways in which we can contribute to social justice.

Social justice is an essential component of ethnoconscious practice. The concept of social justice emerges from the field of philosophy. Definitions of social justice have focused on conceptions of equity, equality, and fairness in the distribution of societal resources. The following definition is taken from the *Encyclopedia of Social Work*:

> ... Social justice can be understood as including economic, social and political equality that is based on egalitarian principles. A primary concern... is with the

oppressive characteristics of injustice, in other words, with the forms of violence used to perpetuate inequality (Van Soest, 1994, p. 1812).

A concern with social justice, therefore, includes a focus on the structures and outcomes of social processes and how they contribute to equality. It places an explicit value on achieving social equity through democratic processes. As a value for our profession it assumes that it is our role to develop policy and practice that contribute to these social goals (Van Soest, 1994).

Social justice is a central organizing feature of multicultural practice because it directly addresses the role and purpose of social work practice with communities of color. It goes beyond sensitivity by positing that if we are to work ethically and effectively we must be advocates for social change. It requires that we take a "mezzo level" approach to our work by 1) making efforts to both assist in the development of individuals and families and impact on the social conditions that contribute to the problems they experience, 2) working with the clients and community to develop a sense of personal control and an ability to influence the behavior of others, and 3) establishing equity in the distribution of resources (Frumkin and O'Conner, 1985; Mizio, 1981; Morales, 1981; Rappaport, 1987; Washington, 1982). The ultimate goal of this approach is to work with disenfranchised individuals and their communities to achieve social justice within the context of cultural values, symbols, and strengths (Kelley, McKay, and Nelson, 1985).

Research suggests that if the development of ethnic-sensitive services do not lead to structural changes in organizations and a greater participation of people of color in the governance of the agency, efforts toward change can be mostly symbolic and marginal (Gutiérrez, 1992; Iglehart and Becerra, 1995). Multicultural organizational development from an *ethnoconscious* approach combines an ethnic-sensitive orientation and an empowerment perspective on practice, and holds promise for creating empowering services, programs, and organizations. It is oriented toward empowerment rather than remediation or adjustment of individual clients and can contribute to the creation of organizations that encourage the empowerment of consumers and workers. These organizations incorporate an empowerment-based perspective in their organization and services, have an explicitly political understanding of their program participants, organization and society, are integrated into the local community, have access to legislative and funding organizations, share and access power through participation with other organizations and are participatory learning organizations (Gutiérrez, GlenMaye and DeLois, 1995; Gutiérrez and Nagda, 1996;

Zimmerman, in press).

The most integrated approach to ethnoconscious services is that of the alternative, ethnic agency. The ethnic agency is a human service organization developed by ethnic minorities to serve the needs of their community. As such it faces the challenges both of organizational maintenance and meeting the primary group functions of the ethnic group (Jenkins, 1989; Kelley, et al., 1985). Ethnic agencies often emerge organically from within the ethnic community in order to meet social service needs and usually have some commitment to impacting community issues and problems (Jenkins, 1989; Mast, 1994; Uriarte and Merced, 1985). Therefore, they have an explicit goal of empowering the community in which they work (Gutiérrez, 1992).

Ethnic agencies exist within all communities of color. The literature documents the presence of child care centers (Jenkins, 1989), senior citizen programs, youth oriented programs (Zambrana and Aguierre-Molina, 1987), mental health programs (Solomon, 1976), and health care clinics (Lee, 1986) which have been developed to meet the needs of specific minority communities. These organizations may focus on the specific needs of one ethnic community or incorporate programs that serve more than one community.

Examples of this work exist throughout the United States. In Detroit, nine community based organizations serving different ethnic and racial communities have come together to form the Michigan Neighborhood Partnership, a coalition that focuses on community and economic development (Michigan Neighborhood Partnership, 1996). This organization provides direct services (such as health care, substance abuse prevention, HIV counseling and outreach, tutoring, ESL programs and adult education) through its member organizations. These direct service programs are created with and by community members to meet the needs and resources of each community. Although these programs are ethnic specific, programs and activities such as conferences, youth camps, and parenting education are developing that bridge ethnic and cultural differences in order to build a sense of community and bring different groups together.

The partnership is also engaged in community and economic development efforts within and between these member organizations. The Comnet Project, which involved all member organizations, was developed to provide Internet access for each organization and to provide training to community members on using this information technology. A manufacturing business incubator is also being developed that will provide support to small businesses in Detroit and help them to grow to maturity (Michigan Neighborhood Partnership, 1996). These projects are built on the social justice foundation of multicultural practice and focus on ways to improve human capital and establish greater equity in the distribution of social and economic resources.

Methods for Multicultural Organizational Development

The ethnoconscious perspective provides a dynamic model for thinking about ways in which our human service organizations can be more representative and responsive to communities. Multicultural oganizational development (MCOD) attempts to transform existing human services organizations through consultation, research, and training to become more inclusive (Chessler, 1993; Resnick and Menafee, 1989; Sue, 1995). The goal is to create a structure, policies and procedures within the agency that support the creation and provision of ethnically competent or ethnoconscious services. A true MCOD approach requires sanction and support from all decision makers in the agency in order to be effective and to achieve maximum change (Chessler, 1993; Sue, 1995).

The existing literature on MCOD has focused primarily on developing models for understanding and analyzing organizations and on methods for moving organizations from an ethnocentric or monocultural approach to one that is truly multicultural (Chessler, 1993; Gutiérrez and Nagda, 1996; Sue, 1995). The emphasis of this approach has been on tools for developing organizational audits, the creation of workgroups and change teams in organizations, specialized training for staff on all levels, and the development of policies that support multicultural work (Bailey, 1998; Chessler, 1993; Gutiérrez and Nagda, 1996). Looking at the organization from multiple levels and recognizing the need for change in many dimensions is emphasized (Bailey, 1998).

Specific methods for building multicultural organizations simultaneously focus on different dimensions or organizational analysis. One model, the 10S model (Bailey, 1998), considers aspects of setting, shared values, skills, staffing, stakeholders, strategy, structure (administration), structure (governance), style and systems as critical dimensions for MCOD. Sue (1995) proposes a three-dimensional model that considers the functional focus of change, the multicultural competencies needed, and the barriers to multiculturalism that exist in the organization. In an extensive review of the literature, Dana, Behn, and Gonwa (1992) identified five essential dimensions to MCOD: agency practices, available services, relationship with the ethnic community, training, and evaluation. Taken together, this literature suggests that the following four dimensions are critical for MCOD practice:

Organizational structure: This involves questions regarding the formal structure of the organization and analyzing the organizational chart and formal policies with a multicultural lens. Another focus is looking at mechanisms for control in the organization. A multicultural organization is one in which there is diversity at all levels of the organization, written policies supportive of diversity, and workers actively involved in different aspects of the organization's work. The formal structure of the organization is less important than clear mechanisms for different groups to contribute to the overall mission.

Organizational culture: In this perspective, organizational norms and expectations are considered as well as relationships within the organization and how things really get done. A multicultural lens on organizational culture considers whether the workplace is open to different standpoints, interpersonal styles, and value systems. An organizational culture that supports learning and growth for staff at different levels would also be supportive of multicultural organizational practice.

Power relations: This perspective recognizes the distribution of power within the organization and takes a synergistic view of power as a dynamic resource that can be generated in the process of social interaction. It recognizes the importance of power on personal, interpersonal, and political levels and assumes that people want to maximize and use their power to achieve organizational goals. In respect to MCOD, this perspective closely considers the distribution of power resources in the organization and the characteristics of those having differential access to power.

Ecology: The focal point of this perspective is the organization in interaction with its environment. It focuses on ways in which the larger community affects the inner workings of the organization. It also explores ways in which the organization reflects the community in which it is located and looks carefully at how external conditions affect internal policy and program changes.

A multicultural organizational audit considers each of these dimensions through a multicultural lens. It asks where the different racial, gender, and ethnic groups are within the formal structure. It considers the degree to which the informal culture is inclusive of differing perspectives and traditions. It looks at which groups have access to formal and informal power resources and looks at the degree to which the diversity in the surrounding community is reflected in the organization and its programs.

This multicultural audit would then be translated into a multicultural change plan. Change would occur on each dimension in relation to the findings of the audit and could be both internally and externally focused. For example, if the audit found that service staff were English monolingual and unable to serve a local Spanish-speaking community, this would be the focus of MCOD work. Similarly, if the audit found that the lack of transportation for people with disabilities in the local community made it difficult for them to work in the organization, then the transportation needs in the community would guide this work.

Some examples from the literature describe ways in which an MCOD approach can be implemented. Jones (1989) describes the implementation of cultural sensitivity training for social work with African-Americans. By beginning training with a clear commitment from the board, administration, and staff to changing their approach to working with African-Americans, the cultural sensitivity program led to a critical analysis of the agency's programs and structure. This created a new structure in which African-Americans were hired into more staff positions and given greater voice within the agency. Similarly, Kelley et al. (1985), in describing MCOD with a Native American agency, found that working with the board, administration, and staff of this organization in a collaborative fashion contributed to the empowerment of workers by enlarging their roles and encouraging professional development. This change in the staff roles improved both direct client services and the agency's status in the community.

Another example of MCOD is the development of a specialized program module within a larger social services organization to meet the needs of a specific ethnic or racial group (Arroyo and Lopez, 1984; Olmstead, 1983; Scott and Delgado, 1979; Watkins and Gonzales, 1982; Zambrana and Aguierre-Molina, 1987). This allows an organization to concentrate its efforts to serving a particular population, although it can also have the effect of marginalizing the needs and priorities of this group by segregating services. A successful specialized service is one that can create and provide effective ethnic-sensitive services while influencing agency wide change.

An example of one way a specialized program can influence agency policy is provided by Olmstead (1983), who describes how a small unit to train ethnic minority social work students in a child welfare agency with a predominantly white staff had profound effects on the services of the agency. Although it was the intention of the agency to provide specialized services to minorities and to train students, administration and staff soon found that the ethnic minority students brought a different perspective to the agency. Their critiques of the program contributed to a change in the orientation of the agency toward greater connection with ethnic minority communities, the use of ethnic-sensitive approaches to direct service work, and a new affirmative action policy which resulted in a greater participation of people of color on the board and in professional staff positions.

Scott and Delgado (1979) describe and analyze ways in which the implementation of a program to serve the Hispanic population moved from marginalization and ineffectiveness to success. Initial efforts to create a specialized program through the incorporation of Hispanic paraprofessionals into a primarily white mental health agency resulted in the marginalization of the program, conflict between the minority workers and white supervisors, and a failure to provide effective services. It was only when the agency hired a bilingual/bicultural Hispanic administrator to design and implement the program that it was successful and accepted by both the Hispanic and social service communities. This demonstrates that unless the administration of specialized services is located within or near the center of power in an organization, it is likely to remain marginal and it effectiveness limited.

Conclusion

The proliferation of literature that focuses on MCOD has moved our thinking about multicultural practice to the organizational level. It has made a significant contribution through the development of tools and techniques for creating organizations that are supportive of cultural diversity and provides a different perspective for understanding organizations. However, in many respects this perspective reflects the pervasiveness of the ethnocentric perspective by continuing to view the "mainstream monocultural" organization with the European American group at its center. This focus would benefit from a perspective that recognizes the work that has been done by ethnic organizations in the creation of truly community based organizations. The methods developed by these organizations can contribute to our understanding of transformational practice.

This paper began with a question: To what degree will our focus be on social control or social justice in an increasingly multicultural world? Will we continue to create programs, policies, and methods that are focused on ethnocentrism? Or will we chose to work toward social justice by building upon the strengths, capacities, and values of the individuals, families and communities with which we work? To what degree will our primary focus be on assisting communities of color to cope with conditions of inequality in culturally sensitive ways or to work with these communities to reduce conditions of inequality?

The new code of ethics of the National Association of Social Workers in the United States suggests that our efforts should be directed toward social justice, empowerment, and collaborative practice (NASW, 1996). However, existing trends in the United States regarding managed care, welfare "reform," and efforts to eliminate affirmative action and to further restrict immigration suggest that working toward social justice will not be easy. Taking the path toward multicultural practice within organizations will require taking risks, speaking out, and challenging current trends. It requires empowering ourselves in our workplaces and daily life so that we can act upon our convictions and professional responsibilities. In order to engage in this critical work we will require support and resources from each other, our professional organizations, and the institutions in which we work. By recognizing the challenges we face, and identifying the means to meet those challenges, we can be effective agents for improving the social conditions in which we all live.

Summary Points

- With globalization, the United States and many other countries are experiencing changing demographics, characterized by increases in ethnic, racial and cultural diversity. This has an impact on the organization of social welfare policies and services.

- Our current perspectives on cultural factors in practice are inadequate for addressing the issues associated with these trends. As our focus has moved from ethnocentrism to sensitivity or cultural competence, we pay inadequate attention to ways in which conditions of inequality intersect with ethnic and cultural difference.

- Our focus on social work has been on the implications of multiculturalism for direct service work, with little attention on ways in which the structure of human service organizations can be supportive of multicultural practice.

- Social justice should be a central feature of multicultural practice. We need to develop human service organizations that work toward social justice for populations that are distinguished by race, ethnicity or culture. This calls for the integration of human and social development.

- Methods of multicultural organization development (MCOD) have been developed to create programs, policies, and services that work for the benefit of communites of color. This practice can be enhanced by learning about methods that have been developed within these comminutes through the provision of community-based social services.

- Partnership is a critical dimension of MCOD. It requires partnership with community members, partnership between non-profit, governmental, and private organizations, and partnership between organizations. These partnerships should be egalitarian and mutually beneficial.

- Organizational audits, which take into account multiple dimensions of organizations, can be helpful in assessing the degree to which an organization is working for the benefit of comminutes of color. These audits can then be used to shape future efforts for organizational change.

- Transforming organizations in this way requires that social workers take risks in their work and exhibit a commitment for social justice and social change.

Note

1. Within the US context, people of color refers to individuals of Native American, African-American, Asian-Pacific American, and Latin American descent. These groups have historically experienced structural inequality based on perceived racial differences.

References

Arroyo, R. and Lopez, S. (1984), 'Being responsive to the Chicano community: A model for service delivery,' in B. White (ed.), *Color in a White Society*. Silver Spring, MD, National Association of Social Workers, pp. 63–73.

Bailey, D. (1998, December), 'The Integration of Multicultural Competency and Organizational Practice in Social Work Education: Recommendations for the Future.' Multicultural Social Work Task Force Meeting, University of Michigan, Ann Arbor, MI, 1998.

Banks, J. (1992), 'Curriculum Guidelines for Multicultural Education,' Social Education, pp. 274–294.

Chessler, M. (1993), *O.D.M.C.O.D.*, PCMA Working Paper Series #42, Ann Arbor, University of Michigan, Program on Conflict Management Alternatives.

Chau, K. (1990), 'A Model for Teaching Cross Cultural Practice in Social Work,' *Journal of Social Work Education*, vol. 26, pp. 124–133.

Cox, T. (1995), *Cultural Diversity in Organizations: Theory, Research, and Practice*. San Francisco, CA, Berrett-Koehler.

Cross, T. (1986), 'Drawing on Cultural Tradition in Indian Child Welfare Practice,' *Social Casework*, vol. 67, pp. 283–289.

Daly, A. (1998), *Workplace Diversity: Issues and Perspectives*. Washington, DC, NASW Press.

Dana, R., Behn, J., and Gonwa, T. (1992), 'A Checklist for the Examination of Cultural Competence in Social Service Agencies,' *Research on Social Work Practice*, vol. 2 (2), pp. 220–233.

Devore W. and Schlesinger, E.G. (1987), *Ethnic Sensitive Social Work Practice*, 2nd ed. Columbus, OH, Merrill.

Dressel, P. (1994), '...And We Keep on Building Prisons: Racism, Poverty and Challenges to the Welfare State,' *Journal of Sociology and Social Welfare*, vol. 21 (3), pp. 7–30.

Dunn, E. (1998), 'Historical Review of US Policy on Diversity,' in A. Daly (ed.), *Workplace Diversity*. Washington, DC, NASW Press, pp. 70–87.

Flaskerud, J. (1984), 'A Comparison of Perceptions of Problematic Behavior by Six Minority Groups and Mental Health Professions,' *Nursing Research*, vol. 33 (4), pp. 190–197.

Frumkin, M. and O'Conner, G. (1985), 'Where Has the Profession Gone? Where Is It Going? Social Work's Search for Identity,' *The Urban and Social Change Review*, vol. 18 (1), pp. 12–19.

Gallegos, J. (1982), 'The Ethnic Competence Model for Social Work Education,' in B. White, (ed.), *Color in a White Society*. Silver Spring, MD, NASW, pp. 1–9.

Green, J.W. (1995), *Cultural Awareness in the Human Services*. Englewood Cliffs, NJ, Prentice-Hall.

Gould, J. (1995), 'The Misconstruing of Multiculturalism,' *Social Work*, vol. 40, pp. 198–205.

Gutiérrez, L. (1990), 'Working with Women of Color: An Empowerment Perspective,' *Social Work*, vol. 35, pp. 149–154.

Gutiérrez, L. (1992), 'Empowering Clients in the Twenty-First Century: The Role of Human Service Organizations,' in Y. Hasenfeld (ed.), *Human Service Organizations as Complex Organizations*. Newbury Park, CA, Sage, pp. 320–338.

Gutiérrez, L., GlenMaye, L., and DeLois, K. (1995), 'The Organizational Context of Empowerment Practice: Implications for Social Work Administration,' *Social Work*, vol. 40 (2), pp. 249–258.

Gutiérrez, L. and Nagda, B. (1996), 'The Multi-Cultural Imperative in Human Services Organizations: Issues for the 21st Century,' in P. Raffoul and A. McNeece (eds.), *Future Issues for Social Work Practice*. Boston, Allyn & Bacon, pp. 203–213.

Gutiérrez, L., Rosegrant Alvarez, A., Nemon, H., and Lewis, E. (1996), 'Multicultural Community Organizing: A Strategy for Change,' *Social Work*, vol. 41 (5), pp. 501–508.

Gutiérrez, L. and Lewis, E. (1999), *Empowering Women of Color*. New York, Columbia University Press.

Iglehart, A. and Becerra, R. (1995), *Ethnic Services: Precedents, Perspectives and Parameters in Social Services and the Ethnic Community* (Chap. 6). Boston, Allyn & Bacon.

Jackson, B.W. and Holvino, E. (1988), *Multi-Cultural Organizational Development*. PCMA

Working Paper Series #11, Ann Arbor, University of Michigan, Program on Conflict Management Alternatives.

Jayasuriya, L. (1992), 'The Problematic of Culture and Identity in Social Functioning,' *Journal of Multi-Cultural Social Work*, vol. 2 (4), pp. 37–58.

Jenkins, S. (1989), 'The Ethnic Agency Defined,' in D. Burgest (ed.), *Social Work Practice with Minorities*. Metuchen, NJ, Scarecrow Press.

Jones, R. (1989), 'Increasing Staff Sensitivity to the Black Client,' in D. Burgest (ed.), *Social Work Practice with Minorities*. Metuchen, NJ, Scarecrow Press.

Kelley, M., McKay, S., and Nelson, C. (1985), 'Indian Agency Development: An Ecological Practice Approach,' *Social Casework*, vol. 66, pp. 594–602.

Land, H., Nishimoto, R., and Chau, K. (1988), 'Interventive and Preventive Services for Vietnamese Chinese Refugees,' *Social Service Review*, vol. 62, pp. 568–484.

Lee, J. (1986), 'Asian-American Elderly: A Neglected Minority Group,' *Journal of Gerontological Social Work*, vol. 9 (4), pp. 103–116.

Longres, J. (1991), 'Toward a Status Model of Ethnic Sensitive Practice,' *Journal of Multi-Cultural Social Work*, vol. 1 (1), pp. 41–56.

Mankiller, W. (1993), *Mankiller: A Chief and her People*. New York, St. Martin's Press.

Mast, R. (1994), *Detroit Lives*. Philadelphia, Temple University Press.

McMahon, A. and Allen-Meares, P. (1992), 'Is Social Work Racist?,' *Social Work*, vol. 37 (6), pp. 533–539.

Michigan Neighborhood Partnership, (1996), *Michigan Neighborhood Partnership: Streetlight*, Detroit, MI.

Midgley, J. (1991), 'Social Development and Multi-Cultural Social Work,' *Journal of Multi-Cultural Social Work*, vol. 1 (1), pp. 85–100.

Mizio, E. (1981), 'Training for Work with Minority Groups,' in E. Mizio and A. Delaney (eds.), *Training for Service Delivery to Minority Clients*. New York, Family Service Association of America, pp. 7–20.

Morales, A. (1981), 'Social Work with Third World People,' *Social Work*, vol. 26, pp. 48–51.

National Association of Social Workers (NASW) (1996), *Code of Ethics of the National Association of Social Workers*. Author.

Olmstead, K. (1983), 'The Influence of Minority Social Work Students on an Agency's Service Methods,' *Social Work*, vol. 28, pp. 308–312.

Ozawa, M. (1986), 'Nonwhites and the Demographic Imperative in Social Welfare Spending,' *Social Work*, vol. 31, pp. 440–445.

Rappaport, J. (1987), 'Terms of empowerment/exemplars of prevention: Toward a theory for community psychology,' *American Journal of Community Psychology*, vol. 15 (2), 121–148.

Resnick, H. and Menefee, D. (1989), *Organization Development in Social Work: A Human Service Partnership*. Paper presented at the Annual Program Meeting, Council on Social Work Education, Chicago, IL.

Rogler, L. (1982), 'A Barrier Model for Hispanic Mental Health Research: New Techniques for the Psychiatric Evaluation and Psychotherapy of Hispanic Children,' *Research Bulletin*, Hispanic Research Center, 5 (4), pp. 1–3.

Rogler, L., Malgady, R., Constantino, G., and Blumental, R. (1987), 'What Do Culturally Sensitive Services Mean? The Case of Hispanics,' *American Psychologist*, vol. 42, pp. 565–570.

Sanchez, G. (1994), *Becoming Mexican-American*. New York, Oxford University Press.

Sarri, R. (1986), 'Organizational and Policy Practice in Social Work: Challenges for the

Future,' *Urban and Social Change Review*, vol. 19, pp. 14–19.

Schoem, D., Frankel, L., Zuniga, X., and Lewis, E. (1994), *Multicultural Teaching in the University*. Westport, CT, Praeger.

Scott, J. and Delgado, M. (1979), 'Planning Mental Health Programs For Hispanic Communities,' *Social Casework*, vol. 60, pp. 451–456.

Simon, B.L. (1994), *The Empowerment Tradition in American Social Work*. New York, Columbia University Press.

Solomon, B. (1976), *Black Empowerment*. New York, Columbia University Press.

Starret, R., Mindel, C., and Wright, R. (1983), 'Influence of Support Systems on the Use of Social Services by the Hispanic Elderly,' *Social Work Research and Abstracts*, pp. 35–40.

Stehno, S. (1982), 'Differential Treatment of Minority Children in Service Systems,' *Social Work*, vol. 27, pp. 39–45.

Sue, D. (1995), 'Multicultural organizational development,' in J. Ponterotto (ed.), *Handbook of Multicultural Counseling*. Thousand Oaks, CA, Sage Publications, pp. 474–492.

Uriarte, M. and Merced, N. (1985), 'Social Service Agencies in Boston's Latino Community: Notes on Institutionalization,' *Catalyst*, vol. 5, pp. 21–34.

Van Soest, D. (1994), 'Peace and Social Justice,' in the *Encyclopedia of Social Work*, Washington, DC, NASW Press

Washington, R. (1982), 'Social Development: A Focus for Practice and Education,' *Social Work*, vol. 27, pp. 104–109.

Watkins, T. and Gonzales, R. (1982), 'Outreach to Mexican Americans,' *Social Work*, vol. 27, pp. 68–73.

Wenocur, S. and Reisch, M. (1989), *From Charity to Enterprise: The Development of American Social Work in a Market Economy*. Chicago, University of Illinois Press.

Williams, L. (1990), 'The Challenge of Education to Social Work: The Case of Minority Children,' *Social Work*, vol. 35, pp. 236–242.

Zambrana, R. and Aguierre-Molina (1987), 'Alcohol Abuse Prevention Among Latino Adolescents: A Strategy for Intervention,' *Journal of Youth and Adolescence*, vol. 16 (2), pp. 97–113.

Zimmerman, M. (in press), 'Empowerment: Forging New Perspectives in Mental Health,' in. J. Rappaport and Seidman, E. (eds.), *Handbook of Community Psychology*, New York, Plenum Press.

4 Inclusive Thinking and Acting

EDWIN HOFFMAN

Introduction

The increasing number of ethnic groups within the population of each European society poses for social workers and their managers the question: What theory and which instruments can be developed for social work practice and its management, in which the notion of 'ethnicity' is firmly embedded? The answer to this question should have a dynamic character in the form of an acknowledgment that people are able to exercise agency in the formation of ethnicity as a constantly changing aspect of their identity.

As a trainer and consultant I will confine my contribution to two aspects: the interpersonal communication level (social workers – clients and managers – employees); here I would like to introduce *a pluralistic, systems-theoretical approach of intercultural communication* (Hoffman and Arts, 1994) and the management level of an organisation with a multi-ethnic workforce and a multi-ethnic clientele, *an inclusive approach of management of diversity*.

I start with a short description of the Dutch context and continue with an analysis of the risks of culturalist and some anti-racist approaches. I go on to elaborate an inclusive model of 'Management of Diversity' and an inclusive model of 'Intercultural Communication'. Lastly, the TOPOI-model is presented as a possible instrument of analysis to detect disturbing cultural differences and misunderstandings in the communication.

The Dutch Context

I write from the context of the Dutch multi-ethnic society with 15 million inhabitants of which about 5% are the officially so-called *'allochthones'*. Allochthones are people who themselves or one of their parents were born abroad. In contrast to the allochthones, *'autochthones'* are the 'original/ native' Dutch (which leaves open the question of how many generations before one is 'pure' Dutch).

Allochthones are migrants from former Dutch colonies, labour-migrants, refugees, asylum seekers and Gypsies. The largest groups are

59

Surinamese (1995: 278,000), Turks (1995: 264,000), Moroccans (1995: 219,000), Arubans and Antilleans (1995: 93,000) (Shadid, 1998: 11). Allochthones are the 'target group' of the Dutch government because they have a weak social-economic position in Dutch society; e.g., disproportionally high unemployment and drop-out rates from school. In 1999, the government launched four action programmes to improve the position of allochthones in regard of youth, unemployment, discrimination and communication. Concerning the citizenship of allochthones, they have the possibility of dual nationality as well as the right to vote and to put themselves forward for local government. Article 1 of the Dutch constitution forbids discrimination and racism. Politically, the extreme right wing political parties are not very significant in the Netherlands. On the other hand, the resistance against the arrival of asylum-seekers is growing.

A last important characteristic of the Dutch political climate is the consensus model or in Dutch the so-called *Poldermodel*: many objectives are achieved by mutual arrangement and consultation.

Risks of Culturalist and Some Anti-Racist Approaches

The demographic context makes it clear that in the Netherlands social workers and their management have to deal with allochthonous clients and colleagues. In general, in the Netherlands most social workers and their managers are really motivated to take on board the ethnic dimension in their daily practice. They ask for concrete information on cultural background, how to recruit more allochthonous personnel, how to manage multi-ethnic teams and how to deal with the misunderstandings and the conflicts they meet in their communication because of the different ethnic backgrounds of clients, colleagues and employees. Monocultural organisations in other countries that are just beginning to take 'ethnicity' on-board may have the same questions and I would like to point out the risks of some approaches of intercultural communication and intercultural management that try to respond to these questions.

Many intercultural communication and management theories (e.g. Hofstede, 1984; Trompenaars, 1993) are current answers to the questions posed by social workers and their management. These studies deal with different national cultures and their characteristics or with dimensions of national cultures like high context and low context cultures (Hall, 1976), power distance, uncertainty – avoidance, collectivism – individualism and femininity and masculinity (Hofstede, 1984). They are important because their intention is to avoid ethnocentrism and racism by giving insight into the diversity of ethnic and national cultures. However, these theories are very risky when taken as indications of how to communicate with people from a different ethnic or national background. This kind of intercultural approach is called *culturalising* (Glastra, 1999) or *culturalist* (Shadid, 1998): the focus is on ethnic or national cultural differences and these cultural problems are considered as the core problem of interethnic living and working together. The culturalist approach reduces the interaction between people from a different ethnic background to an isolated unique microscopic situation and neglects in this way the societal context with historically grown structures of power. This blocks the view of societal processes of dominance and exclusion. Husband (1991) warns that in this way:

> Ethnically sensitive social work practice easily can become a shallow culturally informed modification of service delivery at the client–worker interface. This can take place within existing problem definitions and without challenging existing institutional structures. As such, it easily becomes 'a sophisticated form of paternalistic and institutionally racist service'; which may claim to be client orientated, but could never approximate to being client-led (Husband, 1991: 65).

Another risk is that allochthones are captured in their static ethnic culture and are turned into cultural objects. The culturalising approach suggests that the communication of a person is one-dimensional, determined by her or his belonging to a certain ethnic group. Social workers learn, for example, that with regard to Moroccan or Turkish clients they belong by definition to the out-group; because social workers do not belong to the in-group of the family, Moroccan and Turkish clients have great difficulties in telling them their private, personal problems. Or even more precisely, social workers can get the advice that if they visit a Moroccan or Turkish family at home, a lot of tea will be offered to them. If they do not want any more tea, they have to put the teaspoon on top of their teacup with the convex side up.

This culturalising approach mainly points at the traditional ethnic cultural background of a person and presents this at the same time as static, unchangeable and fixed and fully determining the thinking and acting of people. It neglects the dynamic meaning of daily practices of negotiation, co-operation and conflict resolution: people are not only a product of culture but also producers of culture. Ethnicity is seen not merely as one of several socially constructed identities, but also as an essentially and naturally given identity (Steiner-Khamsi and Spreen, 1996). Together these form the multicultural and multiple 'hybrid' identity that each person has and that is constantly being constructed in interaction with his or her social environment (Hall, 1994; Bhabha, 1996; Hall and Du Gay, 1996). Stuart Hall (1994) uses the concept of a:

> ... post-modern subject, which is conceived without an assured, essential or lasting identity. Identity becomes a 'moving celebration'. It is continuously being built and changed in relation to the different forms in which we are represented or named in the cultural systems which surround us (Hall, 1994: 182f).

The criticism of the culturalising approach applies also to some anti-racist approaches which tend to reduce the multiple self-representations and social identities of individuals to manifestations of imposed collective binary identities like 'black'/'white', racist/anti-racist and perpetrator/ victim (Steiner-Khamsi and Spreen, 1996). Appiah (1995) rejects the 'prison' of this group identity when he refers to the situation in Québec where some inhabitants demand that 'ethnic' Francophones educate their children in French and says:

> I believe ... that in a certain sense the same boundaries are crossed when somebody demands that I organise my life around my 'race' or my sexuality" (Appiah, 1995: 186).

Other risks associated with some of the anti-racist approaches are their moralising character ('the good anti-racists against the bad racists') and the presupposition that racism is the one and only all-embracing explanation for the exclusion of ethnic minorities in interpersonal interactions and in society (Van Dijk, 1987, 1993). Nowadays, the multiple forms of discrimination and privileges are much more important. The attention should be focused on situations, connections and relations in which discrimination and privileges arise and accumulate. There is a need for models that allow for multiple rather than merely binary constructs in order to locate positions in social interactions adequately: for example, a Moroccan person, young, female, well-educated, settled and with high socio-economic status versus a Surinamese-Hindustani person who is elderly, male, less well educated, newly arrived and of low socio-economic status (Penninx, 1988; Bader and Benschop, 1988; Van den Berg, 1992; Steiner-Khamsi and Spreen, 1996).

In my training and consultancy practice I noticed that both a culturalising approach and an anti-racist approach as described above did not support social workers and managers in their daily interactions with people from different ethnic backgrounds. The culturalising and anti-racist approaches lead to generalisations and stereotyping ('All Indos are like that'); to 'exoticising' and the avoidance of interaction ('Communication with an allochthon is too different, too difficult'); passive tolerance ('I have my culture. You have your culture and I respect and tolerate it. Full stop.'); the misuse of culture as an excuse or legitimation ('We are now in the Netherlands and we do it this way'), or on the other hand, ('It is part of my culture that my daughter is not allowed to go to school'); and paralysis ('I am so afraid to make mistakes and to be accused of discrimination or worse, of racism').

An Inclusive Model of Management of Diversity

Because of the preceding risks associated with culturalist and some anti-racist approaches, I developed an *inclusive* model of intercultural communication and of management of diversity. To start with management of diversity: I define management of diversity as a *dynamic* and *continuing* comprehensive managerial process of *quality-care* to develop an organisation whose workforce and clientele are an adequate reflection of the composition of the prevailing society and which does justice to the diversity of norms, values, thinking and behaviour patterns of their employees and clients. The results of management of diversity are a qualitative and quantitative improvement of the product and of the service, and an increased efficiency in adapting to the changes in society (WVC, 1991; Roosevelt Thomas, 1991; Cox, 1993; Human, 1996).

The definition of diversity is not confined to ethnic diversity. Managing diversity focuses on the cultural diversity of all employees and clients and relates to e.g. ethnicity, 'colour', gender, sexual preference, religion and education.

Within an organisation, management of diversity affects all levels (individual, interpersonal and organisational) and all aspects such as the structure and the culture of the organisation. Shadid (1998: 274) mentions three measures that are important to remove obstacles for allochthones and to manage adequately the ethnic diversity of personnel:

1. Enhancement of the recruitment, selection, introduction, participation (in internal communication and decision making) and the career development of the (allochthonous) target groups within the organisation.

2.   Recognition of the ethnic diversity among staff members on the individual level and the level of groups (such as facilities and attention to religious celebrations).

3.   Enhancement of mutual acceptance and intergroup relations on the workfloor (e.g., attention to image building and building of cultural blocks).

Regarding the multi-ethnic clientele it is important:

*   To reach the target groups (e.g. through outreach social work).

*   To enlarge the accessibility of the agency of social work for the target groups concerned. This accessibility relies on the name and image of the agency and on the quality of its services (Hoffman and Hoogsteder 1997).

The guiding principle of my approach to the management of diversity is *Inclusive Thinking and Acting* (Boerwinkel, 1966) based on the principles of *Recognised Equality* and *Recognised Diversity*. The principles of Recognised Equality and Recognised Diversity are inseparably linked: they presuppose and correct each other and they are a condition for each other. The overall aim of *Inclusive Thinking and Acting* is *Quality*, because that is what it is finally all about: the quality of social work, the quality of interpersonal communication and the quality of management.

Inclusive Thinking and Acting, as a result of the linking of the principles of Recognised Equality and Recognised Diversity, may also contribute to finding a way out of the dilemma between, on the one hand, (extreme) universalism, absolutism or monism (e.g. 'The Western, white, Christian, male, rational culture as the norm for all other cultures' or the statement 'Treat everybody the same as a human being') and, on the other hand, (extreme) culture-relativism and particularism ('Communication with people from different ethnic backgrounds is impossible and would end up in ethnocentrism because every local culture is uniquely different and has its own value'). I will explain this in describing the two principles of Recognised Equality and Recognised Diversity.

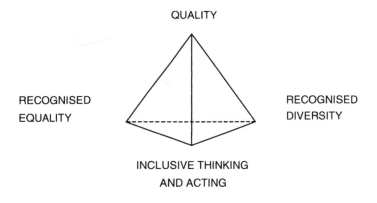

Figure 4.1. Inclusive Thinking and Acting.

The Principle of Recognised Equality

The principle of Recognised Equality refers to the Recognition of *Commonalities*. It refers to what persons within a certain context have in common, such as fundamentally: being human; or within the context of a nation state: having the same citizenship; or more specifically within a social work agency: being social workers, being colleagues or being clients. In that sense all persons within these categories are equal to each other. Within social work organisations the principle of Recognised Equality means that all employees and all clients have the same value irrespective of their ethnicity, gender, sexual preference, ability, social-economic position, religion etc. There is no positive or negative discrimination of persons because of these characteristics. Grounded on Recognised Equality each employee, colleague and client is first and foremost an employee, a colleague or client and *not*, for instance, an allochthon, a Somali, a 'black' person or a person of 'colour'. Social workers and managers sometimes regard clients, colleagues or employees in the first place as an allochthon or as a member of a certain ethnic group. In addition to this, they associate them with less capability or with being problematic. Within an organisation the starting point should be that each person is a worker or a colleague who in principle is motivated, qualified and competent to contribute to the aims of the organisation. Employees and clients, too, sometimes tend to present themselves or to feel addressed in the first place as a member of an ethnic group or as an allochthon and not as an employee, a colleague or a client. This can work out as an obstruction in communication, for instance when criticism is immediately related to one's being allochthon or one's ethnicity, and the criticism is interpreted as discrimination or racism.

In regard to clients, the principle of Recognised Equality means that all clients (irrespective of ethnicity etc.) are entitled to high quality social work. On the other hand, 'in the end', after inclusive thinking and acting (which I will discuss later), social workers may have the same expectations of all clients (irrespective of ethnicity etc.) concerning, for example, following rules, procedures and contracts. One consequence of this is, for example, that specific quality requirements, taking into account inclusive thinking and acting, are maintained and are not reduced on behalf of, for example, allochthones. The latter is a kind of discrimination, though it is sometimes termed 'positive' discrimination (Roosevelt Thomas, 1991).

On the one hand, the principle of Recognised Equality fits the universalistic principle that people share many things in common. On the other hand, Recognised Equality is not the same as the seemingly sincere 'colour-blind' universalistic approach of treating everyone equally, making no distinctions or treating everyone the same because 'we all are human beings'. Treating people equally would impair human dignity. The condition for the existence of human dignity is that every human being is unique, and, therefore, different. That is why the second principle – Recognised Diversity – is so important and is inseparably linked to the principle of Recognised Equality.

The Principle of Recognised Diversity

The principle of Recognised Diversity means recognising *differences*. It applies to the recognition of (cultural) group and individual differences: each employee, each colleague and each client is different and there are differences between groups of employees, colleagues and clients. These differences are *real* differences. As Bhabha (1990: 209) says: 'The difference of cultures cannot be something that can be accommodated within a universalist framework'. We see these attempts at accommodation in culturalist approaches that reduce the allochthonous communities to 'distinct cultures' and abstract from that the cultural competence required of social workers bolting it onto 'professional' values and practices. Not surprisingly, allochthones revolt against this professional and scientific colonisation of their cultures in the name of 'cultural and ethnic sensitivity' (Husband, 1991: 65).

The principle of Recognised Diversity means that an organisation looks for possibilities to meet the individual and group differences among and between its employees and clients. For instance, 'ethnically sensitive social work' will require an awareness of, and responsiveness to, the implications of cultural practices and values that are relevant in interacting with specific client groups (Husband, 1991).

The principle of Recognised Diversity meets the intentions of (cultural) relativism and particularism, i.e., the recognition of differences. But this recognition should *not* imply that, for instance, in social work allochthonous social workers are hired especially and only for allochthonous clients or 'far better' a Moroccan social worker for Moroccan clients, a 'black' social worker for 'black' clients and so on. It also happens in the Netherlands that one teaches special 'intercultural' methods of social work for work with allochthonous clients. It is clear that this would lead to the same risks as mentioned in connection with the culturalist and some anti-racist approaches, because it reduces persons to their 'colour' or ethnic-background.

Inclusive Thinking and Acting tries to avoid these risks and goes beyond universalism and particularism by bringing together in practice the principles of Recognised Equality and Recognised Diversity. See schematic rendition below.

RECOGNISED EQUALITY	RECOGNISED DIVERSITY	
CONTEXT-DEPENDENT COMMONALITIES DIFFERENCES	GROUPS/CATEGORIES DIFFERENCES/ COMMONALITIES	DIFFERENCES
EMPLOYEE	FUNCTION MIGRANT	UNIQUE PERSONS
COLLEAGUE	ETHNICITY SEX/GENDER	
SOCIAL WORKER	SOCIAL ECONOMIC STATUS RELIGION	
CLIENT	COLOUR AGE	
MANAGER	SEXUAL PREFERENCE ABILITY	

Figure 4.2. The principles of Recognised Equality and Recognised Diversity.

Apart from *cultural* differences and differences in needs and interests between individuals and groups, there are of course also *structural* differences in power (positions) such as between manager and social worker and between social worker and client. This power dimension is challenged on the management level by Inclusive Thinking and Acting (see next section) and on the interpersonal communication level by the TOPOI-model (described below).

Inclusive Thinking and Acting

Inclusive Thinking and Acting means to take account of autochthones and allochthones in one integrated perspective. It means thinking and acting in terms of 'we', of 'our colleagues' and of 'our clients' and not exclusively in terms of 'us' (the autochthones) and 'them' (the allochthones) or vice versa. Inclusive Thinking and Acting means that within the interpersonal interaction with employees, clients and colleagues, and within the management of the organisation, (cultural) commonalities and differences are recognised and acknowledged.

Inclusive Thinking and Acting prevents a kind of liberal management of diversity that in fact is, in the words of Lorenz (1997: 3) '... a strategy of corresponding containment of cultural diversity within conditions tightly prescribed by those holding the power to define'. Bhabha, to whom Lorenz refers, explains that when this happens a transparent norm is constituted, a norm given by the host society or dominant culture, which says that 'these other cultures are fine, but we must be able to locate them within our own grid' (Bhabha, 1990: 208). Inclusive Thinking and Acting prevents this and instead creates *hybridity*, a notion introduced by Bhabba (1990). In cultural encounters hybridity is the moment in which the authority claimed by any culture insisting on its purity, is subverted (Lorenz, 1997). In a cultural encounter of a social work organisation providing services for 'others' (the allochthones), the authority claimed by the existing organisational culture insisting on its purity can be challenged by Inclusive Thinking and Acting. This approach diverts attention from the 'other' (from the allochthones) to the hybridity, the heterogeneity of the organisation's culture itself. Inclusive Thinking and Acting achieves hybridity by opening up a new space, a 'third space' in Bhabha's terms (1990). This third space is not only opened up between the organisation's culture and the 'other' cultures, but also *within both of them*. To make this process of Inclusive Thinking and Acting imaginable:

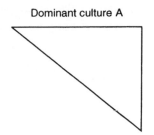

Figure 4.3. Intercultural encounters.

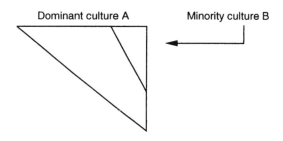

Figure 4.4. Intercultural encounters: Exclusive thinking and acting. A 'Liberal' relativist management of diversity.

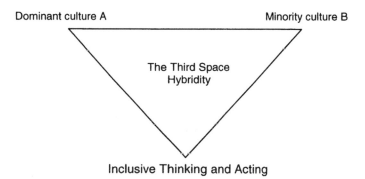

Figure 4.5. Intercultural encounters: Inclusive Thinking and Acting based on the principles of Recognised Equality and Recognised Diversity.

In this third space a process of *'differing'* takes place (Lorenz, 1997: 4). The third space creates a culture as a seat of communication, different-iation, negotiation and argumentation as the only pathway to, in this context, a real pluralistitic social work organisation.

In practice, Inclusive Thinking and Acting and the notion of hybridity mean investigating, testing and, if necessary, adjusting the aims, (power) structures, cultures and methods of the organisation as regards their effectiveness and efficiency for *all* the relevant groups of employees and clients that can be distinguished. It is obvious that this testing and adjusting contributes to the improvement of the quality of an organisation (see Figure 4.1).

Some criteria from an 'ethnic' angle, which an organisation can use for this evaluative research, are:

1. Is the willingness to take allochthonous employees on board within the organisation in proportion to the percentage of the allochthonous popu-lation in the region?
2. How is the representation of allochthones organised within the different functions and on the different levels of the organisation?
3. What are the career opportunities of allochthonous employees?
4. Which allochthonous groups does the organisation reach and how many?
5. With what kind of knowledge, attitudes and skills do employees and the managers interact with and serve clients and colleagues from a different ethnic background?
6. Can allochthonous employees and clients feel committed to the organisation in relation to, for instance, the ethnic composition of the personnel and the teams; the culture of the organisation; the (formal) employees' participation council; the decoration of the building and the rooms (posters, notice-boards); staff activities like anniversaries, parties?
7. How accessible are sources of communication and information for allochthonous employees and clients?

Inclusive Thinking and Acting means further that there is no separate treatment of allochthones solely on the basis of their being allochthonous. Needs and interests of a number of individual employees or clients may necessitate extra facilities and arrangements. Yet, in principle, they have to be open to *all* employees and clients with that need or that interest. Extra facilities and arrangements have to be an integral part of the general system of facilities and interests. In such a way exceptions are presented as general arrangements. To give an example: some (allochthonous) employees like to have a six weeks' holiday because they want to visit their family in their country of origin. If an organisation has the possibility to accede to this request, say, once in two years, then this becomes a general facility for all employees. In practice, it will turn out that especially allochthon employees will make use of this possibility and perhaps some autochthones. In this way, individual needs and interests can work as an eye-opener for the needs and interests of other employees or clients.

It is very important that the term under which 'special' arrangements are being referred to reflects the need or the interest for which they are intended. For instance, interpreters may be made available for clients who have not mastered the Dutch language well enough or a praying room made available for employees who feel the need to pray during the day or to sit alone in silence for a while. The interpreters and the praying room are not simply there 'for the allochthones'. It still happens so often in the Netherlands that public authorities and social workers simply speak of 'allochthones projects', 'activities for allochthones' or 'migrants projects'.

Consequently, if we start from Inclusive Thinking, from the commonality people share (for example *'clients'* or *'employees'*) and then mention the relevant need or interest (*'clients or employees... who have not mastered the Dutch language well enough... or... who like to pray or to sit alone in silence'*), we make the significance of such an arrangement or service clear also to an outsider. This way of naming things ensures that allochthones are not seen as extraordinarily different, that their needs and interests are not seen as exotic or that not all allochthones are regarded as problematic. Furthermore, exclusive thinking is avoided, thinking in the categories of 'us' and 'them' which can additionally convey to autochthones the feeling that all kinds of services and facilities are only obtainable on the grounds of being allochthonous. An inclusive approach does not only reach, in this case, the allochthones who expressed the need or the interest, but also the autochthones who might have the same needs and interests.

The preceding inclusive approach does not exclude specific arrangements for certain target groups. In the case of a prayer room, it is possible for Islamic employees to have their own separate room for praying, but other employees should also be offered the same possibility for expressing their religious faith. What I would like to achieve is the enhancement of the process of 'differing' in the third space and the prevention of exclusive thinking and acting, which excludes people and amplifies segregation along ethnic lines, as is already evident in Dutch society.

An Inclusive Model of Intercultural Communication

Inclusive Thinking and Acting by linking the principles of Recognised Equality and Recognised Diversity is also applicable to my approach of intercultural communication. To support the communication in the third (hybrid) space and to avoid the pitfalls of the culturalist and some anti-racist approaches, I developed the TOPOI-model, an analysis and intervention model for (interethnic) communication. This inclusive model is philosophically grounded in pluralism (Procee, 1991) and theoretically in general systems theory (Watzlawick, Beavin and Jackson, 1967).

A Pluralist Approach to Intercultural Communication

The Dutch philosopher Procee (1991) developed pluralism as his own mix of relativism (particularism) and (communicative) universalism. The essence of his universalism is the idea of the 'unity' in or behind the diversity of empirical phenomena. Universalism assumes a universal and general system of values and norms that applies to everybody.

Relativism is the philosophical conception of 'diversity': the recognition of the specificity of a person, a group or tradition. There are no absolute standards, only local standards are valid. Reality is not uniform but 'pluriform': it consists of different local realities, each with its own interpretations of reality. These local realities are unique phenomena with a value of their own that cannot be reduced to a common foundation. Communication between persons from these different local realities is hardly possible. Mutual tolerance should be a trait of these interactions. Universalism runs up against boundaries when universalism becomes absolutism and monism and overrules local realities. In this way universalism becomes ethnocentric and racist (e.g., when the Western, 'white' rational culture is taken as the standard for the 'other' 'underdeveloped' cultures). Relativism in its turn runs up against boundaries when it leads to passive tolerance and indifference to different cultures (Procee, 1991).

Pluralism tries to go beyond these boundaries of universalism and relativism. It adopts elements from the relativist position that language, knowledge, morals and science are historical products and that people are rooted in cultural traditions; and from (communicative) universalism, that local realities and their cultural products are not totally closed off from each other. Interactions are possible and something new can arise.

Starting from the keywords of communicative universalism and relativism, respectively interactive 'unity' and 'diversity', Procee (1991) develops the key term of pluralism: 'interactive diversity' or 'heterogeneous interaction'.

Pluralist efforts at interaction are important in order to transcend one's own pre-existing frameworks. From interaction something 'better' may result in the sense of more extensive, more adequate schemes of interpretation and a widening of horizons of the participants involved. Pluralist interactions could prevent passive tolerance and the other pitfalls of a culturalist and some anti-racist approaches. Pluralism enhances 'heterogeneous interaction' (Procee, 1991) and challenges us to open up the dialogue and to take mutual responsibility by questioning each other's views and positions (Wildemeersch, 1992).

A Systems-Theoretical Approach to Intercultural Communication

Building on pluralism and in looking for an alternative for a culturalist and anti-racist approach, I developed a *systems-theoretical communication* approach to intercultural communication. My starting point was the research of De Interakie Akademie of Antwerp in Belgium, whose work proceeds pragmatically from general systems theory as developed by Watzlawick (Watzlawick et al., 1967; Baert, 1987, 1991, 1993; Mattheeuws, 1983, 1986, 1988, 1990; Peeters, 1989; Steens, 1993).

Systems theory assumes that a person's communication can only be understood through an understanding of his or her network of social systems: 'colour', ethnicity, gender, age, family, education, religion, profession, region, social economic status etc. Each of these social systems is characterised by a certain culture from which a person can derive a collective or social identity allied to a feeling of belonging. During his life each individual passes through and stays in different social systems. In communicating within these social systems, a person develops a constantly changing multiple, multicultural identity.

> Every individual is composed of a unique combination of different cultural orientations and influences, and every person belongs to many different cultural groups. It is important that we recognize the influences of many cultures on our lives. Based on our heritage and life experiences we each develop our own idiosyncratic multicultural identity' (Kreps and Kunimoto, 1994: 3).

The fact that each person has a multicultural identity makes all inter-personal communication intercultural. So why still the distinction between 'common' communication and intercultural communication?

Another point is that making intercultural communication thematic only makes sense if it is treated as a subdivision of interpersonal com-munication (Gudykunst and Kim, 1984; Bolten, 1995). This also because of the fact that actual communication does not take place between cultures or nations but always in unique interpersonal interactions. In this respect the concept 'intercultural' cannot strictly be connected with the concept communication.

> Cultures are a different level of logical analysis from the individual members of cultures. Cultures do not talk to each other; individuals do. In that sense, all communication is interpersonal communication and can never be intercultural communication. 'Chinese culture' cannot talk to 'Japanese culture' except through the discourse of individual Chinese and individual Japanese people (Scollon and Scollon, 1995: 125).

Because of this uniquely personal character of communication, the multiple multicultural identity of each person, and because of the hetero-geneous character of each social system (also of the systems based on nationality, ethnicity and language), it makes no point to differentiate inter-cultural communication from intracultural 'general' communication. From such a point of view, the addition 'intercultural' is redundant because it adds nothing new to the concept of communication as such. It only repeats what is inherent in each act of communication: there is always the question of different cultural backgrounds.

The question now arises: why stick to the concept of *intercultural* communication? I think it makes sense to keep on talking about intercultural communication if the concept of intercultural communication is not con-fined to communication between people from a different ethnic, national or language background.

Indeed, the cultural background of the interlocutors affects the progress of their communication. But this cultural background can be related to national cultures, ethnic cultures, youth cultures, organisation cultures, gen-der cultures (Tannen, 1986) and so on. The influence of these cultures can be the subject of scientific study or of professional attention during a conversation. It is this communicative approach that I will define as inter-cultural communication. The addition 'intercultural' signals an explicit focus on the cultural aspects that affect the mutual communication between interlocutors. Intercultural communication is *interpersonal communication in which explicit attention is given to the cultural dimensions that affect the communication.* As mentioned before these cultural dimensions can be related to many forms of culture. Interethnic communication, the communication between men and women, the communication between youth from different youth cultures, the communication between people coming from different organisational or departmental cultures are all branches of the 'stem' of intercultural communication.

With this systems-theoretical approach, I hope to achieve a broadening of the horizon in the conversation between people from different ethnic backgrounds. People are not immediately ready to give an ethnic cultural explanation for the behaviour of the other: she or he acts like this because of her or his ethnic background. Nor does the other explain his or her behaviour by saying: 'That is my culture'.

The TOPOI-Model

The TOPOI-model is a pluralist systems-theoretical model in which cultural differences are made operational in five fundamental places or areas of communication where failures of communication may occur: *T*ongue (=language), *O*rder, *P*ersons, *O*rganisation and *I*ntentions. Differences and misunderstandings in communication can be traced back to these five places. The model also offers different strategies for intervention. As was said before, the model is based on the work of De Interaktie Akademie of Antwerpen Belgium where a multi-disciplinary team elaborates pragmatically the axioms of influence (Watzlawick et al., 1967). De Interaktie Akademie has elaborated four of the five axioms of Watzlawick. His fifth axiom of symmetry and complementarity in the definition of relations emerged from later research to be an oversimplification of the second axiom. It does not add anything to the other four axioms (Mattheeuws, 1986). The four axioms are:

1. People influence each other with and especially without words.
2. What I think is true is not necessarily true for another person.
3. Communication is a process of influence that has two levels: that of content and that of relationship.
4. It is not possible to not communicate: all behaviour is communication.

These four axioms are the starting points of the TOPOI-model. Because of my experiences in practice, I added a fifth axiom:

5. Communication is influenced by the organisational context.

I am conscious that this fifth axiom is of a different category from the
original four axioms of the Interaktie Akademie. But the organisational
context is an important separate dimension because of its effects on professional communication with clients.

Based on these five axioms, I developed the five areas of the TOPOI-
model: Tongue (the language of communication and the first axiom), Order
(the second axiom), Persons (the third axiom), Organisation (the added fifth
axiom) and Intentions (the fourth axiom). I chose this sequence because in
Greek TOPOI means 'places': plural of 'place' (as for instance in 'topo-
graphy'). Analogous to this Tongue, Order, Persons, Organisation and
Intentions are the 'places' in communication where we could stop during or
after a conversation in order to trace possible differences and misunderstandings. In this way every 'place' offers a possibility to prevent or detect
misunderstandings.

In the practice of communication, the places Tongue, Order, Persons,
Organisation and Intentions are very tightly interwoven. The places are only
artificially distinguished to make them very clearly identifiable. In actual
communication we have to deal with all these places all at the same time.

The advantage of the TOPOI-model over a culturalist and some anti-
racist approaches is the broad view it offers of communication with people
from a different ethnic background. The TOPOI-model takes account of a
number of questions with which hypotheses can be formed as to where the
communication process possibly goes wrong or has reached a deadlock. The
more hypotheses you can form the more possibilities you have to keep the
communication open or to open it up again. The TOPOI-model does not give
fixed information on ethnic-cultural background beforehand, neither does it
focus on the ethnicity or 'colour' of a person. This means that working with
the TOPOI-model enhances the interaction process in a pluralist direction:
not to be afraid to make mistakes, but to be open and reflective and to work
with the effects of communication. The TOPOI-model also gives space to
the perspective, the view and the self-representation of allochthones themselves (Shadid, 1998; Chen and Starosta, 1996). In other words: the other is
invited to define her identity herself (the area Persons) and to share her
interpretation of the reality, or more concretely, of the situation that matters
(the area Order). Furthermore, the TOPOI-model takes societal power
relations into account, for example by questioning whose language the interlocutors are speaking (the area Tongue); the position of the interlocutors; the

dominant rules, procedures and laws (the area Organisation); and by questioning (in all areas of TOPOI) the influence of the prevailing social representations in the environment on the communication (Moscovici, 1981; Hinnenkamp, 1991).

My approach to intercultural communication entails that in every conversation – also with somebody with a different ethnic background – you can remain yourself, not in the sense of sticking to your values, norms and habits but in the sense of keeping the spontaneity. The deciding factor of your communication is your attitude towards the other. If the attitude is one of effort, concern and sincerity, then you can trust your integrity when things turn out differently from what you wanted. At the same time, it is essential to work with the effects of the communication, because it is always the other who determines the effect of your communication. It is important to be aware and recognise the effect of your communication on the other and to take that as the starting point for the next communication. From this point of view you can – and often this is inevitable – make 'mistakes' in the communication. Interpersonal communication is profoundly influenced by the broad societal context with its prevailing images, ideas and ongoing discourse (the social representations). That is why people are not that free in giving meaning to what they say to and understand of each other. What people say to and understand of each other is not so much a question of wanting to, but rather of *being able to* (Cronen, 1987). This makes communication such a complex process and makes differences and misunderstanding inevitable in any communication. If you realise this complexity of communication (also with someone from a different ethnic background), you can stay calm when the communication reaches a deadlock and try to find out the differences and misunderstandings that disturb the communication. The TOPOI-model can help to detect the disturbing differences and misunderstandings in the communication; it also suggests interventions that can open up the communication process again. I finish with schematic overviews of the TOPOI-model with regard to analysis and to interventions.

Schematic Overviews of the TOPOI-Model

Places in the communication where differences and misunderstandings may occur:

TONGUE (Language)

Meanings : What do the words and the non-verbal language used mean?

ORDER

Views: What is each person's view?

PERSONS

Identities: Who is each person (for him-/herself and for the other person)?

ORGANISATION

Organisation: What is the influence of 'the organisation'?

INTENTIONS

Doing one's best: For what purpose does each person do his or her best?

The TOPOI-model: Analysis of the questions to be detected in interpersonal conversations, of cultural differences, 'discrimination' and 'racism'.

'Places'	Questions
TONGUE	*What do the words and the non-verbal language used mean?*
Meanings	* Which language does each person speak?
	* What does each person say?
	* What does the non-verbal language of each person mean?
	* What are the interpretations of each other's verbal and non-verbal language?
	* What is the influence of the environment on what each person says, does and understands?
ORDER	*What is each person's perspective?*
Views	* What is each view or logic?
	* What is each angle, interest, role, or loyality?
	* What is each frame of reference (opinions, values and norms)?
	* What does everyone have in common?
	* What are the differences?
	* What is the influence of the environment on

everyone's view?

PERSONS
Identities

Who is everyone?
* How does everyone see her-/ himself?
* How does everyone see the other person?
* How is the mutual relationship?
* What is the influence of the environment on how everyone sees the other person?

ORGANISATION
The organisation

What is the influence of the 'organisation'?
* What is the influence of 'one's own organisation' (position of power, function, available time, agenda, aims, rules, agreements, procedures)?
* What is the influence of 'the organisation' of the other person(s) position of power, time-orientation, familiarity with the organisation, procedures, rules...?
* What is the influence of 'the organisation' on the 'wider' environment (positions of power, procedures, available services, manners, organisational culture, facilities, regulations, legislation)?

INTENTIONS
Doing one's best

To what end does each person do her or his best?
* For what purpose and how does each person do her/his best?
* Does everyone notice how the other person is doing her/his best?
* What is 'doing one's best' for the environment?
* How does each person let the other know that he/she perceives that the other person is doing her/his best?
* Does everybody feel recognised in how she/he is doing her/his best?
* Does each person perceive the distinction between intentions and effects of how she/he is doing her/his best?

The TOPOI-model: Interventions to open up for discussion in interpersonal conversations issues of cultural differences, 'discrimination' and 'racism'.

'Places'	Questions
TONGUE *Meanings*	*What do the words and the non-verbal language mean?*
	* Perceive the words and the non-verbal language with several meanings.
	* Investigate the meanings. Explain the meanings.
	* Give feedback. Ask for feedback.
	* Investigate the influence of the environment on the meanings.
ORDER *Views*	*What is each view?*
	* Ask/invite the other to tell her/his view.
	* Listen actively.
	* Empathy: identify with the view and experience.
	* Tell or clarify your own view.
	* Mention the communality and put it foremost.
	* Clarify the differences and leave them standing for what they are.
	* Investigate the influence of the environment on each person's view.
PERSONS *Identities*	*Who is everyone?*
	* Investigate or ask in which role ('as who') the other speaks.
	* Listen actively.
	* Empathy: identify with the view and experience.
	* Reflect and/or clarify which role ('as who') you are speaking.
	* Investigate the environment's influence on how everyone perceives her-/himself and the other person.
ORGANISATION *The organisation*	*What is the influence of the 'organisation'?*
	Interpersonal level:
	* Clarify, explain the own 'organisation'.
	* Reorganise (change) the own 'organisation'.
	* Inquire about the other person's 'organisation'.

* Investigate the influence of 'the organisation' on the environment.
* Management level.
* Management of Diversity.

INTENTIONS
Doing one's best

For what aim does each person do her or his best?
* Investigate for what purpose the other person is doing his/her best.
* Empathy: identify and feel your way (= recognise) into for what purpose the other person is doing her/his best for.
* Show, e.g. tell, (= recognise) that you perceive for what purpose the other person is doing her/his best.
* Investigate what the other person experiences as recognition.
* Investigate where and by whom the other person feels recognised.
* Investigate the influence of the environment on what each other perceives as 'doing one's best'.
* Clarify for what purpose you are doing your best.
* Take a look (and make the other person look) at the effects of how each is doing her/his best.

Summary

This contribution deals with the question how social workers and their managers can take on board the provision of 'ethnically sensitive' services demanded by people from a range of minority ethnic groups. Culturalist and some anti-racist responses to this question risk leading to generalisations and the stereotyping of members of ethnic groups, to passive tolerance, to the abuse of culture or ethnicity as an excuse or legitimation for unacceptable practices, and to paralysis in communication and management. An alternative answer was presented at two levels of social work: an inclusive approach of intercultural communication and of the management of diversity. Based on the principles of Recognised Equality and Recognised Diversity, Inclusive Thinking and Acting opens up the possibility to also take on board ethnic diversity (inclusive that of 'autochthones'). The following are some criteria from an 'ethnic' angle which an organisation can use for inclusive thinking and acting:

1. The willingness to employ a proportional number of allochthonous employees within the organisation.
2. The representation of allochthones within the different functions and on the different levels of the organisation.
3. The career prospects of allochthonous employees.
4. Which allochthonous groups the organisation reaches and how many.
5. The knowledge, attitude and skills of employees and managers to interact with and serve clients and colleagues from different ethnic backgrounds.
6. The possibilities for allochthonous employees and clients to feel committed to the organisation in relation to, amongst other aspects, the ethnic composition of the personnel and the teams; the culture of the organisation; the (formal) employees' participation council; the decoration of the building and the rooms (posters, notice-boards), activities for staff (anniversaries, parties).
7. The accessibility of the supply of communication and information for the allochthonous employees and clients.

Concerning intercultural communication *a pluralistic systems-theoretical* approach was introduced. *Pluralism* resists the closed forms of universalism: monism and absolutism. For pluralism reality is not closed. All interpretations of reality are in principle limited and only partially rational. It is impossible to reach definitive conclusions. Pluralism also opposes 'extreme' relativism which starts from the idea of closed separate cultures. Interaction between people from different cultures is possible and even necessary. Neither culture nor the absolutist and local norms are central for pluralism, but the human being who operates in a multiplicity of relations (social systems). People are historically determined and are socialised beings. As a result, they have a relative, limited 'view' of reality. The key concept of pluralism is 'interactive diversity' which builds on the code words of communicative universalism (interactive unity) and relativism (diversity) respectively. Trying to reach interaction is important for pluralism in order to transcend existing frameworks. From interaction something 'better' has to originate in terms of 'wider', 'more adequate' interpretative schemes and an extension of the horizon of the participants involved.

A concept of intercultural communication derived from systems theory has as its starting point the principle that each person ('allochtones' and 'autochthones') forms part of a variety of social connections (systems) that are all characterised by a certain culture. While interacting with the many social systems in which they find themselves or used to find themselves, people develop a plural, multicultural identity that embraces various social identities. In this respect ethnic identity and 'colour' are 'just' two of the many possible social identities of a person. Depending on their biography and social environment, people will put one or more social identities to the fore. The plural and multicultural character of everyone's identity causes each interpersonal communication, with or without ethnic-cultural differences, to be intercultural in character.

Apart from this widening of the culturalising and anti-racist angle, on the basis of systems theory, system thinking offers a circular idea of communication: communication as a process of continuous mutual influencing, both between the people involved and between those people and the wider social environment. Social representations and social perspectives, being the concept of the above-mentioned influence of the social environment, connect the micro-event of interpersonal communication with the macro-event of society.

Starting from systems theory and from a dynamic and heterogeneous concept of culture, I have developed a new definition of intercultural communication. So far, through a largely culturalising approach, intercultural communication has only been understood to mean communication between people of a different ethnic, national or linguistic background. However, looking at this on the basis of systems theory, as I have shown above, all communication (also amongst members of the same ethnic group) is by definition intercultural. From such a perspective, the addition of intercultural is superfluous because it adds nothing new to the idea of 'communication'. It simply repeats what is common to all communication: that in communication there is always a question of different cultural backgrounds. The cultural background of the people communicating always influences the course of their communication. This cultural background can be related to many cultures such as national cultures, ethnic cultures, youth cultures, organisational cultures and gender-specific cultures. The influence of these cultures on communication can be an object of scientific research and a point of attention during a conversation. In my opinion, the question of intercultural communication arises in everyday (often professional) communication when one or more of the persons communicating pay explicit attention to the cultural factors (from many dimensions) that influence their communication. Intercultural communication as a scientific field of study investigates the influence of cultural factors on communication. It is this *approach* to communication that I want to call intercultural communication. The addition 'intercultural' means the explicit attention (academic and professional) paid to the cultural aspects that influence mutual communication between people communicating. Thus, I reach the following definition of intercultural communication: intercultural communication is *communication in which explicit attention is paid to the cultural dimensions that influence communication.*

For the practice of social work the TOPOI-model is an instrument of analysis and intervention to discover and tackle differences and misunderstandings in communication. The TOPOI-model is based on the axioms of influencing which were first proposed by Watzlawick et al. (1974), and four of which have been worked out by the Interaktie Akademie (Mattheeuws, 1986). The five areas of TOPOI are in fact communicative specifications of 'culture' and 'discrimination'. In other words, in interpersonal communication 'culture', 'cultural differences', 'discrimination' and 'racism' can be observed, worked at or made a subject of discussion by looking at the way in which they manifest themselves in the areas of Tongue (Language), Ordering, Persons, Organisation and Intentions of communication.

References

Appiah, K.A. (1995), 'Identiteit, authenticiteit, overleving, multiculturele samenlevingen en sociale reproduktie', in C. Taylor (ed.), *Multiculturalisme*. Meppel, Boom, pp. 172–189.
Bader, V.M. and Benschop A. (1988), *Sociale Ongelijkheid en Collectief Handelen, Deel I, Sociale Ongelijkheden*. Groningen, Wolters Noordhoff.
Baert, D. (1987), 'De persoon in een systeemtheoretisch ontwerp', in A. Mattheeuws and D. Baert (eds.), *Psychotherapie, Psychologische Theorieën, Systeemtheorie*. Antwerpen, V.St.P.
Baert, D. (1991), 'Identiteit en identiteitsontwikkeling, een poging tot systeemtheoretische benadering. I, theoretisch zoekwerk', *Systeemtheoretisch Bulletin,* vol. IX (2), pp. 64–91.
Baert, D. (1993), 'Identiteit en identiteitsontwikkeling, een poging tot systeemtheoretische benadering. II, de ontwikkeling van identiteit', *Systeemtheoretisch Bulletin,* vol. XI (4), pp. 277–300.
Bhabha, H.K. (1990), 'The third space', in J. Rutherford (ed.), *Identity, Community, Culture, Difference*. London, Lawrence and Wishart.
Bhabha, H.K. (1996), 'Culture's In-Between', in S. Hall and P. Du Gay (eds.), *Cultural Identity*. London, Sage, pp. 53–61.
Boerwinkel, F. (1966), *Inclusief Denken. Een Andere Tijd Vraagt een Ander Denken,* Hilversum/Antwerpen, Paul Brand.

Bolten, J. (1995), 'Crossculture, interkulturelles Handeln in der Wirtschaft', in J. Bolten (ed.), *Schriftenreihe Interkulturelle Wirtschaftskommunikation*. Berlin, Verlag Wissenschaft und Praxis, pp. 25–43.

Chen, G-M. and Starosta, W.J. (1996), *Intercultural Communication Competence, A Synthesis. Communication Yearbook*. London, Sage, pp. 353–383.

Cox, T. jr. (1993), *Cultural Diversity in Organizations: Theory, Research and Practice*. San Francisco, Berrett-Koehler Publishers.

Cronen, V. (1987), 'Het individu vanuit systeemtheoretisch perspectief', *Systeemtheoretisch Bulletin*, vol. 3, pp. 167–197.

Glastra, F. (ed.) (1999), *Organisaties en Diversiteit*. Utrecht, Lemma.

Gudykunst, W.B. and Kim, Y.Y. (eds.) (1984), *Methods for Intercultural Communication Research*. Beverly Hills, CA, Sage.

Hall, E.T. (1976), *Beyond Culture*. Garden City, New York, Anchor.

Hall, S. (1994), *Rassismus und Kulturelle Identität*. Hamburg, Argument-Verlag.

Hall, S. and P. Du Gay (eds.) (1996), *Cultural Identity*. London, Sage.

Hinnenkamp, V. (1991), 'Talking a person into interethnic distinction. A discourse-analytic case study', in J. Blommaert and J. Verschueren (eds.), *The Pragmatics of Intercultural and International Communication*. Amsterdam, John Benjamins Publishing Company, pp. 91–111.

Hoffman, E. and Arts, W. (1994), *Interculturele Gespreksvoering*. Houten, Bohn Stafleu Van Loghum.

Hoffman, E. and Hoogsteder, J. (1997), 'Management van interculturele dienstverlening', in J. Hoogsteder and J. Verhoeven (eds.), *Van Allochtonenbeleid Naar een Integrale Aanpak van Kwaliteitsmanagement*. Nijmegen, Instituut voor Inter-Etnisch Management, pp. 36–60.

Hofstede, G. (1984), *Culture's Consequences, International Differences in Work-Related Values*. Beverly Hills CA, Sage.

Human, L. (1996), *Contemporary Conversations*. Senegal, Gorée Institute.

Husband, C. (1991), '"Race", conflictual politics, and anti-racist social work. Lessons from the past for action in the 90s', in Central Council for Education and Training in Social Work, *Setting the Context for Change*. CCETSW, London, pp. 47–71.

Kreps, G.L. and Kunimoto, E.N. (1994), *Effective Communication in Multicultural Health Care Settings*. Thousand Oaks/London/New Delhi, Sage.

Lorenz, W. (1997), 'Hybridity as the basis for the practice of citizenship' (internal paper). Cork, University College.

Mattheeuws, A. (1983), 'Omtrent sociale perspektieven', *Systeemtheoretisch Bulletin*, vol. I (3), pp. 13–25.

Mattheeuws, A. (1986), 'Systeemteoretische vraagtekens bij partnerrelatieterapie', *Systeemteoretisch Bulletin*, vol. IV (3), pp. 140–162.

Mattheeuws, A. (1988), 'Systeembenadering en kommunikatieteorieën', in *Leren en leven met groepen*. Alphen aan den Rijn, Samsom, pp. A1500: 1–33.

Mattheeuws, A. (1990), 'Het spel der vanzelfsprekendheden', *Systeemteoretisch Bulletin*, vol. VIII (4), pp. 255–287.

Moscovici, S. (1981), 'On social representations', in J.P. Forgas, (ed.), *Social Cognition. Perspectives on Everyday Understanding*. London, Academic Press, pp. 181–209.

Peeters, F. (1989), 'Het besef van invloed en zijn varianten', *Systeemtheoretisch Bulletin*, vol. VI–II (1), 2–25, Antwerpen, Interaktie Akademie.

Penninx, R. (1988), *Minderheidsvorming en Emancipatie; Balans van Kennisverwerving ten Aanzien van Immigranten en Woonwagenbewoners 1967–1987.* Alphen aan den Rijn, Samsom.

Procee, H. (1991), *Over de Grenzen van Culturen.* Meppel, Boom.

Roosevelt Thomas, R.R. Jr. (1991), *Beyond Race and Gender.* New York, AMACOM.

Scollon, R. and Scollon, S. (1995), *Intercultural Communication: A Discourse Approach.* Oxford, Blackwell.

Shadid, W.A. (1998), *Grondslagen van Interculturele Communicatie.* Houten/Diegem, Bohn Stafleu Van Loghum.

Steens, R. (1993), *Menselijke Communicatie. Een Zoektocht naar Haar Complexiteit.* Interaktie Akademie, Antwerpen.

Steiner-Khamsi, G. and Spreen, C.A. (1996), 'Oppositional and relational identity, a comparative perspective', in A. Aluffi-Pentini and W. Lorenz (eds.), *Anti-Racist Work with Young People.* Lyme Regis, Russell House.

Tannen, D. (1986), *That's Not What I Meant! How Conversational Style Makes or Breaks Your Relations with Others.* New York, William Morrow.

Trompenaars, F. (1993), *Riding the Waves of Culture.* London, The Economist Books.

Van Boxtel, M. (1999), *Kansen Krijgen, Kansen Pakken.* S'Gravenhage, Ministerie van Binnenlandse Zaken.

Van den Berg, H. (1992), 'Racisme onderzoek en discourse-analyse', *Migrantenstudies,* vol. 8, pp. 38–60. Houten, Bohn Stafleu.

Van Dijk, T.A. (1987), *Communicating Racism: Ethnic Prejudice in Thought and Talk.* Newbury Park, Sage.

Van Dijk, T.A. (1993), *Elite Discourse and Racism.* Newbury Park, Sage.

Watzlawick, P., Beavin, J.H. and Jackson, D.D. (1967), *Pragmatics of Human Communication.* New York, W.W. Norton and Company.

Wildemeersch, D. (1992), 'Vorming in de multiculturele samenleving. Antwoorden op de oproep van de vreemdeling', *Vorming,* vol. 7 (2).

WVC (1991), *Modellen voor Intercultureel Management.* Den Haag, Ministerie van Welzijn en Volksgezondheid.

PART II:

COMMUNITY-ORIENTED
MODELS OF PRACTICE

5 The Social Pedagogical Model in the Multicultural Society of Germany

FRANZ HAMBURGER

Introduction

Migration is a common phenomenon and occurs naturally in history. The resulting social diversity is an everyday consequence that can generally be managed in the routines of everyday life, yet it is repeatedly defined as an intractable issue in political confrontation. The political character of these debates shows that questions of difference and diversity constitute issues of political power.

To examine the consequences of migration from a social pedagogical perspective, we must first establish the degree to which social pedagogy has a responsibility at all in this area and determine its special contribution to the definition of the problem of migration. We will do this first by explaining the concept of social pedagogy with reference to Paul Natorp's (1968) definition of the prerequisites for social pedagogical action. We will then compare this concept with a brief description of professional practice to provide concrete reference points for further debate. Rather than simply affirming such interventions, a social pedagogical perspective retains a critical stance and seeks to elucidate the problematic implications of narrowing social pedagogical practice down to a question of culture alone. Such criticism leads to the development of alternative perspectives on the problem of culture and their constructive use in a pedagogy of recognition.

This supports my hypothesis that although there is not just *one* model of social pedagogy in dealing with the consequences of migration, social pedagogy nevertheless provides a coherent critical perspective on the tasks involved.

Social Pedagogy

Social pedagogy is a field in the educational and social sciences whose subject matter is all 'pedagogical' activities and institutions that shape the relationship between individuals and society. The earlier restriction of the field to 'everything that is education but is neither school nor family' (Bäumer, 1929) has proved in many ways to be too narrow. From this view the modality of educational intervention focuses too narrowly on work with children. Instead the field of social pedagogical interests extends to inventions such as support, counselling, supervision, planned and structured communal living, the provision of information, social resources and material assistance, reflection and work involving formation, planning and publicity.

It has also become problematic to define social pedagogy as belonging institutionally to the field outside the family and the school, as many tasks in, for example, the area of child welfare, involve the family (social pedagogical family assistance). It also has to be recognised that schools themselves can give rise to *social* pedagogical tasks (e.g., in the form of school social work). It has, lastly, proved difficult to allocate social pedagogy to any one particular discipline because institutions for the disabled, adult education and vocational training programmes and recreational and media pedagogy all require and perform social pedagogical tasks.

Social pedagogy has become a social reality in modern society and has expanded enormously; this has produced its own problems for the discipline (Winkler, 1995). How should we conceptualise its specific task and special function and how should we formulate its relationship to society and its different parts? Modern societies attribute to social pedagogy a central regulatory function on account of its very wide mandate for addressing the relationship between individuals and society. It has become necessary to bring social pedagogy's 'production of normalcy' into everyday and very general contexts in these societies in which bonds that had previously been unquestioningly regarded as natural and traditional have 'vaporised'. Both the individualisation and the socialisation of people are products of processes that need to be organised by society. Social pedagogy plays a key role in modern society well beyond that of providing emergency assistance for people in difficult situations and the disciplining of difficult individuals. It provides the prerequisites for life in a society as such by functioning as an instrument of organised socialisation.

Definitions of social pedagogy focus on the relationship between individuals and society. This relationship constitutes a fundamental category in all social sciences. Very different definitions exist to describe this relationship more precisely. If we accept in principle that individuals and society are mutually interconnected and at the same time independent of one another, we can speak of a dialectical relationship. Regardless of whether we think of the individual's basic independence from society as conceptualised in terms of a drive, a basic need or an act of willing, individuals always confront society as subjects. This shapes their individuality in the socialisation process. The dyadic mother-child relationship in early childhood provides a good illustration of this. It can be understood as social interaction according to the model of the 'primary dialectic' (Riegel, 1981). The total unity of mother and child dissolves at the birth of the child. After that they are on the one hand objects for each other in as much as the child identifies with the mother and she in turn regards the child as object of her care. On the other hand they also gradually become subjects for each other because both learn to experience themselves as independent of each other. Given the right conditions they learn to form in one sense a unity and in another to be simultaneously autonomous of each other. Individuals have in a similar way become part of society through socialisation. However, in this very process of socialisation they learn to regard themselves as autonomous individuals. Conflicts in the dynamics of interactions between individuals and society give rise to the questions posed by social pedagogy, for which this discipline then in turn seeks productive solutions. Social pedagogy, therefore, also finds its limits both in the subject's ultimate refusal to be made objectively available and in society's internal logic.

Normative Assumptions of Social Pedagogy

On closer examination the task assigned to social pedagogy proves to be the task undertaken by pedagogy generally. Paul Natorp (1968) develops his definition of social pedagogy by starting with the differentiation of the human will. This will can best be understood as the quintessence of individuality, of that which sets itself in opposition to society. This individual will is, however, by no means void of content but expresses itself always in concrete terms and is thus dependent on adopting given social and cultural perspectives.

> The concept of social pedagogy thus involves the fundamental recognition that an individual's education is socially defined in every significant aspect, just as the human formation of social life depends fundamentally on a corresponding

education of the individuals who share this social life. This needs to be taken into account in defining the ultimate and most comprehensive function of education for the individual and for all individuals. The subject matter of this scientific discipline are, therefore, the social conditions of education and the conditions for the formation of social life. We consider these to constitute one single rather than two independent tasks. Society exists only as a union of individuals, and this union in turn exists only in the consciousness of its individual members. The final law is thus necessarily one and the same for both individual and society (Natorp, 1968: 9).

The correspondence that Natorp assumes exists between the logic by which individuals and that by which societies develop (he uses language as an example of how we can express both the individual will and generally recognised knowledge) can, however, only be assumed if the same conditions are valid for all individual expressions of the will and of self-consciousness, and if they all partake in a communal pool of 'intellectual property'. This can only come about by the removal of force and oppression since 'we can only speak of a community of willing and the formation of this willing by the community when each person interacts with the others as an equal and learns how to will the same freely with equivalent results' (Natorp, 1968: 6).

Natorp clearly overlooks the fact that society may at times confront individuals sharply as a system of rules and compulsion. However, if this power relationship is not simply to be imposed, it must be counterbalanced by the recognition of equal rights and a relationship free of force. The leitmotiv of the social pedagogical model is, like that of the political discussion on migration, the demand for equality, which is made controversial by the very need to accept and recognise differences between people, differences that migration magnifies.

Social Work in Practice

Institutionalised forms of social work with immigrants in Germany are differentiated according to the legal status of the immigrants. Political and legal criteria thus structure the conditions of social intervention here, too, and give it a particular function. However, in actual practice, social work intervention need not limit itself to this allocated task. It can transcend it and increase its social and political effectiveness by establishing networks. Work with immigrants today is performed in a multi-dimensional 'scene' in which self-help organisations, spontaneous initiatives and elected representative bodies co-operate with the professional social services but at times also work at cross purposes. As was already the case in Jane Addams' Hull House in Chicago at the turn of the century (Müller, 1982; Eberhart, 1995), social work, community politics, cultural and educational work, intervention and prevention all come together in work with immigrants.

Social Work with Migrant Workers

The recruitment of '*Gastarbeiter*' in Germany (foreign workers were regarded as 'temporary' guests') created an obligation to provide bare, essential social services. This obligation was based, on the one hand, on functional considerations of expediency ('frictionless integration') and on the other, on the terms of the EEC Treaty. Social counselling centres were established, managed by the *Arbeiterwohlfahrt* (the welfare organisation of the labour movement, taking responsibility for Turkish, Yugoslav, Moroccan and Tunisian migrants), the *Deutsche Caritasverband* (the German Catholic Welfare Organisation for Italian, Yugoslav, Spanish and Portuguese workers) and the *Diakonisches Werk* (the Protestant equivalent, for Greek migrants). In the early 1990s, there were approximately 600 social counselling centres with a total of 1,000 counsellors.

In the counselling centres, issues present themselves in the following order of frequency: 1) employment and social welfare payments, 2) psycho-social problems, and 3) legal questions specific to immigration (cf. Hamburger, Koepf, Müller and Nell, 1997). The preponderance of questions concerning material welfare demonstrates that social counselling is still a necessary task in the form of counselling specific to workers. In addition to counselling, the centres perform important functions in mediating access to institutions and professional services and co-operation with associations and self-help organisations.

The discovery of the 'problem of foreigners' during the 1970s led to the creation of hundreds of projects, initiatives, associations and self-help organisations. Among them were organisations providing services for foreigners as well as those providing services by or in association with foreigners (Karsten, 1984). This range of projects dealt primarily with educational problems of the second generation and frequently combined educational, cultural, advisory and social work. During the 1980s, the 'foreigner scene' expanded to include associations of self-help organisations on the one hand, and designated specialists for issues concerning foreign nationals, foreign advisers and intercultural bureaux on the other. Designated specialists for foreign nationals (*Ausländerbeauftragte*) are members of a local administration mandated to deal with questions concerning migrants and to resolve conflicts. Advisors (*Beiräte*) are elected representatives who do not have legislative, only advisory functions. They exercise their powers through communicative means by articulating and representing publicly the interests of foreign nationals. Intercultural bureaux take up the tasks of the designated specialists and follow them up in developing action programmes on how the 'indigenous' and the migrant populations can learn from and with each other in order to reduce conflicts in the community. During the 1990s, the institutions of the standard social services became increasingly more receptive to immigrants both as users and as employees.

Immigration also caused changes in the provisions in the field of child and family welfare. Although reception and integration into kindergartens have been considered to play a special role in promoting integration ever since the time when families joined the individual migrant workers and right through to the present day, this area is not satisfactorily regulated. Most regrettably, kindergartens seldom promote the use of the mother tongue. Children and young people of foreign origin become users of social peda-gogical institutions such as crèches, day care centres, playgroups, homework projects, residential homes, social work and legal support services and social pedagogical vocational training programmes in ever greater numbers. Social problems in particular parts of the city (sub-standard neighbourhoods in the old parts of town centres, large housing estates and residential areas near industry) get defined to a large degree as 'problems associated with foreigners'.

Work with Refugees

Social assistance for refugees was initially provided primarily by initiatives of spontaneous groups, often in conjunction with voluntary welfare associations which also played an active role. Social work with refugees more specifically became necessary in the central reception centres and group shelters for asylum seekers in each of Germany's *Länders*. The central contradiction here is that, according to the criteria governing policies for asylum seekers, officially social work should not be aimed at promoting linguistic and social integration – so that rejected applicants can still be removed from the country – whereas the internal logic of providing meaningful support always seeks to promote 'integration' in the current environment.

Work with refugees usually involves the following tasks:

- psycho-social support in dealing with traumatic experiences during the escape,
- motivation and support towards self-help,
- assistance in linguistic and professional training, and
- organisation of support groups in the community and public information campaigns to combat xenophobia.

As most refugees are active individuals who have learned to deal with challenging situations, social work in this field had to reorient its methodology significantly. Rather than directing the work at the refugees themselves, it becomes necessary to target and break down barriers to integration in society (prohibitions on employment, housing regulations and the like) and xenophobic structures. Society's reaction to the presence of immigrants often creates the very effects social work later has to cure.

Work with Returning Emigrant Germans (Aussiedler)

The social policy context for social work with returning emigrants of German ethnicity is significantly more favourable than for work with other immigrants. The German law on citizenship, which is based on the concept of ethnic origin, has made it possible to develop outstanding integration programmes. At the same time, a series of legal changes have tightened regulations governing descendants of emigrants who wish to immigrate and made their access to Germany more difficult. Emigrants (*Aussiedler*) can still count on a wide variety of support programmes. In 1998, there were 25 programme areas for everything from the reimbursement of 'return-travel expenses' to pension plans. Special attention was paid to assistance for educational and professional integration, linguistic support, vocational training for young emigrants and for insurance payments. In implementing these programmes the *Länder*, cities and communities, employment departments and care providers, private foundations, adult education centres, charitable associations and associations for displaced persons all play an integral part. The different groups and organisations responsible have developed differentiated programmes for young emigrants involving academic and vocational training, language assistance and social pedagogical programmes, target group-oriented community work and employment initiatives.

Culture or Rights?

This shows that in the practice of this broadly based field of social work, as in work with immigrants as a whole, lasting access to the labour market is a key factor in promoting integration. At the same time, this factor is influenced by the individual's level of education and the strength of his/her motivation to integrate ('cultural capital') while social integration in the sense of the recognition of factors promoting a feeling of belonging are also significant. Unemployment, the awareness of a lack of opportunities and the experience of rejection reinforce the internalisation of marginalising self-definitions among immigrants and foster the creation of sub-cultural milieux. In addition to providing access to the resources made available by integration programmes, social work must then make additional efforts to improve opportunities (for example by finding training positions through social work in vocational schools) and to promote the identification with the host society through 'relationship work'.

These tasks confront social work also with the non-intended consequences of its own institutionalisation. The particular form in which social work in Germany became institutionalised in the context of the 'voluntary sector' of welfare organisations from its very beginnings had a decisive influence. Only a small part of German social work services is the direct responsibility of local authorities (social assistance and part of youth and family support services). The bigger part is located in the voluntary sector corresponding to the prevailing cultural profile of Germany in terms of the dominant religions, the labour movement and the free and alternative social movements. The division of responsibilities for labour migrants was implemented according to these existing cultural sectors. In addition, the nationality of the service users became a criterion for their allocation to services. Welfare services were meant to organise themselves along the lines of the languages spoken by the different groups of immigrants, a measure that was supposed to have enhanced their accessibility.

A second reason for the specific manner in which established cultural criteria influence work with migrants in Germany can be found in its political culture. The terms 'race' and 'folk' have become lastingly discredited by their function in Nazi ideology and are, therefore, impossible to use in serious political and scientific discourses, quite apart from the fact that they do not have any analytical quality anyway. For the representation of the assumed 'difference' of migrants, only the concept of culture was, therefore, available which has meanwhile taken on inflationary proportions in everyday discourses as well as in pedagogical and social science debates. All perceived differences get subsumed under this concept and we can, therefore, speak of the 'culturalisation' of social work.

The Central Problem: Culturalisation

The pedagogical discussion in Germany has, without much critical debate, settled on a central interpretative formula that suggests that the problems of migration are simply or primarily cultural conflicts. Despite frequent warnings not to reduce the immigrant question to one of ethnicity, an intercultural pedagogy has become established that understands individuals as bearers and representatives of a (national) culture. This reduction of the multi-dimensional character of social issues to a single category is the result of the creation of an uncritical academic representation of the practical identification of a problem and the subsequent actions required. I will illustrate the problem for both research and practice with an example.

In a study Eberhard Nölke (1996) examines the experiences of a young Turkish woman (Esra) who has been given accommodation in a self-governed residential community for young people. In an interview, she reported conflicts with other women living in the home:

> ... *little things really – I mean, that I really – ah, cannot cook and that sort of thing, because I can't really, I can't cook German things, because I have always cooked Turkish up to now and the women there have never eaten Turkish food – and that always caused trouble and so on – and I, how shall I say? – when I cooked, then the kitchen was not clean and so on and so forth – and little things like that...* (Nölke, 1996: 657).

The young Turkish woman Esra separated from her family because there she had suffered constant violence from her father. But in the community, which had been arranged for her by the Youth Department, there are constant conflicts between her and the other female residents. One of the themes of this conflict is also cooking and the cleanliness and tidiness of the communal kitchen.

This passage in the interview with Esra is summarised in the commentary under the heading of 'cultural differences between her and the young German women that became apparent in everyday life' (Nölke, 1996: p. 658).

We need to develop an alternative interpretation for this. In general terms, it might read:

This is an interpersonal conflict based on a personal and/or racist rejection of one person by others rather than on cultural differences. The people involved resort to the instruments available to them for an interpretation which would legitimate the conflict. Cooking is a conflict situation in residential homes and in the case described here led to conflict for many reasons identified by Esra. According to *her* presentation, her Turkish way of cooking was one of the reasons. This may however have been simply an easy way for the German young women, about whose behaviour we actually know nothing, to justify their rejection. (We will disregard whether and in what way it is possible to cook Turkish food in a residential home and what this means.) For Esra, in turn, her self-presentation, viz. that she has been rejected because she cooks 'Turkish', also represents an opportunity to neutralise what may be personal problems and to attribute her problems to an 'external' characteristic for which nobody has direct responsibility. (For more on such exculpatory processes in intercultural partnerships, see Wießmeier, 1993.)

The interpretation that Esra 'has been marginalised by the young people because of cultural differences that became apparent in the "little things" of everyday tasks *because she is different*' (my emphasis) (Nölke, 1996: 659), should, therefore, be modified so that cultural differences can no longer be presented as social facts. For the scientific interpretation of this case was based on the underlying assumption that cultural differences are the actual origins of such conflicts. Instead, a differentiation is necessary between cultural belonging as objectively evidenced, first of all, by language, and the interpretation of this belonging. For cultural belonging and identity are not unambiguous facts, neither in the self-identification ('I am a member of this cultural group'), nor as an external ascription ('Esra is a young Turkish woman'). Instead, we are dealing with the product of constructions and interpretations which can differ from situation to situation. When communication flows easily, similarities become emphasised ('I am a young woman like you'), when conflicts become acute the focus moves to separate, mutually exclusive identities ('I am German, you are Turkish, and a third option between us is impossible'). In multi-cultural societies the command over such rules governing the allocation of identities, modified to suit different situations, is part of the particular behavioural repertoire of those young people who have to fight for positions of recognition and identity in everyday contexts. Especially among young people who come into contact with social service institutions, this behaviour pattern is quite pronounced. In a group of young people who for various reasons no longer live in their families of origin, the ascription of the role of 'outsider' to an individual can add to the cohesion and stability of the rest of the group.

The case involves a second element worth discussing. Esra has left her family 'to escape violent attacks by her father' (p. 657). The social worker responsible explained her instruction that Esra should not be allowed to come home as late as the German young women by referring to the supposed necessity of bringing her up in the 'Turkish tradition', following a discussion with Esra's father. The social worker's approach here is in itself unusual but it also leads to increased conflict and finally to the reception in a residential place. Esra cannot understand 'Turkish upbringing' as reflected in the requirement to come home earlier ('because it was a German home – German young women, German staff and German surroundings generally – and I could not be brought up to be Turkish there – and I did not even want to be brought up Turkish'; p. 659), and we have no difficulty understanding this as she is being treated as a bearer of the characteristic 'Turkish culture' rather than as an individual. This reification of the interaction between the pedagogical reference person is – presumably – the result of stereotypes internalised by the professional as part of intercultural training, as we may doubt that the social worker's behaviour was motivated simply and directly by the wish of a father whose violence the daughter was seeking to escape.

The social worker's action, trapped in culturalist stereotypes, became a central cause of conflict. She disregarded Esra's personal wish to be treated like the other girls and took her bearings instead from the images and assumptions she had formed of Turkish culture. Given the conflictual context of the residential community, Esra is unable to find the kind of protective solidarity in the social worker that would free her from the role of the outsider. The actions of the social worker also confirm the behaviour of the other young women of the residential community by providing additional 'legitimate reasons' to treat Esra as 'different'. Consequently, Esra is forced to leave the residential group after a short while.

We wish to show two things with this reinterpretation: Firstly, 'intercultural' interactions involve complex processes, which can usually be analysed on more than one level. The available interpretative category 'culture (conflict)' which actors use in their interpretations of themselves and of others can have various functions and meanings. The acceptance of such categories as the main reference point for one's interpretative scheme, expressed with all authenticity, can easily become a most problematic construction. Secondly, the fixation on (inter-)culturalism that can currently be observed in so many training centres for pedagogues and which has become established as a norm in academic discussions, is itself a source of conflict, because the cultural stereotypes with which it operates obstruct a clear perception of the actual paradoxes arising in interaction, as Nölke (1996) analysed in exemplary fashion (see also Hamburger, 1997).

The identification of a cultural difference as national or ethnic ('Turkish') merely makes stereotypical attributions easier. Such a view does not promote a deeper understanding of those differences. This applies particularly to the category 'ethnos'. The term 'ethnicity' by contrast can be analysed as a fragile product consisting of attributions and self-interpretations with differing functions and meanings in specific situations. 'Ethnicity' is an object and not a tool of academic investigation while the experience of space, time and society associated with the process of migration constitutes the backdrop for an appropriate interpretation, which may then also take the use of ethnic attributions into account.

Social Pedagogy as Culture within Cultures

The knowledge involved in ethnic attributions and ethnicity is itself a part of culture. It becomes, therefore, necessary to reflect on the concept of culture itself. Furthermore, the concept of culture as such cannot strictly be reconciled with multi- or interculturalism. The concept in its most general meaning implies the totality of human knowledge and human practices, which cultures create over against nature. Culture as such is thus an unending totality that is constant, knows no precise borders, remains fluid, active and self-referential. Culture is reflexive and permanently recreates itself through this reflexivity. Culture is not hierarchical. It is a multi-level non-hierarchical system with loose internal connections. Culture as such is general. All exclusionary distinctions are secondary.

This is particularly true of the obvious distinction between different languages and religions. Culture is comprehensively general; it contains also the rules of translation which help to overcome divisions, as well as the knowledge of the principles within the languages and religions on 'either side' according to which borders are drawn. At the same time, culture does not hover above the different religions and languages. Instead, it is almost completely contained within them. Languages and religions only limit the reflexivity and openness characteristic of culture to the extent that they define themselves by drawing distinctions that divide or exclude. In this way, specific meanings and beliefs crystallise out, and these forms of congealed knowledge then in turn become the material and object of cultural reflexivity practised by translators, interpreters, refugees of conscience, religious critics, theologians and linguists.

If generality characterises the concept of culture as such and specificity the individual partial cultures created by distinctions, the dynamic within culture arises from the dialectic between its claim to generality and the claim to distinct cultural expressions by cultures differentiated in terms of language and religion, tradition and knowledge. The diversity of cultures and the generality of culture itself as well as the reciprocal relationship between culture and the cultures form hence the 'conditions of normality' under which humans live and do not represent an exceptional situation. Reflecting on the ordinary awareness of the different kinds and forms of cultures in which individuals live and on one's own unique, individual culture gives quite immediate access to these insights.

This renders the consequences of migration, in as much as they raise cultural issues, accessible as normal, everyday problems. Communicating explicitly over the knowledge employed in these contexts makes underlying intentions transparent and the resulting actions acceptable – unless they were designed to humiliate, restrict or injure individuals. Divisions that are defined by inequality and injustice cannot be transcended by acts of understanding and, therefore, negate the existence of culture. A 'battle of the cultures' can indeed exist if the cultures concerned have themselves become cultureless, because they have shut down the process of cultural self-reflection contained within them and succumbed instead to dogmatism. Such cultures are particularly eager to link themselves to economic and military imperialism.

Unlike the differentiated cultures, culture as such facilitates reflections on universal validity, i.e. on claims aimed at our common humanness and humanity. This element is also contained in the various cultures, and reflecting on their relative specificity thereby fosters an awareness of particular ties and obligations to specific individuals.

Pedagogy's goals have changed fundamentally since the Enlightenment. It is no longer possible to believe that an education in and towards a particular culture is the only correct one. The Enlightenment had destroyed the self-conception of the Christian tradition as the culture that represented the universal and that should, therefore, be passed on unquestioningly. It had thereby opened up the tension between culture as such and the different cultures. Education was thereafter to be understood as education in one of the cultures (or rather in a particular culture) to achieve culture as such. As the critical evaluation of the Enlightenment has shown, the Enlightenment was of course itself tied to a particular cultural tradition. Nevertheless, it made available the tools for this critique so that it could also be used to criticise the ties to a particular ideology by any educational system or approach, such as national education.

Issues of Recognition

'Recognition' plays an important role in relations among states. The habits of ritualised and formal behaviour and etiquette that sometimes seem so ridiculous do have a deeper significance in making possible interactions among states as equals beyond the incompatibilities and differences in political organisation, cultural tradition and political and economic status. They are based on the mutual recognition of autonomous states. The increased diversity migration creates makes the 'dilemma of difference' (Kiesel, 1996) even more obvious and a pedagogy of recognition even more important. This recognition should relate to:

- the autonomy of individuals and the obligations they undertake to other individuals,
- the equality of citizens and their democratic rights, and
- justice as the prerequisite for equal opportunities in democratic participation.

This means that social pedagogical practice must play a particular role in policies and in pedagogical approaches dealing with foreigners, in addition to many other tasks. As long as children in Germany are regarded and treated as foreigners who lack basic civil rights, an intercultural upbringing is impossible. Only under the conditions of equality and autonomy can respect for difference be prevented from turning into condescending pity for the 'poor children of foreigners'. Self-determination is a precondition for the possibility of education, but non-nationals continue to be denied the right to freely choose where they want to live. It may be possible to accept limits to the right to self-determination for a short time, but they are unbearable as a permanent condition. One of the results is also a critical assessment of the way intercultural pedagogy defines individuals primarily as representatives of a particular culture and in a sense as representatives of particular characteristics. Max Horkheimer fittingly formulated the criticism of such 'culturalist' attributions:

> To treat people a priori not as individuals, as persons, but generally and primarily as Germans, Blacks, Jews, foreigners or Mediterraneans, to assume

without evidence that they lack any faculty to judge for themselves and deserve therefore no consideration as persons in their own right, is barbaric (Horkheimer, 1985: 191–192).

It is commonplace and unproblematic to attribute traits to cultures – by way of giving them or oneself ethnic significance – as long as such comments remain flexible, do not stigmatise the individual and recognise the multiple aspects of each individual's identity. This means that intercultural education, which in this sense refers to particular cultures, repeatedly renders itself superfluous and works to suspend itself, as it is directed at the creation of culture as such and at 'culturedness'.

Lastly, a pedagogy of recognition involves working towards participation in educational and training processes. Success in the education system is no longer unheard of among children of immigrants and they now have a and educational success. However, the majority still remain excluded from further education opportunities and there is a danger that an ethnic underclass will become established. Not everyone is equally affected by dwindling employment opportunities in society; immigrants and unqualified workers are particularly affected. These two characteristics are linked by a lack of opportunities in the labour market. Furthermore, immigrants can become completely marginalised when the discussion of violence and crime becomes linked to their status as foreigners. More than ever is it our primary pedagogical and cultural duty to make success at school and in vocational training possible for all young people.

Summary

Social-pedagogical interventions are meant to support individuals in making the social and cultural world their own. It offers a space and opportunities for social relationships in a manner that protects individuals in their experimenting with different modes of this acquisition and that allows them to (re)gain access to social belonging. In the case of migration this relates particularly to the language and culture of the host country context and to the social interaction and the identities and roles through which recognition can be experienced. And lastly, social-pedagogical intervention as a means of taking a position politically relates to the legal status of migrants who, in their status as foreigners, are excluded from essential rights and particularly from rights of self-determination. In relation to members of the indigenous population, social pedagogy has the same mandate to support the process of accepting society as it presents itself and of themselves as part of this society. They have to come to terms with the reality of a multi-cultural society by changing their image of society and regarding Germany no longer as 'the state of the Germans' but as a country composed of a population of diverse origins and traditions. Wherever this reality is being negated, ethnocentricism turns into racism. Racism is the decisive barrier that prevents migrants from accepting Germany as their social reality.

References

Bäumer, G. (1929), 'Wesen und Aufbau der Öffentlichen Erziehungsfürsorge', in H. Nohl and L. Pallat (eds.), *Handbuch der Pädagogik. Band 5: Sozialpädagogik.* Langensalza/ Berlin/Leipzig, Beltz-Verlag, pp. 3–26.
Eberhart, C. (1995), *Jane Addams (1860–1935). Studien zur Vergleichenden Sozialpädagogik und Internationalen Sozialarbeit, Band 9.* Rheinfelden/Berlin, Schäuble-Verlag.
Hamburger, F. (1997), *Kulturelle Produktivität durch Komparative Kompetenz.* Mainz, Institut für Sozialpädagogische Forschung e.V.
Hamburger, F., Koepf, T., Müller, H. and Nell, W. (1997), *Migration. Geschichte(n), Formen, Perspektiven.* Mainz, Landeszentrale für politische Bildung Rheinland-Pfalz.
Horkheimer, M. (1985), 'Nachwort zu: Porträts deutsch-Jüdischer Geistesgeschichte (1961)', in, *Gesammelte Schriften, Band 8.* Frankfurt am Main, Suhrkamp-Verlag.
Karsten, M.-E. (1984), *Sozialarbeit mit Ausländern.* München, Kösel-Verlag.
Kiesel, D. (1996), *Das Dilemma der Differenz. Zur Kritik des Kulturalismus in der Inter-kulturellen Pädagogik.* Frankfurt am Main, Cooperative-Verlag.
Müller, C.W. (1982), *Wie Helfen zum Beruf Wurde. Eine Methodengeschichte der Sozialarbeit.* Weinheim/Basel, Beltz.
Natorp, P (1968), 'Erziehung und Gemeinschaft. Sozialpädagogik', in Röhrs, H. (ed.), *Die Sozialpädagogik und Ihre Theorie.* Frankfurt am Main, Akademische Verlagsanstalt, pp. 1–10.
Nölke, E. (1996), 'Strukturelle Paradoxien im Handlungsfeld der Maßnahmen Öffentlicher Ersatzerziehung', in A. Combe and W. Helsper (eds.), *Pädagogische Professionalität.* Frankfurt am Main, Suhrkamp-Verlag, pp. 649–677.
Riegel, K.F. (1981), *Psychologie, mon Amour. Ein Gegentext.* München/Wien/Baltimore, Urban und Schwarzenberg.
Wießmeier, B. (1993), *Das 'Fremde' als Lebensidee. Eine Empirische Untersuchung Bikultureller Ehen in Berlin.* Münster/Hamburg, Lit-Verlag.
Winkler, M. (1995), 'Die Gesellschaft der Moderne und ihre Sozialpädagogik', in H. Thiersch and K. Grunwald (eds.), *Zeitdiagnose Soziale Arbeit. Zur Wissenschaftlichen Leistungsfähigkeit der Sozialpädagogik in Theorie und Ausbildung.* Weinheim/München, Beltz-Verlag pp. 155–183.

6 Social Development as a Model of Social Work Practice: The Experience of Zimbabwe

EDWIN KASEKE

Introduction

This chapter examines the use of a social development model in the practice of social work in Zimbabwe. It begins by defining social development before making a case for a social development model in Zimbabwe. The chapter then looks at the operationalisation of social development in Zimbabwe.

Social Development Defined

The term social development emerged as a result of dissatisfaction with a development model that puts undue emphasis on economic growth at the neglect of social factors. Economic growth had not necessarily resulted in an improvement in the welfare of the people. Thus social development emerged as an attempt to draw attention to the importance of social factors in the development process. In view of this, it is, therefore, not surprising that there is no precise definition of social development. Dominelli (1997: 29) agrees that the term is diverse and she defines social development 'as a dynamic way of organising resources and human interactions to create opportunities through which the potential of all peoples – individually and collectively, can be developed to the full'. With this definition, Dominelli sees social development as a model that can be used to address the problem of poverty and underdevelopment.

Another definition of social development is provided by Midgley (1995) who perceives it 'as a process of planned social change designed to promote the well-being of the population as a whole in conjunction with a dynamic process of economic development' (Midgley, 1995: 25). Thus, Midgley sees social development and economic development as interdependent. In other words, social and economic factors of development reinforce each other and no meaningful development can occur without due regard being given to both factors. Midgley's definition emphasises that social development is a process of change directed at conditions that prevent groups and communities from realising their potential.

The two definitions point to the fact that social development as a model of practice underscores the importance of macro policies in changing those conditions or structures that undermine the welfare or well-being of the people. The social development model, therefore, challenges the status quo with a view to ensuring that the environment becomes more responsive to human needs. It is also clear from the two definitions that developing countries provide sufficient scope for implementing a social development model.

As Midgley (1995: 70) observes, 'social development does not have a well-developed body of theory'. However, the modernisation theory of development is often used to understand the causes of underdevelopment. According to the modernisation theory, traditional values and institutions create conditions of underdevelopment. The modernisation theory argues that underdeveloped societies should be transformed into modern societies using the experiences of the developed countries. Rostow's theory as explained by Midgley (1981), that all societies should pass through the common stages of economic development, is pertinent. The modernisation theory also assumed that the benefits of economic development would trickle down to the people in the form of employment, higher wages and social security. This then would improve the standards of living.

The starting point for the social development model is that the modernisation approach has failed to transform developing countries. The benefits of economic development have not trickled down to the majority of the people. Instead the wealth is concentrated in the hands of a few people while the majority live in absolute poverty.

Social development is different from community development in that it puts more emphasis on macro-level policies and intervention strategies, unlike community development which focuses on the micro-level. Social development also calls for the active participation or intervention of government, unlike in community development where the government takes a passive role and expects communities to determine and implement the changes they need to see at local level without reference to the centre. Another major distinguishing characteristic between social development and community development is that unlike community development, social development concerns itself with making rights accessible to all. As Dominelli (1997: 37) observes, 'a new vision of social development, therefore, has to be rooted in making certain rights accessible to every individual on this planet regardless of who they are or where they are'. Social development, therefore, takes a global perspective.

The value base of social development is informed by the belief in the worth and dignity of the human being. Consequently, it considers all human beings as equal and who should, therefore, be given equal opportunities for realising their potential. Furthermore, social development seeks to ensure that individuals have access to resources necessary for meeting basic needs and under conditions that do not undermine their self-esteem. The pursuit of social justice and egalitarian ideals is at the core of the social development model.

The principles of social development are related to social work in that what social development seeks to achieve is also what social work seeks to achieve; namely, the concern with improving human well-being. In improving human well-being, both social development and social work recognise the need to make human rights accessible to all in the interest of equity and social justice. Thus, they both seek to empower the people and as Dominelli (1997: 35) observes, 'this may mean challenging existing social relations and changing the distribution of power and resources'. Both social development and social work are concerned with harmonising the relationship between individuals and their environment. The maintenance function of social work is, however, seen as being out of step with the social development model because it perpetuates the social exclusion of the poor and vulnerable groups.

The Case for a Social Development Model in Zimbabwe

In order to appreciate the case for a social development model in Zimbabwe, it is necessary to understand this within the context of the country's colonial history. Zimbabwe was colonised by the British in 1890 and the colonial government immediately adopted a policy of racial segregation. The policy of racial segregation promoted the supremacy of the white population whilst marginalising the African population. For instance, the colonial government adopted what is referred to as the 'white agriculture policy' designed to promote agricultural activities undertaken by the white settler community by providing them with extension services, land and credit facilities (Stoneman, 1981). The same services and facilities were not made available to the

African population. In fact, the African people had their land appropriated under the Land Apportionment Act of 1930. In pursuance of the white agricultural policy, the colonial government enacted the Maize Control Act of 1931 which stipulated that African farmers were not to receive the full market value of their crops (Stoneman, 1981).

This white agricultural policy had the effect of destroying African agriculture and by so doing destroying the African population's source of sustenance. The resultant problems of landlessness, impoverishment and overpopulation forced rural people to migrate to urban areas in search of income-earning opportunities. Unfortunately, the urban areas were not ready to receive such an influx and migrants had difficulty in securing employment, shelter and food. These people easily became destitute in the urban areas and were subject to the intervention of social workers. Unfortunately, the task of social workers became that of repatriating the urban destitute to their rural homes. Of course, this did not solve the problem of poverty; if anything, it only aggravated the problem. In this respect, social workers were simply operating as agents of social control.

It should be noted that as far as the Africans are concerned, land has cultural, social, economic and political significance. It is the land that defines the identity of the African people and provides the link between the living and the dead. It is also for this reason that the land issue was the rallying point for the war of liberation. It is, therefore, not surprising that many African people are still bitter that they were forcibly removed from the land of their ancestors. They are also still bitter that about 4,600 white farmers from the white population, which constitutes about 0.8% of the country's total population, own about 43% of the land in Zimbabwe. This has sharpened the racial divide in Zimbabwe. However, unlike the situation in Western countries, the colonial legacy in Zimbabwe has resulted in a situation where the minority white population dominates the majority African population. The majority population has political power whilst the minority population has economic power. The minority, therefore, uses their dominant economic power to resist redistributive policies.

The implementation of the economic structural adjustment programme in 1991 accentuated the problem of poverty in Zimbabwe. The poor performance of the economy and a growing debt burden forced the government to accept the International Monetary Fund and World Bank prescription for ailing economies, that is, structural adjustment. Structural adjustment entailed restructuring the economy to achieve sustainable levels of economic growth, which would ultimately improve the living standards. The structural adjustment programme has impacted negatively on the welfare of the people. Of particular concern is the worsening of the unemployment problem. Both the public and private sectors have been retrenching their workers on a larger scale. A total of 60,000 workers had lost their jobs by the mid-1990s (Kaseke, 1998). The liberalisation of the economy is forcing local enterprises to compete with their foreign counterparts, resulting in their being driven out of business. Apart from worsening the problem of unemployment, structural adjustment has also resulted in high inflation and steep price increases. Added to this is the burden of cost recovery occasioned by the need to reduce the budget deficit, which means people now pay for social services.

This is not unique to developing countries only, but parallels can be drawn with the experiences of some Western countries where there has been pressure on welfare regimes to yield to economic considerations. Dominelli (1997: 30) cites the example of Britain which had its own brand of structural adjustment called 'Treasury control', and this resulted in a situation where 'social policies and welfare provisions were subordinated to economic exigencies'.

When social work was introduced during the colonial period, it represented a wholesale transfer of social work models from Britain. Social work was introduced initially for the benefit of the white settler community (Kaseke, forthcoming). The idea was to enable the white settler community to enjoy the same services enjoyed by their kith and kin in Britain. It was felt necessary to extend social work services to the indigenous population only at a later stage. However, when social work services were introduced to the indigenous population, they were inferior and only served to perpetuate their marginalisation. The intervention strategies were mainly directed at the urban population at the neglect of the rural population. There was, therefore, a deliberate neglect of the rural population on the assumption that their needs were simple and easily satisfied within the traditional structures.

The intervention strategies were remedial in orientation and only offered palliative measures. The intervention strategies assumed that social problems were caused by the failure of individuals to adjust to their environments, particularly within the context of rural-urban migration. It was believed that new migrants in the urban areas had problems adjusting to their new environment. As Midgley (1981: 105) observed, 'Social problems are conceptualised in social work as individual maladjustments, and it is the social worker's primary goal to treat these emotional difficulties and problems by interpersonal relationships'.

Casework was used as the main method of intervention, the focus being on enabling the individual to realise adequate social functioning. However, this mode of intervention does not enhance adequate social functioning as it assumes that the individual is to blame for his/her problems when in many instances the problem can be attributed to the environment. This is why Kaseke (1991: 44) argues that 'social work has not been able to differentiate between individual and social causation'. Consequently, inappropriate intervention strategies have been applied with too much emphasis placed on helping individuals cope with their social problems and thereby suggesting that there is nothing that can be done to alter their circumstances.

Social workers are frustrated to discover that the social problems they are handling emanate from ignorance and underdevelopment yet they are unable to address these problems. As a result, social workers have been dealing with symptoms rather than the root causes of the problems. This realisation has made Ankrah (1986: 33) conclude that the residual model of social work is a 'deficient vehicle, not only to change the material welfare of poor rural people, but to address the larger issues of social development'. Thus, to change the material welfare of the poor, there is need for intervention at both the macro and micro levels.

At independence, it was felt that social work in Zimbabwe needed to transform itself so that it could contribute to the material welfare of the poor. For instance, the traditional practice of providing public assistance to destitute members of society has failed to make an impact on the amelioration of poverty. This is because social workers have tended to provide public assistance as an end in itself rather than as a means to an end. Consequently, public assistance has failed to improve the circumstances of the beneficiary populations. The issue of exit strategies for the recipients of public assistance has not been given sufficient attention. Although there have been attempts to introduce community development as a vehicle for promoting development at the local level, these have not been successful owing to the government's failure to empower communities for self-reliance. It should be appreciated that self-help initiatives are successful in instances where deliberate efforts are also made to build the capacity of communities for self-reliance. Local development efforts need to lock into a national framework for social change; the social development model can provide such a framework. Thus, the social development model represents a shift from the residual model. A social development model sees the role of social work as that of facilitating social change and ultimately enabling individuals to realise their potential.

Social Development Operationalised

The implementation of the social development model has revolved around developing strategies for improving the material welfare of the poor. In this regard, social workers have become agents of social change, enablers and facilitators of development. As Dominelli (1997: 35) observes, this 'requires social workers to reinterpret their professionalism – away form the detached bureaucrat or technician into the well-informed activist who cares about and for others'.

The poor and marginalised groups have been specifically targeted with a view to enhancing their productive capacity. With respect to the rural poor, it has been accepted that the root causes of their poverty include land-lessness or inadequate land and the lack of access to credit facilities and extension services. Social workers have joined hands with churches, human rights organisations and the rural poor themselves to lobby government to address the land issue. Although the land issue was the principal cause of the war of liberation, this problem has still not been seriously addressed, nineteen years after independence. At independence, the government announced that 62,000 families were to be resettled, but only 45,000 had been resettled by early 1989. The government has attributed the slow pace of land reform to the problem of resources, but many are convinced that the government lacks the political will to address the land issue. This is, however, set to change as the government has designated several farms for resettlement, indicating a new level of political commitment, although it is doubtful whether the government has the means to pay for the farms. It is disconcerting to note that the ruling elite is benefiting from land originally earmarked for landless peasants. Thus, lobbying efforts should also be directed against this growing phenomenon if social justice and egalitarian ideals are to be realised. It is, therefore, important to provide social workers with lobbying and advocacy skills.

Whilst social workers have not directly lobbied national institutions that provide credit to smallholder farmers, they have nonetheless mobilised rural communities to form mutual aid societies in the form of rotating savings and credit schemes. These promote savings that are shared by members on a rotational basis. They also provide credit facilities for the members. The savings and loans are being used by rural communities as capital for their agricultural activities and are also used to meet the health and education needs of families. This has enabled rural communities to enhance their productive capacity and thus provides an escape route out of poverty.

The impact has, however, been minor, as only a few have joined these schemes. The challenge for social workers is to mobilise more people to join these schemes and to link the marginalised communities to appropriate resource systems that can provide seed money and technical support.

Efforts to improve the material welfare of rural communities are constrained by the fact that land is idle for half of the year owing to too much dependence on rain-fed agriculture. The majority of rural people have no access to irrigation facilities that would make it possible for them to utilise their land throughout the year. Although the government is support-ing the construction of small dams countrywide, the pace is so slow that many rural communities will remain without irrigation facilities for many years to come. Some non-governmental organisations, however, have sourced funds from the donor community to support dam construction. Local communities are often required to contribute their labour as a way of encouraging them to participate in the development of their communities and also to help avoid the development of a dependency syndrome. The cardinal principle in social work of doing things with and not for the communities is observed.

Social workers and other development workers recognise that the construction of dams for irrigation purposes is a long-term goal. For the short-term, they have recognised the need to promote non-farm income-earning opportunities. Consequently, community workers employed by the Ministry of National Affairs, Employment Creation and Co-operatives and those employed by non-governmental organisations are mobilising rural communities to set up income-generating projects in order to supplement incomes derived from agriculture. This makes an important contribution in reducing the problems of unemployment and under-employment in rural areas. An important activity undertaken by community workers is that of assisting individuals, groups or communities to prepare project proposals and undertake feasibility studies for their intended projects.

Community workers also assist by linking individuals, groups and communities to appropriate resource systems that provide skills training and start-up capital for the projects. Furthermore, community workers mobilise the rural communities to improve infrastructure such as roads, bridges, clinics and schools. Emphasis is not only on programmes or projects that directly improve the material welfare of rural communities, but also on those programmes and projects that indirectly contribute to an improvement in the material welfare of the poor.

The impact of these measures to improve the material welfare of rural communities has been quite minimal because of poor funding of the activities by the Ministry of National Affairs, Employment Creation and Co-operatives. The poor funding precludes community workers from traversing the breadth and width of the country and from providing reasonable start-up capital for projects. Although non-governmental organisations have been more successful than the government, their impact has been compromised by the fact that they tend to confine their activities to more or less the same districts, leaving some remote parts of the country virtually untouched. This is partly responsible for the uneven development in the country.

The decision by the government to implement the economic structural adjustment programme brought with it new challenges for social workers, even though they were not part of the initial decision-making process. The government of Zimbabwe anticipated that structural adjustment would have a negative impact on the welfare of the people through unemployment, steep price increases and cut-backs on social services (Government of Zimbabwe, 1991). Consequently, social workers in the Department of Social Welfare were asked to put in place measures to cushion vulnerable groups against the social costs of structural adjustment. The Department of Social Welfare set up the Social Development Fund whose objective was to provide food, money and assistance with the payment of education and health fees. The food money was targeted at low-income urban households with incomes of Z$200 and below per month, whilst assistance with payment of education and health fees was targeted at retrenched workers, unemployed persons and households with monthly incomes not exceeding Z$400 (Kaseke, 1993).

Whilst the Social Development Fund was intended to improve the well-being of vulnerable groups, the realisation of this objective was compromised by the poor design of the programme. The targeting system renders the Fund unable to capture the most needy members of society because the costs of accessing the Fund are high; as a result the poor are unable to access the benefits (Kaseke, 1993). As argued by Chisvo and Munro (1994: 19) the Social Development Fund 'is a passive mechanism that waits for potential beneficiaries to come forward and apply for benefits. This approach in itself effectively (though inadvertently) excludes many of the poorest and most vulnerable members of the target population'.

Because of poor funding, the Social Development Fund is unable to honour its commitments in time. Consequently, it is always in arrears, there-by forcing schools and hospitals to demand payment from people who are not supposed to pay. As a result, children from poor households end up dropping out of school. As the harsh economic conditions continue to bite, the government is increasingly finding itself unable to protect the poor. As a result, many have begun to question the government's commitment to the welfare of the poor, particularly at a time when the government is fighting an unnecessary war in the Democratic Republic of the Congo. Sadly, social workers are reluctant to use their advocacy and lobbying skills to pressure the government to spend money on programmes and projects that could improve human well-being. Social workers have also failed to cause the government to revamp the Social Development Fund so that it becomes more responsive to the needs of the poor.

The Social Development Fund also has an employment and training programme targeted specifically at retrenched workers. These are workers who are declared redundant. The aim is to assist retrenched workers to create their own employment by embarking on small to medium-scale enterprises. The programme offers loans to retrenched workers to start their own business, but the retrenchees have to make a contribution of 10% of the capital needed. Before they embark on their business ventures, they have to undergo training to acquire the relevant skills. The impact of this programme in improving the material welfare of retrenched workers has been minor because most of them fail to raise the 10% contribution. The programme was also narrowly conceived as it confines itself to the new poor, that is, those who have become poor because of retrenchment. As Kaseke (1998: 262) observes, the employment and training programme could have made a greater impact if it had not confined itself to assisting retrenched workers only.

An Assessment

Although there has been no systematic evaluation of the social development model, it is apparent that social workers in Zimbabwe have not fully implemented the social development model. This can be attributed to two major reasons. First, the implementation of structural adjustment has placed the government in a vulnerable and dependent position where it no longer has a free hand in determining its economic and social policies. Consequently, largely external forces are determining policies. There is, therefore, limited space for social workers. Second, social workers themselves have been slow in shaking off their old mantle, particularly those employed by government.

Furthermore, social work education has not sufficiently prepared social workers for social development roles. There has been too much emphasis in the past on preparing students for remedial social work. However, in the last few years, the social development model has had some impact on the curriculum of the School of Social Work in Harare (the only institution providing social work education in Zimbabwe). The curriculum provides an opportunity for students to understand the concept of social development, its objectives and how these can be realised. It also enables students to make a critical analysis of traditional social work practice models. The curriculum also focuses on socio-economic development, rural development and project planning and management. Our social work graduates, however, have realised that the implementation of their progressive ideas is often constrained by agency policies and the rigidity of central government.

Despite these shortcomings, there is some consensus among social workers that social work should move away from its traditional maintenance function which has tended to perpetuate the marginalisation of the poor and vulnerable groups such as women and persons with disabilities. Empowerment of the poor and vulnerable groups has become a topical issue among social workers, but the results have not been outstanding, largely because empowerment is not being addressed in a holistic manner. Consequently, progress in one aspect of the people's lives is undermined by lack of progress in other aspects.

Empowerment also rests on the capacity of social workers to take on an advocacy role. Although there have been half-hearted attempts at advocacy, social workers together with marginalised groups have attempted to draw the attention of government to unmet needs in communities in the hope that efforts will be made to improve their circumstances. These have, however, met with mixed fortunes.

Social workers can be more successful in this area if they can increase the tempo of their advocacy and lobbying roles. Advocacy and lobbying should result in the creation of an enabling environment, that is, an environment that makes it possible for individuals, groups and communities to realise their potential. This is the biggest challenge for social workers in Zimbabwe.

Conclusion

The discussion has shown that while Zimbabwe has made a start in the implementation of a social development model, it has a long way to go before the objectives of social development can be fully realised. Successes in the implementation of a social development model have been more on the micro than macro level. There is, therefore, a need for social workers to influence social policies with a view to ensuring that policies are responsive to human needs. Zimbabwe's problem of underdevelopment requires both micro- and micro-level intervention. The macro-level policies such as those associated with structural adjustment are impacting negatively on human well-being, and social workers need to assist local communities in articulating their concerns and problems and drive home the message that structural adjustment undermines human welfare.

References

Ankrah, M. (1986), 'The Practicum after a Decade', in J. Hampson and B. Willmore (eds.), *Social Development and Rural Fieldwork.* Proceedings of a Workshop Held on 10–14 June, Harare, *Journal of Social Development in Africa,* pp. 62–73.

Chisvo, M. and Munro, L. (1994), *Review of Social Dimensions of Adjustment in Zimbabwe 1990–1994.* Harare, UNICEF.

Dominelli, L. (1997), 'Social Work and Social Development: A Partnership in Social Change', *Journal of Social Development in Africa,* vol. 12 (1), pp. 29–38.

Government of Zimbabwe (1991), *Social Dimensions of Adjustment.* Harare, Government Printer.

Kaseke, E. (1991), 'Social Work Practice in Zimbabwe', *Journal of Social Development in Africa,* vol. 6 (1), pp. 33–45.

Kaseke, E. (1993), *A Situation Analysis of the Social Development Fund.* Harare, Ministry of Public Service, Labour and Social Welfare and UNICEF.

Kaseke, E. (1998), 'Zimbabwe', in J. Dixon and D. Macarov (eds.), *Poverty: A Persistent Global Reality.* London, Routledge, pp. 248–264.

Kaseke, E. (forthcoming), 'The State of Social Welfare in Zimbabwe', in J. Dixon and R.P. Scheurell (eds.), *The State of Social Welfare: The Twentieth Century in Cross-National Review.* Westport,CT/London, Greenwood Publishing Company.

Midgley, J. (1981), *Professional Imperialism: Social Work in the Third World.* Heinemann Educational Books Ltd.

Midgley, J. (1995), *Social Development: The Developmental Perspective in Social Welfare.* London, Sage.

Stoneman, C. (1981), 'Agriculture', in C. Stoneman (ed.), *Zimbabwe's Political Inheritance.* London, Macmillan Press, pp. 127–150.

7 Social Work Education with Migrants and Refugees in France

TASSE ABYE

Introduction

The objective of this chapter is to present a model of positive action, aimed at the advancement of this issue of migrants and refugees in relation to social work education and practices, implemented within the Institute of Social Development at Canteleu.

To start, I wish to offer some clarifications to allow a better understanding of the general context in which this kind of action takes place. First, this chapter is derived from a process which produced a framework for building a model of action concerning the relationships between 'social work and immigrants and refugees in France'. This model of action is still being developed and makes no claims to being a model of practice with general validity. With the benefit of hindsight, further improvements can be made. It will, therefore, be presented with all its shortcomings as a basis for further discussion, critique, improvement or even rejection.

Secondly, I would like to dispel the ambiguity that is often implied in the concept of 'model of practice'. Models of practice are, in the jargon of social work, most frequently associated with models of practical experiences favouring particular 'clients' (the beneficiaries) of social work and having more or less diverse features. In our case, 'the clients' of the action present diverse characteristics and have various social positions. The action developed within the framework of our project aims not at a category or a group of people, but at a particular situation in which different categories of people or institutions are implicated. Consequently, we are dealing simultaneously with multiple aims and actors. The objective of this project is an attempt to elaborate and implement a model of global action in the field of social work regarding the issues specific to the social and occupational integration of migrants and refugees in France.

Our model of practice does not answer the question: How can we carry out social work interventions among immigrants and refugees?' but rather: How can we generalise the issues specific to that population for social work as a whole? Or, to put it differently again: How can we create the basic conditions for the development of social work intervention in that field? This project is, therefore, at the forefront of social intervention. The main reason for implementing this action is our estimation that social work in France does not address, in a structured way, the different issues specific to immigrants and refugees when aiming to achieve social and occupational integration. Although there is no general lack of concern in social work for this issue, this defect could be explained partly by the lack of specific methodologies in social work training. The specific characteristics of French policy regarding immigrants and refugees explain the wider deficits of current social work and will therefore be presented first before dealing with the field of social work and the project more specifically.

The Context

Migration and Policies on 'Minorities' in France

The French political and philosophical position regarding ethnic minorities has a strong influence on social work training as well as on social intervention in general. The French position is anchored in the history of how the nation-state was constituted. Indeed, if the homogeneity of populations is in principle not necessary for the existence of the nation (Schnapper, 1991), this seems to imply that the insistence on the homogeneity of populations is a product of the specific French republican conception of the nation-state. The firm determination of the holders of 'legal legitimate power' to assimilate the minorities to the 'superior' republican and 'universal' culture, which sometimes included the use of force, is based on the pretence that 'the culture' in question has no ethnic basis. One of the explanations most often put forward for the refusal to recognise ethnic minorities in France is that France is the Nation-State par excellence, and consequently, the nation of individual integration (Schnapper, 1992). Moreover, it is always a matter of 'good manners' among theoreticians to present the concept of the French nation in opposition to others; for example, the German nation (Brubaker, 1992; Schnapper, 1992). The former is regarded as a political nation without any reference to ethnic identity whereas the latter is regarded as essentially based on ethnic identity. If it is true that there is opposition between these two countries relating to differing ideologies, most often this contrast is exaggerated when we come to comparing rights, not only in a formal sense but also in regard to the everyday reality of immigrants in the two countries.

Unlike some other countries of the European Community such as Sweden, Italy or Ireland, which prefer to define themselves as countries of emigration but have been changed into countries of immigration only very recently, France denies that it is a country of immigration. Our lack of awareness of the integration process of populations from foreign origin can be attributed to the existence of a common national ideology. 'The systematic disregarding of immigration and of integration mechanisms has been, in this case, one of the ways that allows national unity to be maintained' (Schnapper, 1991). The will to strengthen the national unity prevented France from seeing that it is made up of multi-ethnic populations. Even today few research results in human science recognise that France is a multi-ethnic country. Those who attempt to introduce into the French debate the question of ethnicity find the shadow of an American reading of French realities cast on them. The most radical researchers, who in France count as 'communitarians', feel most often 'obliged' to take rhetoric precautions in order not to be accused of being 'Americanist'. Moreover, they 'do not contest the principles of individual citizenship either, even if they now find it insufficient to integrate the new populations' (Schnapper, 1998). The recent controversy, described as critical by Bernard and Weill (1997), involved Tribalat (1997), who carried out a study on the integration of immigrants using the criterion of ethnic membership and ethnic origin, and Le Bras (1997, 1998) who blames Tribalat for questioning the republican model. In Le Bras's opinion, nationality is the only acceptable criterion. This controversy is very instructive regarding the French situation. For Tribalat, the consideration of ethnic memberships or ethnic origins of French people coming from the 'recent' immigration (less than four generations) provides evidence for French society being multicultural. The presentation in ethnic terms of the descendants of those former immigrants, who now have French nationality, shows for Le Bras a logical error because of the notion of French descending from foreign people has no significance (Le Bras, 1997). In his view a person is either French or foreign. The significance of this debate is that it goes far beyond a discussion between two demographers about a question of statistical techniques used in demography and indicates a general polarisation of models of thinking available in France on this matter.

However, taken as a whole, the considerations developed above do not lead us to infer that the French republic is on the side of injustice and inequality in its intentions. Far from it, the principles of justice, equality and brotherhood remain the foundation of French society (even if some people want to come back to them and make them to be heard more strongly). The non-recognition of ethnic minorities in France does not stem from the intention to discriminate against a minority; we can even say that this lack of recognition of ethnic minorities represents for some people the principle of 'the struggle against discrimination'. It is in the name of equality for all, brought about by individual integration, that the existence of ethnic minorities is denied. Nevertheless, the very attractive principle of the French universalism meets with limitations as soon as someone tries to exercise individual and collective citizenship rights. Many investigations have shown that immigrants are the victims of daily and grave discrimination, even in areas till recently considered as the best facilitators of republican integration, for example the workplace and school (Bataille, 1997). The inequalities with regard to employment and accommodation are by far the clearest. School, which had played the most important role as a tool of integration of children of immigrants into the national society, becomes more and more contested in its capacity to achieve this aim.

The project presented here, though demonstrating the importance of the recognition of ethnic minorities, was initiated above all with a view to correcting the gaps between the principle of equality represented by universal principles and the reality of daily-observed inequality. Far from proposing a reappraisal of the universalist founding principles, we prefer on the contrary to adopt a perspective that attempts to implement the very intentions of universalism in practice. We suggest that it is possible to practise a form of universalism that does not exclude, for instance, women or ethnic minorities. In other words, it seems to us that we cannot be satisfied with either a universalism that is only a utopia where we never reach our goal, or with a fossilised culturalism with essentialist trappings. We are conscious of the contradictions that this kind of project shows, contradictions that are inherent in every action having as its objective to correct the gaps between the intentions of universalist principles and practical experiences. The actions that we carry out in the framework of this project make sense only in relation to observed daily discriminations compared with universalist principles and intentions. In a situation of real equal opportunities and in the absence of mechanisms of institutional racism, such actions would be unnecessary. This project is, therefore, a project waiting for the right moment to become obsolete.

This project is not the only experience of its kind in France. There are other initiatives aimed toward correcting the discrepancies between claimed principles and daily practice, even if they are not labelled as such (except in the case of ZEP (*Zone d'Education Prioritaire*) – Educational Priority Zone, which clearly declares itself as this type of action). Examples of such initiatives are measures that favour the disabled or are designed to promote the equality of women. However, while it seems simpler in individual cases to select beneficiaries by using 'objective' criteria (such as gender and income level) or 'subjective' criteria (that nevertheless have analytical power), in France today there is no way to define which people belong to or come from a particular ethnic minority. Indeed, there is no direct way to deduce ethnic membership; the only possible distinction is that between French and non-French nationals. For this reason, the actions we wanted to carry out in this project came up against difficulties of implementation rather quickly.

Social Work in Relation to Immigrants and Refugees

As is the case in other fields, social work in France does not recognise the existence of ethnic minorities. In other words, social work in France does not acknowledged the existence of specific problems faced by migrants. However, while there are many non-governmental organisations working with migrants and refugees, there are only two important organisations related to public authorities working with migrants and refugees. The first, the Social Action Fund (*Fonds d'Action Sociale – FAS*), is the main instrument of social intervention. For a long time it concerned itself, among other objectives, with the building of accommodation for immigrants. The second is the Social Care Department for Immigrants (*Service Social d'Aide aux Emigrants – SSAE*), a department whose aim is to carry out social work among immigrants. In these two cases, the population targets are historically migrant workers, which means foreigners, at least in principle (in recent years the FAS have clearly enlarged their target groups to French people from migrant origin). With the exception of these two structures, which take into account the administrative status of immigrants and refugees, it seems that in most cases social workers on the whole do not raise questions that explicitly acknowledge the ethnicity of the users of services. The leitmotiv of social workers is 'all people are identical to me and if there are differences, these are only differences of ability, and are of an individual nature'. Nevertheless, the observation of their practice and the analysis of their discourses show that social workers often operate with notions that distinguish the 'French' French from others, that is to say, from French 'having immigrant origins'. Moreover, we have often met social workers or student social workers who, when discussing French people of immigrant origin, refer to them as foreigners (Abye, 1994). However, framing them in this way does not automatically imply a sensitive and structured practice that considers the specific features of immigrants.

The lack of systematic reflection and subsequent development of models of practice in this field has important consequences for social work intervention with the populations concerned. Indeed, practice is more often based on individually constructed 'knowledge', which sometimes does not go beyond common sense; that is to say, the level of prejudice, which can appear to be positive or negative. In the framework of social assistance with the social and occupational integration of people from immigrant origin, social workers do not take into account the dimension of racism and discrimination faced by these population groups when seeking accommodation or employment. It is not uncommon that social workers regard the immigrant's successive failures to obtain jobs, for instance, as the result of the immigrant's personal deficiency when it actually stems from existing racism. Instead of recognising the fact that these groups encounter racism and discrimination problems, social workers often only consider problems in terms of communication skills. Consequently, they tend to recommend 'a training programme for personal presentation', or a programme to ameliorate their capacity to communicate in which immigrants must enrol to enhance their level of communication. In this case, as in others, as mentioned above, the solution seems to be found only at the level of personal deficits of the immigrant.

While it is sometimes possible that some immigrants do indeed show 'deficits' with regard to the perfect command of appropriate communication codes of 'the republic', it is amazing that no other perspective is taken into account, in particular that of racism. This possibility is not even considered as a hypothesis of work with a view to diagnosing problems that immigrants find in their social and occupational integration. However, it seems to us that acknowledging existing discrimination enables us to carry out research in other directions and to position the problems encountered in a different context. Thereby, we can avoid questioning the abilities of people, a response that can easily end up becoming internalised by the victims. It is against this background of questions and observations that the following project attempts to develop a model of global action and to apply it to an educational institute for social work.

The Project [1]

By taking advantage of a 'window of opportunity' offered by the implementation of an EU Community Initiative Programme (*Programme d'Initiative Communautaire – PIC*), and more particularly, one of its constituents, INTEGRA, we were able to get a handle on the issues of racial identification. This programme included among its aims to pay particular attention 'to actions dealing with needs specific to immigrants and refugees'. Furthermore, for the first time, this was a programme directed at social workers as an important link in the steps taken to integrate immigrants and refugees. The framework of the INTEGRA programme, among the numerous options offered, enabled us to assemble three conditions that we regarded as indispensable for the completion of our project. First, it recognised unequivocally that ethnic minorities (immigrants and refugees) encounter specific problems as far as social and occupational integration is concerned. Secondly, it offered the possibility to carry out actions in favour of social workers and recognised that the latter were necessary for setting up social policies in that field; and thirdly, it encouraged the participation of the beneficiaries. It is true that in some countries of the European Community, the development of actions in favour of populations defined as ethnic minorities is 'common'; the INTEGRA project can then build on continuity. In the particular case of France, this initiative could be regarded as a 'rupture' with previous practices of 'designation'. Indeed, the specifically French projects and programmes commonly refer, for instance, to a particular geographical areas as targets of social policies. We speak then of action in favour of underprivileged suburbs, priority areas for education, etc. instead of action in favour of ethnic minorities (immigrants); the living quarters are supposed to confer common characteristics on their population. This difference of designation is not only a semantic difference. As demonstrated above, it is an ideological difference as well, and we shall see still more how far this generates different modalities of work.

This project has been inspired by and benefited from practices carried out in other countries, in particular a project in Great Britain conducted by the Central Council for Education and Training in Social Work[2] and the 'Project of Five' in the Netherlands dealing with interculturalism (Abye and Eckmann, 1998). Furthermore, it draws on several experiences in France, of which two in particular have been based at the Institute of Social Development (Project for education and training of professional animators and Project for pre-education and training of four hundred young people). Those two projects at the national level were aiming to promote social workers coming from four hundred deprived suburbs.

From Intuitive Observation to the Study of the Actual Situation

Several reports and observations regarding the relationship between immigrants with social work in general were available at the start of this project. Indeed, because of the transformations brought about by labour migration turning into permanent residence, and this during an economic crisis, social workers are now more frequently in contact with immigrants and refugees than in the past. This situation is strengthened by the increasingly important role social workers are supposed to play in assisting populations that are regarded as being in some kind of difficulty in the process of social and occupational integration. Among the populations considered at risk, immigrant populations are strongly represented. Indeed, for a number of years a significant number of them have been experiencing difficulties with economic, social or cultural integration. What seemed to be 'working relatively well' in France for earlier immigrants (coming from European countries) seems now less and less functional when applied to populations from countries considered to belong to the Third World and more particularly from former colonies. Indeed, the transformation of labour migration into permanent residence migration, of immigration of young and single men living alone in isolated workers' hostels turning into a much more visible form of immigration of the familial type living among 'native' populations, does not occur without stirring up problems. Today, even if not everybody recommends the same solution, it seems, nevertheless, that there is a consensus that republican integration of the French style no longer produces the desired effects, or at least, that the mechanisms are seized up. In that particular context, as underlined above, the role and the mission of social workers assume more significance in the work with these populations.

The implementations of innovative practice in that field therefore necessitate deep transformations of social action in general and of social work in particular. If establishing an imaginative and coherent social policy is one of the conditions of success for an ambitious policy of integration, it cannot be carried out without modifications in social work practice and in the contents of training, which prepare future social workers. The project that we have carried out was therefore intended to play a large part in the success of this indispensable transformation. Certainly, it limited itself to the field of education and training for social work, but it was designed as a step and not as an end in itself. From the different reports, observations and limitations arising from this kind of intervention, we have determined five sometimes simultaneous and sometimes consecutive but interconnected axes of work around which we have constructed this project relating to the following five aims:

- To develop methodological tools for social workers in training relating specifically to the situation of immigration and refugees, which would also be of relevance to future and presently practising social workers.
- To train and increase the awareness of the teachers of our institute to use methodological training tools for social work education and social action developed in the framework of this project.
- To train social workers to be able to apply appropriate methods when working with immigrants and refugees.
- To promote access of members of ethnic minorities and refugees to social work education and training.
- To carry out, from the four previous aims, actions of comparison, co-operation and exchange with agencies and professionals who work with immigrants and refugees in several European countries.

Before being able to carry out our project as a whole and to carry on with our defined aims, we were obliged to proceed from reports drawn up in an intuitive way to a report based on an inventory and statement on the situation based on a deeper analysis. In that capacity, we have therefore put into place staff groups which produce official reports from different perspectives. These reports generally confirm the intuitive notions explained above. In addition, they enabled us to be more precise in certain fields, and principally to know better the different external partners of our institution which are necessary and indispensable for the success of our project.

Lack of Theoretical and Practical Considerations in Social Work Education

The principal characteristic of aspects of the methodology of action in social work education that take into account problems specific to migrant populations is that they are informal and very local. Most frequently, it becomes a matter of offering optional strategies depending on the goodwill of the students. Hence, when training in this subject is given to students there are few or no participants (Bensaadoune, 1998). The dominant concept of 'all people are the same' and that there is 'no need for specific methodology concerning ethnic minorities' is based on the refusal to stigmatise immigrants and refugees and seems to be the expression of a 'state republican position infused with humanism'. Nevertheless, this hides the fact that immigrants and refugees experience difficulties precisely because they are immigrants or refugees.

This attitude and approach are more or less general among programme heads at the Institute, which has prevented the internal development of 'a set of methodologies for action' which could be 'taught'. Neither has it been possible to apply and adapt curriculum units to methodologies developed elsewhere. A review of the resource centre with a view to evaluating the different existing resources (books, magazines, brochures, manuals, news-papers) shows this question to be of least concern and represents certainly the most important blind spot of the whole training system. The setting up of training in this subject matter, in a formal and a structured way, is therefore a lengthy job requiring the mobilisation of the whole Institute and its external partners. Indeed, the introduction of 'new' contents of training implies deeper modifications of all the contents of the existing training programmes. As with every modification, it generates resistance, at least because it requires additional work to introduce changes to 'well oiled' practices. This anticipated resistance is reinforced by the existing powerful ideological base that legitimises the entire social system.

Nevertheless, to achieve the three aims – 1) to build a specific method-ology of action, 2) to train trainers to teach this methodology, and 3) to train students in competent social work – the whole staff have now been working together for more than two years. This includes librarians, teachers, re-searchers, administrators and training designers; in short, all corporate bodies of the Institute. At the time of writing, we have built two modules of training that were carried out within the framework of the training of Social Service Assistants and Specialised Educators. Three other modules are now constructed to complete the whole range of measures taken for professional training. Our action aims therefore simultaneously at several objectives, including multiple external as well as internal partners to the Institute, that is to say different actors in the field with whom we are working within the framework of our social work training. Indeed, it would be useless in our case to implement a high quality curriculum on methodology around this issue if it were not supported by a sufficient number of staff inside the Institute and above all by external partners. Social work students will spend more than half their training time with external partners as practice teachers. Nevertheless, this action would be incomplete unless we also attempted to carry out corrective actions to make up for the lack of social workers coming from immigration groups.

A Time Limited Positive Discrimination Approach

In the studies we conducted in the course of our general inquiries, the almost total absence of 'immigrants and refugees' among trained social workers in courses leading to the social work diploma – *Educateur Specialisé, Assistant de Service Social*[3] – seems to be a recurrent feature. In other words, for more than ten years we have seldom observed the recruitment in that field of students coming from 'visible minorities'. This intuitive observation is difficult to substantiate because schools offering social work training do not have information on the ethnic composition of the student population in their files of registration. We are conscious that the use of the concept of a visible minority is very debatable and it gives only partial information about the situation of immigration populations. Nevertheless, it seemed to give a clue, which requires clarification by means of other kinds of verifications.

The absence of visible minorities could be due to many different reasons. Nevertheless, we think that in the conditions of admittance in schools of social work, two types of barriers prevent access for immigrants and refugees. The first is that the selection exam excludes them while it privileges those who have perfect command of the French language and grammar. The second, which concerns social resources (relations), tends to benefit those who have a dense social network. Indeed, in contrast to university requirements[4] for which the possession of the French baccalaureate is the only condition for enrolment in practically all courses, in the framework of social work education the baccalaureate, while being indispensable, is not sufficient. In order to qualify, candidates who hold a baccalaureate must pass an additional selection exam given by every school under the authority of the state. Indeed, because the number of free places is limited in relation to the number of candidates, the selection exam has over the years become very selective and competitive. The number of candidates is sometimes ten times higher than the number of places available. While places financed by the state are reserved for those who head the list (in the jargon of the schools, called the 'quota'), a limited number is available to those who have at least average marks (10/20) and have an employment contract. The latter can be admitted to training provided they have an employer or a future employer ready to pay the school for the cost of the training (they represent the so-called '*hors quota*'). In the case of the above Institute, there are more than 1200 candidates and about 110 places in the 'quota' financed by the state and about sixty '*hors quota*' places financed by employers.

The selection is carried out in two parts. All students have to meet the first requirement, which is the written exam. The essential aim of this exam is to check the use of the French written language, so that candidates could proceed to apply to the second part of the selection process, which is an interview dealing with motives for studying social work[5]. Until 1998, the rule was to average points obtained in these two tests to classify future students. It is, therefore, evident that candidates who are more proficient than others in the written French language had a considerable advantage in the selection process. As indicated above, it was not enough for social work candidates to know the French language well; they had to be among the best in wording techniques and grammar to be admitted. Of course, this type of exam 'endorsed' the formal principle of the 'equality' of all students!

From the initial stages of our project, we attempted, albeit in a rudimentary way, to evaluate how many immigrant candidates present themselves to the selective entry to two training courses in social work which are considered 'mainstream' (social service worker and specialised educator). We carried out a 'pre-study' on the available information at our school during the four years (1994, 1995, 1996 and 1997). The aim of the 'pre-study' was to identify candidates born in foreign countries and/or those who were born in France but from parents born in foreign countries. Indeed, whereas the registration files show nothing about the ethnic origin of the candidate, they nevertheless inform about place of birth; pictures are included in the files as well as the name of the family. In addition, certain candidates present birth certificates in which the places of birth of the parents are indicated. The interpretation of the results obtained in the 'pre-study' is difficult in that it does not yield hard information but only gives an indication of the approximate number of candidates from visible minorities. The four years of the sample period are not representative; information obtained from one school alone does not reflect the reality of what is going on in other institutes and in the whole national territory. The 'pre-study' cannot claim to have general validity; it is valid only in the specific case mentioned. Any attempt to generalise seems to be inappropriate; nevertheless with all due caution, the findings can be considered as an indicator.

Our results of that small survey were the following: the number of candidates who met our selection criteria – indicators for selection that we used in a cumulative way – for the past four referenced years was 153, 162, 180, 177. The total number of candidates was 1150, 1210, 1235, 1266, respectively. In other words, the proportion of candidates that the chosen criteria indicate as being from immigrant origin and as those who are clearly identified as foreigners oscillates between 13.3% to 14.5% for the four years concerned. For every one of those years, their rate of success in the exams is 3.9%, 3%, 2.2% and 3.3%, respectively. This means that only an average of 3.1% of candidates from immigration or refugee backgrounds succeed in breaking through the barriers to start training. Among those who succeed we find, in the four years, only three people of foreign nationality at the time of the final exams. The discrepancy in the number of accepted candidates between those coming from an immigration background and the others is significant. Indeed, the percentages of persons admitted among these latter are 16.7%, 15.7% and 15% respectively; this represents an annual average rate of 15.7% against 3.1% for those having immigrant origins.

With a view to opening these training courses in social work to visible minorities and refugees, we set up three types of 'corrective' and simultaneous actions. First, and most important, were the changes relating to the conditions of selection introduced in that process; the second was the implementation of a pre-course training programme intended to help candidates to prepare for competitive examinations for entry to social work schools. The third was the construction of a network in conjunction with associations of immigrants so that the latter could inform future candidates of the conditions of selection and sponsor some young people to help them enter training within the framework of '*hors quota*' places.

Modifications in the Conditions of Selection: Advances and Resistance

The most important modifications relating to conditions of selection that had been introduced in 1998 at our Institute was the relative re-equilibrating of the importance of written exams. As pointed out above, in the past it was the accumulation of marks obtained in the written exam and the interview dealing with the candidate's motives that determined the classification of future candidates. Since 1998, the only function of marks obtained in the written exam is to determine if candidates are eligible to apply to the subsequent interview. This means that since the introduction of these modifications to the selection procedure, students who have obtained at least an average mark (10/20) can apply to be interviewed as before, but the marks obtained on the written exam cannot be added to the marks obtained in the interviews. In other words, the meter is reset at zero and only the marks obtained in the interview on motivation are taken into account for the classification of the candidates. We hope that with this change, conditions for selection will be based less on excellence in writing and grammar and more on other qualifications that the interviews are intended to bring out.

Although it is too early to give a final verdict on the impact of this action after only a year, we can already see some changes, albeit very slight, in the composition of candidates entered in the academic year 1998–1999. Nevertheless, because we did not reflect on the purpose and conditions of the interviews in collaboration with the interviewers, the results we are obtaining do not seem to match our expectations. As the interviewers are the same people and act more or less on the same principles as in the past, our hypothesis is that they try to compensate for the changes in the new system, which give less weight to the written exam, by screening the candidates primarily for qualifications of a scholarly type. It therefore seems evident to us that important work has to be done with the persons responsible for defining the selection requirements and interview guidelines, and with those who carry out the selection interviews.

A Pre-Training Programme and the Construction of a Support Network

To set up a pre-qualifying training programme that prepares for better success in the competitive selection process presented us with several problems of a methodological, ideological and practical nature.

To say clearly and publicly that we carried out a preparatory course designed 'only' for ethnic minority causes, in the case of France, problems of an ideological nature, as indicated above. Not only are the institutions apparently unready to take the plunge (or rather a step forward), but also immigrants themselves do not always want to be identified as such. How could we make a selection of future candidates for pre-training considering that the places available are limited to 25 people per year in the framework of this project? Even in this project, where immigrants are clearly and unambiguously the targets of the programme, we encountered great difficulties in its implementation. We had to adapt the project to find a solution. Although our solutions were not completely satisfactory, they gave interim answers and achieved some results.

Our first task was to establish links, to put in place a network with associations working for or with immigrants. These networks sponsor young people and send them to us directly so that they can enrol in pre-qualifying training. Some associations sent us young people who do not come from immigrant origins but who were already working with ethnic minorities in deprived suburbs. We have, within the limits of the places available, opened a third of the places to this latter category in order to avoid the feeling of 'ghettoisation' in training. The second level of the problem is that the organisation of this kind of training was often premised on an assumed deficiency of the beneficiaries. As with many similar training courses, it seems that if the situation is not clearly debated among participants and organisers, there is a risk that the difficulties arising from the lack of resources (in this case financial ones, i.e., the limited places available in social work education due to budget restrictions imposed by the state on schools of social work) will be transformed into a 'deficiency' inherent in the candidates. Furthermore, the general deterioration of the employment situation in the last twenty years in France and in other European countries, coupled with the promising job market for social workers has meant that training in social work attracts more and more people. Many of the candidates have already attended universities in other fields and have a certain cultural knowledge that enables them to succeed more easily in competitive examinations. The general rise of the levels of studies at the selection point, therefore, restricts entry to such schools to those who are holders of a baccalaureate. In the training programme, under the heading of pre-qualifying courses, we organised all this information. This has, therefore, been the subject of discussion and of work with people coming to be registered. At this stage of our project, the results of pre-training seem encouraging. Already, among 25 candidates who have completed the first course and submitted themselves for the selection process, 16 succeeded in the selection exams and have subsequently entered the training programme for social work this year. We hope that the rate of success for candidates coming from the next pre-qualifying course will be as high or even higher in coming years.

Conclusion

We are conscious of how difficult the transfer of our experience and plan of action is. Indeed, it would have been necessary to detail the whole range of actions taken more fully and to discuss them more deeply. Two constraints have weighed heavily. The first is the space that we were obliged to give to the presentation of the political and social context of France in relation to the problems specific to immigrants and refugees. The second relates to the detailed descriptions of the specific context of social work, in particular, the conditions for selection. We considered that without the descriptions of these two elements, our strategies and conditions of action could not be clearly understood. Nevertheless, we underline that the implications of our co-operation with European partners[6] are of prime importance for the success of our project. Indeed, in places where the partners already have a working culture in the field of social action and ethnic minorities, we were able to use the experience they had gained and therefore avoid making some of the errors and blunders that are quite frequent in projects of this kind. Also, through this project we have attempted to develop a model of action that on the one hand, distinguishes itself from an approach that is essentially 'culturalist' and tackles the problem of minorities only at the level of culture. This would imply that culture was static and not subject to modifications with time and in relation to other available cultures. On the other hand, it distinguishes itself from a type of universalism that remains rhetorical with affirmations of equality without recognising that these affirmations never actually change the current reality. We are conscious of the contradictions of an approach of this type. The aim here is not to present a new theoretical approach but, through experimentation, to augment the thoughts and ideas that contribute so much to the search for a new perspective.

A major development in France is the introduction a new bill on the parity of men and women in politics. This bill seems to herald a change in the traditional universalist conception which did not admit until now that type of action. It remains to be seen what consequences will arise from this for dealing with ethnic minorities.

Notes

1. The implementation of this project was due to the hard work of many colleagues. They are alphabetically Christine Bâtime, Yamina Bensaadoune, Manuel Boucher, Elizabeth Cordier, , Jacques Jouanne, Rose-Marie Keller, Catherine Legrand, Evelynne Dupont Lourdel, Christelle Rabanelle and Yvonne Thomas.
2. I take the opportunity to thank Naina Patel for her advice and for having given me the benefit of her experience in the implementation of this type of project. On this matter see CCETSW (1991).
3. On the issue of social workers from immigrant origin, see the work of Jovelin (1993, 1996).
4. Except competitive examinations necessary to enter specific schools called '*grande écoles*' or similar and the selections for certain courses during study programmes (for example medicine, and pharmacology). On this matter see the work of Pierre Bourdieu (1989).
5. In schools where the selection is based principally on the social experience of the candidates and not on being the best in the French language, the results of admittance are completely different from the majority of schools. Only very few schools select candidates this way.
6. The transnational partners of our project are: Fondazione Silvano Andolfi, Italy; The Olofström kommun, Sweden; The National Youth Foundation, Greece; Net Step Project, Finland, The University of Kent, England.

References

Abye, T. (1994), *Diagnostic local de sécurité: ville de Grand Couronne, sous la direction de Guido.* De Ridder, Laboratoire d'étude et de recherche sociale, Institut du développement social, Canteleu.

Abye, T. and Eckmann, M. (1998), *Interculturaliser les écoles sociales? Réflexions à propos du 'Projet Néerlandais des Çinq'.* Rapport pour la conférence d'ECSPRESS, Ostrawa.

Bataille, P. (1997), *Le racisme au travail.* Paris, La découverte.

Bensaadoune, Y. (1998), *Observatoire, état des lieux de la formation. Étude des pratiques de formation concernant la question de l'immigration à l'Institut du développement social.* Canteleu, Institut du développement social.

Bernard, P. and Weill, N. (1998), *Une virulente polémique sur les données 'ethniques' divise les démographes.* Paris, Le monde.

Bourdieu, P. (1989), *La noblesse d'État: Grandes Ecoles et esprits de corps.* Paris, Les Editions de Minuit.

Brubaker, R (1992), *Cititzenship and Nationhood in France and Germany.* Cambridge MA, Harvard University Press.

CCETSW (1991), *Setting the Context for Change.* London, Central Council for Education and Training in Social Work.

Commission Européenne (1997), *Emploi-Integra, parcours d'insertion sociale et professionnelle en faveur des exclus.* Luxembourg, Emploi et Affaires Sociales.

Jovelin, E. (1993), 'Les travailleurs sociaux d'origine étrangère. Destins professionnels et choix du métier', *Revue Française de l'Enfance. Expansion Scientifique Française*, n°4.

Jovelin, E. (1996), 'Les assistants sociaux d'origine étrangère. Repli professionnel ou vocation?', *Revue RAMALA/CEFISEM* n° 19.

Le Bras, H. (1997), 'L'impossible descendance étrangère', *Population* n°5, pp. 1173–1186.

Le Bras, H. (1998), *Le démon des descendances: Démographie et extrême droite.* Paris, Edition de l'aube.

Schnapper, D. (1991), *La France de l'intégration. Sociologie de la nation en 1990.* Paris, Editions Gallimard.

Schnapper, D. (1992), *L'Europe des immigrés. Essai sur les politiques d'immigration.* Paris, Editions François Bourin.

Schnapper, D. (1998), *La relation à l'autre: Au coeur de la pensée sociologique.* Paris, Gallimard.

Tribalat, M. (1997), 'Les populations d'origine étrangère en France métropolitaine', *Population* n°1, pp. 163–219.

PART III:

MAINSTREAMING SOCIAL WORK PRACTICE WITH DIVERSE CLIENT GROUPS

8 Linking Our Circles

RICHARD P. BARTH

Introduction

Race, culture and ethnicity can be amongst the most important assets that social workers and clients draw on in their efforts to produce desired outcomes. Understanding the importance of racial, cultural, and ethnic identity to our clients and to ourselves can serve as an asset in our work. Yet, there is no question that the extent to which, and way in which, we emphasize these differences can also hinder what we do. This chapter provides some examples from the children's services in the United States that illustrate some of the challenges of providing effective services across racial divides. Part of the message from these efforts to protect children and to see that they have permanent homes is that when race and ethnicity of children unduly influence service provision, poor services may result. In addition, policy makers may intervene to reduce the emphasis on race and culture in decision making about services receipt. Finally, the chapter concludes that acknowledging differences between us and our clients should not paralyze us or keep us from reaching out, as much helping can be accomplished across racial and ethnic divides.

Looking at the Issue

The reader should understand the filter through which I look as I struggle with the issues of ethnic sensitive practice. Until this last year, I was a Northern Californian, having been a student or faculty member at the University of California at Berkeley for 21 years. California is a study in diversity – indeed the University of California at Berkeley's student body has had no ethnic group with more than 39% representation for many years. Californians have struggled with the uses of race in public policy in ways that few other citizen groups have struggled, and have passed a state constitutional amendment that prohibits the use of race in public policy – basically, ending affirmative action programs. By constitutional amendment, they have also severely curtailed bi-lingual education programs (programs which taught children in English and Spanish for many years). Although

138 Beyond Racial Divides

social work and higher education groups were against these changes, the support for these measures was broad-based and communicates that the public may be more concerned about emphasizing our similarities than our differences. This is not to suggest that this is the 'correct' world view, but it is certainly humbling. And, there is no doubt that there is yet no optimal emphasis of our differences and similarities.

My research has also taught me about race and culture and has focused on child welfare services with particular interest in foster care and adoption. I have been involved in state and national policy making with regard to the use of race and culture in child welfare decision making and have come to understand the delicate balance between the benefits of celebrating differences between people of varied descents and the risks of allowing those differences to capture us and keep us from providing maximum protection and opportunity for all children and their families.

Ethnic Differences and Evidence-Based Practice

One of the ways we must become careful analysts of racial and ethnic differences is to better understand the meaning of those differences with regard to the receipt of services. So in the U.S. we often find that African-American and Native American (but not Latino) children are placed out of their homes at a rate that is disproportionate to their membership in the general population, and this is often reason for concern. Indeed, policy makers sometimes have used the evidence of disproportionate service receipt to challenge service providers to change their approaches – inferring that this practice is racist, at worst, or unfair, at best. When our federal government asked the Children's Bureau (which administers federal child welfare services policy in the U.S.) they pulled together a work group that generated, in early 1999, a draft of 'Outcomes for State Child Welfare Services' (US DHHS, February 2, 1999). In that document there is a proposal that one of the permanency related outcomes that states should track is to 'reduce the disparity of length of time in foster care between children of color and Caucasian children'. Although the outcome indicator does not clarify whether increasing the length of time in care for Caucasian children is as desirable a way to reduce the disparity as is reducing the time in care for 'children of color,' it really does not matter; neither approach is desirable unless it is clear what happens to children afterward.

That is, we should not base human services policy on the appearance of fairness; we must base it on evidence that our clients are getting what they need. If the risks for children of color are different from the risks for Caucasian children, then they will need different services to protect them against those risks. Policies and practices that move us beyond racial divides should be most careful not to ignore real differences in risk for the appearance of equality. The ultimate goal is to provide equal opportunity for safety and development, not a client-base that is racially balanced.

Also, for older children, reducing the length of stay may reduce the benefits of protection that those stays produce. For African-American children (whose lengths of stay are not especially similar to other 'children of color' except American Indian children) the risks of mortality and incarceration following premature returns from foster care may be greater than they are for Caucasian children. We know, for example, that African-American children die of child abuse at a rate three times higher than that of other children (Collins and Nichols, 1999; Herman-Giddens, Brown, Verbiest et al., 1999; Seigel, Graves, Maloney et al., 1996) – a difference that appears to be greatly reduced by foster care. They are also far more likely to end up in the correctional system.

If their risks from being out of foster care are so much greater, why should their lengths of stay be the same? This is just one example of how a child welfare services performance indicator that takes no consideration of outcomes that occur for children after they receive child welfare services could lead to a dangerous disregard for the well-being of African-American children.

For in our research we have shown that children of color who receive fewer services are substantially more likely to go on to have worse outcomes than white children. More specifically, African-American and Latino children who were investigated for child abuse and neglect after age 7 were two times more likely to later enter the California Youth Authority (CYA), California's most secure detention facilities for youth, than were white children. Yet when those children of color receive ongoing services their likelihood of entering CYA was cut in half and equaled the rates for white children who received services (Jonson-Reid and Barth, 2000; Jonson-Reid and Barth, in press). Presumably those children who received ongoing services had higher levels of family problems and were at greater risk of poor outcomes. Assuming that this higher level of risk was the likely basis for their receipt of services, yet they ended up, following those services, with half the rate of subsequent incarceration, we can see how important the services were to protecting their futures. Apparently, the families that had their cases closed and then ended up having their children incarcerated were provided with less services than they needed.

Although we do not have all the reasons for these case decisions, our interviews with child welfare decision makers suggest a grave concern about over-involvement or unfair involvement in the lives of minority families. Thus, a lack of comfort with minority families and a lack of confidence in the benefits of the services we offer for those families may result in poor practice. If those workers believe that ethnic sensitive practice involves minimal intervention, then this misunderstanding can have very serious consequences. We may risk underserving families of color far more than we do overserving them (Rose, 1999).

We also examined the likelihood that children in foster care or after foster care would die from such preventable deaths as homicide, child abuse and neglect, accidents and fires. We found that the likelihood of dying from all causes and from preventable causes was higher among African-American children than than among children in foster care or in the general community (Barth and Blackwell, 1998). Also, among children of color of different age groups, the likelihood of dying from preventable deaths after foster care was higher than it was during foster care.

These studies suggest how important it is not to assume that greater rates of admission to foster care or longer stays in foster care – which contribute to disproportionality – are necessarily harmful to children. Indeed, although there are many ways to reduce the use of foster care, these ways must be judged against the higher standard of providing safety and protection for children and the effects for the community resulting from inadequate levels of intervention.

We must not move beyond racial divides by overlooking the differences in experiences and needs that our children have. We should not assume that the differences found in service patterns are always a result of racism or of misunderstanding cultural or ethnic strengths. Some of these are also a response to underlying vulnerabilities that may have a basis in racism but which exist in the current realities of children's lives. In an odd way, the super-sensitivity of service providers to risks and to communities that they do not understand can work to the benefit of children by resulting in more thorough assessments. Carol Jenny and her colleagues (1999) prepared a well-publicized paper showing that white children with skull fractures were more likely to have them undiagnosed and then subsequently die than were children of color. This was interpreted by some as an indication of racist practice – that is, that service providers are more suspicious of African-American families than of Caucasian families. A more direct interpretation is that Caucasian children received less benefit from service providers than other children. Moving beyond racial divides then also requires that we not underestimate the needs of children or other service recipients because they are on the same side of the divide as we are.

An important study of Finnish war children (Räsänen, 1999) shows the challenges that children face even as they later become adults whose language ability distinguishes them from the communities around them. For many of these children good, warm, caring relationships served as protective factors to reduce the disadvantages experienced through their repeated and disruptive migrations between Finland and Sweden. We know too little about the way that children and youth experience race and culture, to be sure, but preliminary evidence suggests that younger children are quite open to receiving social support across racial divides. Apparently these young Finnish refugees understood and accepted the love and support offered to them. Such assistance across cultural lines is vital to helping children understand that they are part of a social compact that is far larger than their own geographic racial community.

Sensitivity to Ethnic Realities

Ethnic-sensitive social work practice requires knowledge of the likely impact of the ethnic reality of those with whom we work, and requires commitment to the social work values of helping people to enhance the quality of their lives (Devore and Schlesinger, 1997). In Bruyere's chapter (this volume) much information is provided to help persons working with varied populations to develop a framework for use in achieving the goals of ethnic sensitive practice. The scheme of life of the Anishnabe people reminds us that we all have our own cognitive and affective schemes that have substantial influence on decisions we make as social workers. I know that I was struck by the central role of the spiritual life in the Anishnabe world view and how focused I have been on the cognitive, affective, and physical outcomes of children's services. His work shows me that my work has a significant shortcoming.

Gord Bruyere also brings illumination to our quest for ethnic-sensitive and socially competent practice by eloquently describing the wisdom-making process itself. This begins with a vision – a vision in which we choose to engage the learning process and identify what it is that we wish to learn. In time, according to the Anishnabe way, we develop skills and self-knowledge. With vision, time, and knowledge we can take wise action.

The vision for First Nations peoples in Canada and ethnic groups around the world is to increase self-governance. This desire often arises from a profound sense of injustice, abuse, and isolation. The quite understandable reaction by minority group members to such historic mistreatment may be a hostile and mistrusting approach to working with persons of the dominant culture. Yet without the collaboration and support of the resource rich and ethnically sensitive members of the dominant culture, the odds against achievement of social and economic success for ethnic minorities are overwhelming.

Policy Relevance

Social policies and local practices in the U.S. have too often sharpened the lines between ethnic groups in ways that have resulted in greater disadvantage for these groups. As a case in point, the American policy of nearly requiring that African-American children had to be placed in African-American adoptive homes resulted in greater discrimination against African-American children who subsequently had their chances of adoption cut in half and experienced long delays in foster care while same-race adoptive placements were sought (Avery, 1998; Barth, 1997). Whereas preferences for same-race or same-culture placements make sense, when these preferences become categorical and rigid they threaten the welfare and progress of historically disadvantaged groups. In the American case, activists from the civil rights community argued for a federal law to greatly limit the use of race or culture in foster care and adoption placements.

This was accomplished (and such a law was passed), but we now must operate with a public policy that has become rigid and excessive in its own way (Brooks, Barth, Bussiere, and Jackson, 1999). The Multiethnic Placement Act and its amendments now prevent the routine use of race for making any placement decisions for foster children. This means that it is illegal to match children to foster homes or adoptive homes even when families of their ethnic or cultural background are already available to receive them, if there are unmatched families who had previously entered the available pool of adoptive homes. A fundamental lesson learned from this experience is that when social workers become rigid in practices to accommodate ethnic differences, they may be overruled by those who believe that we have become indiscriminate in our practices.

Celebration without Separation

Alternative visions to such a rigid multiculturalism are available. David Hollinger (1995) calls for a *postethnic perspective* to better articulate and deliver the lofty goals of multiculturalism. Although I do not like the name 'postethnic' very much, I do agree with the primary principle he articulates – basically, that race and culture should be sources of celebration not separation. This perspective pulls together and supports certain elements of multiculturalism and criticizes others. Hollinger's postethnic perspective favors voluntary over involuntary affiliations, views talent as a component of all communities, calls for us to be determined to make room for new communities, and promotes the celebration of people's different ethnic and racial backgrounds. The postethnic perspective affirms the last generation's recognition that many of the ideas and cultural practices, once taken to be universal, are specific to certain cultures. We must recognize the ways in which these practices differ from local traditions but do not diverge from our safety or care-giving standards. A postethnic perspective celebrates the cosmopolitan elements of multiculturalism but cuts against pluralistic tendencies of multiculturalism to draw our lines and boundaries around ethnic groups – boundaries designed to preserve them but that may have the reverse effect. A postethnic perspective cannot solve all our policy and practice problems but can provide a long-term framework for its analysis.

Gord Bruyere's poetic descriptions of the Anishnabe schemes of life help us to gain a sense of comfort that could be helpful should any of us be called on to provide services to Anishnabe families. Such comfort is the basic element in ethnic sensitive practice. A growing body of research shows that the greatest risk from service providers is that they will do too little in the way of intervening to assist people from different cultures rather than that they will do too much. My colleagues and I have reviewed the research on services to children that addresses the issue of race and found children of color in the United States are routinely underserved (Courtney, Barth, Berrick et al., 1996).

Concerns about the Safety and Well-Being of Children are Universal

In Gord Bruyere's words, it is critical to listen to the perspective of others and to be both a teacher and a learner; and we must also, in his words, 'trust in what we know'. In many cases, what we know is that a significant risk to a child's physical, cognitive, affective, and spiritual well-being can be confirmed by other family or community members. Concerns about the safety and well-being of children tend to cut across race and class lines. Whereas moving children to avoid temporary harm may result in modest longer-term risks, we also know from recent research on the biochemistry of the brain that children can suffer permanent limitations in their capacity to process information and emotion if they are allowed to experience chronic deprivation.

A caring non-blaming environment provides protection against the dangers of murderous environments and traumas of change and family disruption (Räsänen, 1999). This is consistent with a significant body of research indicating the benefits of stable foster care and adoption placements (Barth, 2000; Berrick, Needell, Barth, and Jonson-Reid, 1998), even when these are cross-ethnic or cross-racial placements (Brooks and Barth, 1999).

This does not suggest that there are no iatrogenic effects of foster care, nor can these findings rule out the possibility that children placed in homes with less cultural familiarity will do less well. This is just not necessarily so. Racial and ethnic identity and politics does not have equal importance to all individuals at all times.

Finally, Gord Buyere's discussion of the Circles of Life reminds me of Edwin Markham's verses in 'The man with the hoe', cited in Hollinger (1995). Marham writes,

> He drew a circle that shut me out –
> Heretic, rebel, a thing to flout,
> but love and I had the wit to win
> we drew a circle that took him in.

We certainly must go as far as necessary to draw circles that bring others in to the mainstream economic and social life. Ethnic sensitive social work practice certainly must do this in a way that integrates safety, respect, and inclusion.

Conclusions

- We can affirm the cultural histories and experiences of children without becoming so sensitive to them that we begin to believe that they are the central organizing principle for the development of services for children.

- We can value cultural, geographic, and family continuity for children without overlooking the potential benefits of planned and caring discontinuity.
- Our responsibility to our children can be one of the greatest reasons to move beyond racial divides and to be sure that we surround them with linked circles of caring.

References

Avery, R. (1998), *Public Agency Adoption in New York State: Phase 1 Report. Foster Care Histories of Children Freed for Adoption in New York State: 1980–1993.* Ithaca, NY, Cornell University.

Barth, R.P. (1997), 'Effects of race and age on the odds of adoption vs. remaining in long-term foster care,' *Child Welfare*, vol. 76, pp. 285–308.

Barth, R.P. (2000), 'Adoption services,' in M. Kluger and P. Curtis (eds.), *What Works in Child Welfare Services*. Washington, DC, Child Welfare League of America.

Barth, R.P. and Blackwell, D.L. (1998), 'Death rates among California's foster care and former foster care populations,' *Children and Youth Services Review*, vol. 20, pp. 577–604.

Berrick, J.D., Needell, B.N., Barth, R.P., and Jonson-Reid, M. (1998), *The Tender Years: Toward Developmentally Sensitive Child Welfare Practice*. New York, Oxford University Press.

Brooks, D. and Barth, P.B. (1999), 'Adjustment outcomes of adult transracial and inracial adoptees: Effects of race, gender, adoptive family structure, and placement history,' *American Journal of Orthopsychiatry*, vol. 69, pp. 87–105.

Brooks, D., Barth, R.P., Bussiere, A., and Jackson, G. (1999), 'Implementing the multi-ethnic placement act,' *Social Work*, vol. 44, pp. 167–178.

Bruyere, G. (1999), 'Making circles: Renewing First Nations ways of helping.' Paper presented at the conference 'Beyond Racial Divides: Ethnicities in Social Work Practice', Stockholm, Sweden, April 22–24.

Collins, K.A. and Nichols, C.A. (1999), 'A decade of pediatric homicide – A retrospective study at the Medical University of South Carolina,' *American Journal of Forensic Medicine and Pathology*, vol. 20 (2), pp. 160–172.

Courtney, M.E., Barth, R.P., Berrick, J.D., Brooks, D., Needell, B., and Park, L. (1996), 'Race and child welfare services,' *Child Welfare*, vol. 75, pp. 99–137.

Devore, E. and Schlesinger, E.G. (1997), *Ethnic-Sensitive Social Work Practice*. Columbus, OH, Charles C. Thomas.

Herman-Giddens, M.E., Brown, G., Verbiest, S., Carlson, P.J., Hooten, E.G., Howell, E., and Butts, J.D. (1999), 'Underascertainment of child abuse mortality in the United States,' *The Journal of the American Medical Association*, vol. 282, pp. 463–467.

Hollinger, D. (1995), *Postethnic America: Beyond Multiculturalism*. New York, Basic Books.

Jenny C, Hymel, K.P, and Ritzen A. (1999), 'Analysis of missed cases of abusive head trauma,' *Journal of the American Medical Society*, vol. 281, pp. 621–626.

Jonson-Reid, M. and Barth, R.P. (2000), 'From maltreatment report to juvenile incarceration: The role of child welfare services,' *Child Abuse and Neglect*, vol. 24, pp. 505–520.

Jonson-Reid, M. and Barth, R.P. (in press), 'From placement to prison: The path to

adolescent incarceration from child welfare supervised foster or group care,' *Social Work*.
Räsänen, E. (1999), 'Finnish war children.' Paper presented at the conference 'Beyond Racial Divides: Ethnicities in Social Work Practice', Stockholm, Sweden, April 22–24.
Rose, S. (1999), 'Reaching consensus on child neglect: African American mothers and child welfare workers,' *Children and Youth Services Review*, vol. 21, pp. 463–480.
Siegel, C.D., Graves, P., Maloney, K., Norris, J.M., Calonge, B.N., and Lezotte, D. (1996), 'Mortality from intentional and unintentional injury among infants of young mothers in Colorado, 1986 to 1992,' *Archives of Pediatrics and Adolescent Medicine*, vol. 150 (10), pp. 1077–1083.

9 Minority Ethnic Elderly: Ageing with Care

NAINA PATEL

Introduction

Who has sent old age?
Strength in the body disappears,
Work progresses in slow motion
But I like the "ladoos"(cakes)
And the idea of visiting places – an adventure.
Faith in god and belief in oneself will see that this adventure comes
There is so much to see and learn!
Shantaben, aged 79 years

So begins the quote to the UK entry in a publication, *Living and Ageing in Europe* (Patel and Mertens, 1998). It illustrates the reality of many Black and minority ethnic (BME) older persons as being neither passive nor in-active as they age. This chapter outlines some of the key developments in care and the challenges that await us as the numbers rise in the context of the current care position. It should be noted that while many aspects outlined below are relevant to the UK, they are also applicable to other countries in Europe. This is not simply in relation to cultural, linguistic and religious differences, but also experiences generated as a result of elders being a minority, 'migrant' and /or refugees. Such a background explains the external forces in society that determine opportunities, life chances and consequent adjustments minorities may make, successfully or not. For example, it was one aspect of this recognition, racism, which the European Parliament regarded as significant in European countries and thus declared 1997 as the *European Year against Racism*. In 1998, an action programme was instituted to establish the European Monitoring Centre on Racism and Xenophobia.

In this chapter, we first consider who the BME older people are with an explanation of the main issues and developments in the 1980s to 1999[1] – a nineteen-year period. The issues and developments span policy and service considerations in the provision of care to BME elders. We explain that the go-slow approach of care providers for elders in many countries and the consequent responses by BME elder organisations can only reinforce the view that BME are marginal to society. The citing of the frequent myth that they wish to return home in their old age prevents society looking at BME elder groups as permanent citizens. Moreover, without understanding their complex life and living and ageing as a dynamic process, the issue of BME elders gets frozen into a care concept of 'needs' to the exclusion of other areas. The needs are then bound purely into a static notion of culture, language and religion.[2]

We should stress that all is not well for the majority of older people and much needs to be done to improve the quality of care. Our focus is on BME elders and the UK, although other EU countries show similar trends in the characteristics of BME and in their responses to this group. For example, the recently produced film by the CNEOPSA team (1999) showed that irrespective of BME elder composition, the issue of dementia and BME care challenged policymakers, health and social care professionals and planners in all four EU countries selected: Finland, Spain, Netherlands and the UK. However, in some areas the UK is ahead, and so a focus on this one country can also act as an indicator of the need to progress further in BME elder care.

The key questions to be asked in BME elder care are: Do we seek parity with majority elder care or do we seek alternatives? How are developments structured into the economy when examining the issue of 'separate vs. mainstream' services? Are the developments such that we are locked into the debate of asking for 'more of the same'; i.e., a question of *quantity* rather than *quality and appropriateness*? The examination of policy and service developments spanning nineteen years enables us to explore these questions analytically.

Demographic Trends

A Black and minority ethnic presence in the UK is not a recent phenomenon – with the Irish coming in the 16th, 17th and 18th centuries and the Jews, the Poles and other minority groups in the late 19th and 20th centuries. The migration of people from the Caribbean and Indian sub-continent mainly dates from the post-WWII period. According to the 1991 Census, there were some 3.2 million minority ethnic people constituting some 5.5% of the total population in the Great Britain. Their presence extends to most districts of Great Britain and Northern Ireland, making the UK a multi-ethnic society.

Table 1 below shows the distribution of the population in Great Britain according to age and ethnicity. It shows the relative youth of the minority ethnic population compared with the White population and the diversity in patterns of ageing amongst different ethnic groups. Nevertheless, over 4% of minority ethnic people are over 65 years of age compared with 16% of the White population. Of a total of some 8.8 million people aged 65+ years, 130,000 are from minority ethnic groups. In the 85+ age group, minority ethnic groups account for 3,871 people from a total population of 830,678.

If we consider the share that minority ethnic and White groups, respectively, make of the total population in different age ranges, we find that minority ethnic groups make up 13.6 and 4.2% of the 45–64 and 65+ age ranges, respectively, compared with 19.2 and 19.3% for the corresponding age ranges for White groups (Owen, 1996; Warnes, 1996). This means that in the next decade there will be an increased percentage of minority ethnic people reaching retirement age, resulting in a considerable change in the present profile described above. These trends can also be seen in several European countries (Patel and Mertens, 1998).

Table 1: Age breakdown of ethnic groups in Great Britain, 1991.
(Based on data adjusted for Census under-renumeration. Original table not corrected.)

Ethnic group	Total population	Percentage of total population					
		Age 0-4	Age 5-15	Age 16-24	Age 25-44	Age 45-64	Age 65+
White	52,893.9	6.5	13.0	12.9	29.3	19.2	19.3
Ethnic minority groups	3,117.0	11.1	21.7	16.4	32.9	13.6	4.2
Black	*925,5*	*11.1*	*18.0*	*16.5*	*33.8*	*15.4*	*5.1*
– Caribbean	517.1	7.6	14.1	15.3	33.4	21.8	7.7
– African	221.9	11.8	17.1	17.0	42.7	9.5	1.8
– Other	186.4	20.1	29.6	19.3	24.6	4.4	1.6
South Asian	*1,524.3*	*10.9*	*24.6*	*16.5*	*30.5*	*13.5*	*3.9*
– Indian	865.5	8.9	20.5	15.5	34.9	14.9	5.2
– Pakistani	491.0	13.2	29.2	17.9	26.1	11.3	2.4
– Bangladeshi	167.8	15.1	31.9	17.9	20.8	12.7	1.5
Chinese and other	*667.2*	*11.6*	*20.1*	*16.1*	*36.9*	*11.4*	*3.8*
– Chinese	162.4	7.1	16.0	18.4	41.4	12.7	4.4
– Other - Asians	204.3	8.0	16.2	15.1	43.6	13.7	3.1
– Other - Other	300.5	16.4	25.0	15.5	29.9	9.2	3.9
Entire population	**55,969.2**	**6.7**	**13.5**	**13.1**	**29.5**	**18.9**	**18.5**

Source: Owens, D. (1996), p. 116.

The Socio-Economic Position

The diversity in age distribution, location concentrations – some 45% of all minority ethnic groups reside in Greater London (Owen, 1996), and London has the largest share of BME elders (PRIAE 2000) – and gender differences reflect the pattern of migration and settlement. This process has also determined the social and economic position of today's BME elders. Their social and health care needs cannot be understood without reference to their experience of employment, housing and income.

The early surveys from the Policy Studies Institute (1977, 1984) explained the unequal distribution of BME workers in the 1970s (i.e., the elders of today) by sector and industry, as being due to differences in labour requirements between various industries and discrimination by employers and unions. Once in jobs, discrimination in earnings followed suit. The disparity in earnings as regards 'working period' as well as the length of working life, coupled with known under-claiming of welfare benefits, account for the differences in pensionable income (Askham, Henshaw and Tarpey, 1995; DSS, 2000). For the emerging generation of elders, we must add the effects of long-term unemployment and continuing lower rate of participation in non-state pension schemes: 62% for Black and Indian workers compared with 69% for White workers. For other groups the figures are as low as 43 to 53% (London TEC Council, 1999). These factors may contribute to the use of services in many centres by BME elders beginning from the age of 55 years. This has serious implications for policy since there may be 'early ageing' amongst this group. PRIAE's recommendation to the Royal Commission on Long-Term Care stressed that this aspect should be 'shifted' with proactive developments rather than be accepted as the norm (Patel, 1999).

BME elders face a range of health problems, and mainstream health and social services have been inadequate in meeting their needs (Bhalla and Blakemore, 1981; Patel 1990; Pharoah, 1995; Askham et al., 1995; Lindesay, Jagger, Hibbett, Peet and Moledina 1997; Patel, Mirza, Lindblad, Amstrup and Samoli 1998; Patel, 1999). Also, compared with White groups, elderly Afro-Caribbean and Asians show evidence of a higher frequency of health services use, including general practitioners (GPs). However, frequency of contact with GPs and hospitals does not necessarily reflect the quality of treatment received. Again we find a similar patterning of ill health and disadvantage as experienced by BME elders in other European countries (Kokshoorn, 1998; Patel and Mertens, 1998).

The latest Murray and Brown Survey from the government (DH, 1998) provides us with information on policies, strategies and practice in the care of Black elders by social services departments. This survey adds to the empirical studies conducted in the last 18 years. For health we have considerably less information, although the *CNEOPSA* study (Patel et al., 1998) presents a new area hitherto neglected: research and practice agenda on managing dementia care. The Askham et al. (1995) and Pharoah studies (1995 at ACIOG) provide a wealth of information on the responsiveness of health professionals to provide 'appropriate' care to BME elders.

Ageing with Care: Evidence from the 1980s

The eight major empirical studies conducted in the 1980s that we examined (Patel, 1990) showed conclusively that BME elders need and demand care services. Moreover, the mainstream care sector is identified as being responsible for meeting this demand. But it is responsible with the qualification that services must be appropriate, accessible and adequate to be regarded as 'effective'. So requiring a particular type of food, being able to exercise religious and spiritual practices, having access to day centres that are in appropriate locations and are accessible the entire week, having staff who can understand and communicate appropriately, being able to live with dignity in a residential or sheltered home free from racial abuse from residents or staff, having privacy when bathing, and so on – these are not 'special' requirements. They are not even choices. They are basic requirements which you and I probably take for granted.

The central point here is about meeting 'specific' racial, cultural, religious and linguistic needs as a result of *ordinary* and not *special* requirements. The main difference we would suggest is the experience of racism generated during the life of BME elders.

The critical issues in providing care concern: a) the ability of mainstream providers to plan, design and provide services that are appropriate, accessible and adequate; and b) the competence of staff to provide effective services made possible through referrals, assessment and its management.

From the eight studies supplemented with the results of the national study in 1995 by Askham et al. (1995) and Pharoah (1995), we concluded *then* that differences in needs were not being recognised at a time when the number of BME elders was growing. Progress remained 'patchy, ad hoc and piecemeal'. So, for example, in primary health care services, the employment of health workers linked with social workers and specific personnel working with BME elders was critical in removing barriers to information, communication and access to services. However, the issue remained whether this critical chain of personnel between the care system and BME elders had sufficient power to affect the necessary changes required in decision making and in the allocation of resources to affect the required developments.

We also commented from the studies examined in the 1980s that in the absence of mainstream care provision, self-help projects were being established to respond to BME elders' immediate needs. The projects operated with shoestring budgets, temporary structures in staffing and accommodation and rising demands. In reality, BME elder centres had become the *'primary'* providers of care (i.e., a substitute for the mainstream) rather than a *'secondary'* provider (complementing mainstream services). We analysed that such organisations were financially supported and positively viewed by mainstream health and social services because they provided a 'buffer' against direct criticism of failure to provide services by the mainstream. Since they are characterised by small budgets, often on a short-term basis, with poor infrastructure, a 'fringe' provision is created which in a climate of financial stringency can be trimmed, cut or stopped, as shown by various authors (Patel, 1990; Atkin, 1996).

The mainstream lack of adequate responses to BME elders' care can be explained by considering how the providers focus on apparent cultural attributes and equity. The experiences of BME elders reflect racial and cultural stereotyping when the issue of care and welfare is considered. Amongst these are: 'We treat everyone the same'; 'Our service is open to all'; 'Providing for special needs is discriminatory – it is racism in reverse'. These arguments have all been used when adjustments in the existing mainstream care for cultural responsiveness are called upon. Such mainstream services would be day care, meals delivered at home for the housebound, residential services and health care.

Let us briefly consider the continuing racial stereotype of 'extended families provide care', where the popular image is that an extended network of 'families within families' provides care and socio-psychological support. Hence, 'They look after their own.' Strangely, such virtues are married to another stereotype of 'overcrowded households'. Family structures are continually changing in all our societies as they adjust to internal and external conditions; minority ethnic families are not immune from this process. The important question is not whether extended family structures exist[3], but whether minority ethnic elders are receiving the necessary forms of care from the social, health and housing systems, irrespective of the nature of the family structure. 'They look after their own' is a useful myth and constitutes a cost-effective evasion, maintaining the status quo in services. The myth is sadly operationalised by many professional staff, including social workers and doctors, who do not refer BME elders to existing services, believing that their needs are best provided for by the presence of extended families. In the absence of such families, for BME elders *no referral* to services means *no assessment* of their needs, hence, *no services*. The myth essentially determines the eligibility criteria for services, not the rights or needs of BME elders. Even when BME elders are referred, there is still the next hurdle of being appropriately assessed and of there being appropriate services. In PRIAE's report to the British government on 'who gets what service', we argued that *any eligibility criterion that is good for minority use will also be good for majority users*. But the government's Fair Access initiative will be limited in effect if the issues at the a) pre-entry stage (information, knowledge of services), b) entry stage (fair access/ eligibility criteria) and c) post-entry stage (service availability, appropriateness and quality) are not effectively addressed in policy, planning and professional agendas engaging with BME elders and their organisations (PRIAE, 1999).

A Contrast – Evidence from the 1990s

In the UK, the then Conservative Government passed the National Health Service and Community Care Act 1990, which was implemented in 1993. This introduced the mixed economy of care with purchaser – provider split in the health services. The key objective was to make sure that users live in the community as independently as possible. Flexibility, choice, users' and carers' involvement were some of the overriding concerns of this policy, as was the intention to consult with minority groups in putting together a purchasing strategy (called commissioning role). This emphasis follows from the 1989 White Paper, *Caring for People*, which stated:

> The Government recognises that people from different cultural backgrounds have particular care needs and problems. Minority communities may have different concepts of community care and it is important that service providers are sensitive to these variations. Good community care will take account of the circumstances of minority communities and will be planned in consultation with them (Department of Health, 1989: 10–11).

So How Did This Work in Reality?

For the answer, we turn to two main reports, the first from the Department of Health and the second from the CNEOPSA Project study on dementia, both published in 1998.

We will first consider the Government's own inspection of social services in a report entitled *They Look After Their Own, Don't They?*, written by Murray and Brown (1998). We briefly summarise their findings below.

- Regarding *policies, strategies and planning*, the inspection found that in the main there was reference to minorities but specific issues relating to elders were often absent. Where there was mention, 'best practice' included examples of effective joint planning between health, social services and minority ethnic elders' organisations; ethnic record-keeping and monitoring systems routinely used by staff; and 'race' and ethnicity treated as integral to policy planning and delivery rather than being marginalised.

- On *communication and information*, it found that some organisations had produced information in languages accessible to minorities, or communication strategies were being developed with those communities and clear guidelines were issued for staff. These are all essential to enable BME elders who cannot communicate in English to access services.

- For an elder to receive care services, *assessment and care management* is critical. The report stated that assessors' skills in anti-discriminatory practice, cultural sensitivity and giving confidence to elders' and their carers to exercise 'choice' are significant in determining eligibility of services and the determination of a care package. Here it found that best practice included advocacy for elders and their carers, participation of elders in their assessments and care plans and minority ethnic staff working in teams that assess and manage care plans.

- The effect of the Community Care Act was to ensure that the users (BME elders in our case) have *effective* services. For our target group, responding to cultural, social, linguistic and spiritual considerations are *ordinary* and not special needs that have to be met differently to constitute *effective* practice.

The report pointed out the following. On *service delivery*, it noted that there were 'genuine' attempts by mainstream authorities to respond appropriately to minority elders' needs. However, the progress made was variable. The report noted that:

> ... service choice was limited in the majority of Local Authority areas and the eurocentric nature of the service provision meant... basic services like meals-

on-wheels were provided in an inappropriate manner (Murray and Brown, 1998).

The report recognised the critical role played by BME organisations in service provision, while acknowledging the difficulties in funding and infra-structure. As to best practice, it found examples of 'effective' working with minority ethnic organisations and support to them; residential care homes where staff could communicate in appropriate languages and food was pre-pared in accordance with residents' cultural requirements; direct partici-pation in service delivery by staff who shared the same cultural background as the elders; and positive images built up through reminiscence work.

The report is extensive. But, the above gives us some insight into the scale of work still required to meet the principles outlined in the quote cited above on Community Care and BME groups. We can conclude from reading the vast recommendations on the overall rate of care developments to BME elders in the late 1990s that 'some authorities are making good progress, some are doing a little, and others are not doing anything at all' (Patel, 1999: 276).

In the analysis we made in the 1980s (Patel, 1990), we termed this go-slow approach as 'ad hoc, patchy and piecemeal'. The 'go-slow' approach suggests that, undeniably, some progress is being made. Indeed, our con-tention is that we know quite well which models of care work and which do not. But there is an urgent need to accelerate progress in this emerging area. At the same time, we cannot deny the conclusion reached above, that there is a trend of neglect in the context of rising numbers of BME elders. Further-more, the very title of the Government report, *They Look After Their Own, Don't They?*, though ironical, suggests a recurring theme in the employment of cultural and racial stereotyping, which we explained above for the 1980s. Such experience of care to BME elders is not restricted to the UK alone. Gaunt (1998) reaches a similar conclusion for Sweden on the *primary* care role played by BME elder organisations and the need for resources. He writes:

> Minority ethnic groups cannot operate their services without economic sup-port from the municipality...will this in future mean that some minority ethnic elderly will go without care just because the minority ethnic related association they belong to was not successful at lobbying? (Guant, 1998: 115).

These care experiences to a variable degree extend to other European countries as well (see Patel and Mertens, 1998).

A Focus on Dementia/Alzheimer's Disease

Our second study covers the research undertaken by the project 'Care Needs of Ethnic Older Persons with Alzheimer's' (CNEOPSA, 1999; Patel and Mirza et al., 1998), based at PRIAE. The project is concerned with dementia and minority ethnic elderly, and examined the UK, Denmark and France in the initial study (Patel, et al., 1998) and later, the Netherlands, Spain and Finland (CNEOPSA, 1999). Here, we take up only the salient points covered in both publications. The purpose of the CNEOPSA Project was to establish country profile and country practice with future agendas mapped in terms of research, developments and professional practice. For complete details the reader is advised to refer to the publications Patel et al. (1998) and CNEOPSA (1999). We worked with the following paradox (Marshall, 1997) and found it to be true for all the countries examined: 'The world of dementia is colour-blind and the world of minority ethnic organisations is dementia-blind'.

We briefly explain the main points on dementia in the UK and our focus on minority ethnic organisations below.

Dementia in the UK: Epidemiological Profile

Prevalence According to Age

By the year 2001, 15% of the UK population will be over 65 – representing more than one in six people. Since Alzheimer's disease increases in frequency as we get older, it will become a greater concern for society in general. Table 2 shows its prevalence in different age groups in the UK (in Barnes, 1997).

Table 2: Prevalence of dementia in the UK.

Age (years)	Prevalence by age
40-65	1.0% (1 in 100)
65-70	2.0% (1 in 50)
70-80	5.0% (1 in 20)
80 plus	20.0% (1 in 5)

Prevalence amongst Ethnic Minorities

Information on the prevalence of Alzheimer's disease in BME groups is scanty and research suggests that it is a 'hidden problem' as opposed to being a 'non-existent' one (Brownlie, 1991). However, some estimates can be made. Figures from the 1991 census showed that there were 97,100 people from ethnic minority groups in Britain 65 years and over (not adjusting for under-renumeration). If we assume a similar ratio of one in 20 for the general population (see Table 2), then there are an estimated 5,000 people from ethnic minorities with Alzheimer's disease in the UK (from Alzheimer's Society, UK; Owen, 1996; see also Barnes, 1997).

Country Practice: An Examination of One Aspect of the UK Study – Minority Ethnic Organisations

If the management of care needs of BME elders with dementia is to be properly addressed from the point of view of policy and the capacity of organisations to plan and provide care, then our examination of this area must begin with the critical players. Therefore, our main questionnaire concentrated on BME organisations catering for the elderly. A shorter questionnaire was also developed and aimed at professionals working with BME elders with dementia. Furthermore, some data relating to family carers were also generated so as to give a more complete picture of the system of care.

Methodology – General Approach

The interviews were conducted with minority ethnic residential or day care organisations between June and September 1997. Twelve organisations were interviewed using the questionnaires, all of which catered for ethnic minority older people. Ten of these interviews were conducted face-to-face with managers, with a visit to the organisation itself to establish rapport, and two were conducted via the telephone. There were a number of criteria and considerations in choosing the organisations for this study:

- Ethnicity spread – to cover a number of different ethnic minority groups, including Afro-Caribbean, Chinese, Polish, Asian and Jewish.

- Geography – organisations from selected cities of England and Scotland were chosen to reflect the demographic spread of ethnic minorities in these countries.

- A cross-section of day centres and residential homes were questioned.

- The criterion that all organisations should have contact with minority ethnic elderly with dementia and that they were managing some form of care was crucial.

The questionnaire itself consisted of 34 questions grouped into three broad categories relating to specific issues:

- *Background on the organisation* – who the main service users were and the services provided by the organisation.

- *Dementia* – where the organisations' referrals had come from, diagnostic issues and issues on the care provided.

- *Ethnicity and dementia* – views on barriers facing minority ethnic elderly in receiving care, factors important to them in care, examples of (good/bad) practice and, finally, similarities/differences between dementia in people from the majority ethnic population and minority ethnic elderly using an "indicators of well being" list (Kitwood and Bredin, 1992).

- *Carers* – the issues concerning carers and the recommendations and areas of improvement considered as important now and in the future, as observed by managers of the organisations interviewed. We considered this separately from organisations and supplemented it by two case studies, which shed light on the issues important for carers.

Summary of Results

The following are the main findings from this study on organisations:

- *Language* – dementia suffers and their families who do not speak English face problems at every stage when trying to obtain care.

- *Information* – minority ethnic families are unable to communicate with care professionals or are not able to access information on what services are available to them.

- *Culture* – many cultures fail to recognise that dementia is an illness. Because of this, issues are not addressed and dementia is accepted as an inevitable part of growing old. Cultural problems also account for families tending to look after the person with dementia themselves and not trying to get outside help. This leads to the person coming to the attention of care professionals later in the illness.

- *Complexity of the care system* – minority ethnic people with multi-faceted illnesses such as dementia who are, in addition, disadvantaged by language and the cultural stigma associated with disease in old age, face huge problems in negotiating a very complex system that involves several agencies, each with their own methods of working.

- *Funding for care provision* – the inadequate and short-term nature of funding is a particular problem for day centres and voluntary organisations, which impedes their ability to provide services. Since day centres may for various reasons (see above) be better placed to provide care for BME elders with dementia than are residential centres, this is yet another barrier that they face.

- *Specialist organisations* – analysing the current context of care for BME elderly and the critical position of minority ethnic organisations in providing this care, a recommendation for further specialist organisations as an area of development appears to be a sensible pragmatic solution. These organisations are already on the ground providing such care. Not only do such organisations recognise the current unmet need in these communities, but also it is estimated that in the near future there will be higher numbers of older people from such communities (see country profile section in Patel et al., 1998; CNEOPSA, 1999).

- *Training, and materials development* – it is clear from these findings that organisations want training ('specialist advice and support' in working with professionals) and 'appropriate' resources to support existing materials in how to care for people with dementia and to reach a better understanding of the clients' culture and background.

- *Policy and research* – all organisations regarded these two areas as equally worthy of immediate development.

A Brief Consideration of Barriers to Services

Every organisation involved in the study agreed that there were barriers. In the case of day centres, there were seven different identifiable barriers. Although language and communication, lack of resources (e.g., assessment facilities) and information, and the stigma of the illness being a form of madness are obvious highlights, the barriers extended to this group by professionals are particularly worrying. General practitioners were unable to explain the illness and often sent people home; hospitals and social services departments appeared to have 'no time' for patients; and the methods and tools used by professionals were inappropriate and their attitudes were interpreted as racist. Moreover, the complexity of the system itself was seen as a barrier, since services are scattered rather than housed under one roof, and this, in combination with a lack of communication between different service providers, posed multiple hurdles, exacerbating the scale of the problem for vulnerable people. It also suggests that there are no simple answers, whether practical or otherwise, to providing adequate care for BME elders with dementia.

As expected, there were fewer barriers perceived by residential homes, but these included communication, culture (the notion that the client was 'begging' was difficult to alleviate) and staff, since they did not share the same cultural/linguistic background as the person(s) with dementia or they viewed them through stereotypes.

As regards overcoming barriers, both types of organisations appear to be taking appropriate steps. In common, both are using equal opportunities legislation in the interests of persons with dementia. They are raising awareness and explaining dementia 'personally' by obtaining more information from experts/Alzheimer's associations, and by having more contact with families. In addition, day centres are doing outreach work in the community and acting as advocates for sufferers. The suggestion from many day centres was that voluntary community organisations should be involved more, partly because they are trusted by minority ethnic groups, but also because they can act as a 'one-stop-shop' where minorities can access various services, and thereby obviate the complexities of the system.

Discussion and Analysis

Barriers and Solutions

The findings above point to the effective role-played by BME organisations in managing the care of their members with dementia.

The findings also show that such organisations are facing several barriers, but are making efforts to overcome some of them. To understand the critical role played by such organisations, we will begin by stating that, in the absence of appropriate health and social service provision, such organisations have met minority elderly's needs. They have played a *substitute* role, essentially becoming the *primary* providers of care since there was no pre-existing provision of services to our target group.

Given this structural context, and the rising numbers of BME elders, it is all the more remarkable that the organisations we interviewed were *actually* responding to the 'new' problems of BME elders with dementia. Earlier, we presented the barriers they identified, the difficulties they managed, the range of approaches with which they were familiar, and the clear recommendations that they put forward as being necessary to improve care and achieve the indicators of relative well-being for their members with dementia. From this, two clear conclusions have emerged: 1) there is scope and potential for BME elder organisations to be the major providers of care for BME elders with dementia; and 2) policy makers and professionals should support such developments.

A Proposal for Progress

Supporting Minority Ethnic Organisations Specialising in Dementia Care: the CNEOPSA-Satellite Model

The introduction of community care, with its market-oriented reforms, has altered the service provider balance: BME organisations have had to engage with the changes and enter into contracts or obtain grants as *providers* of care, supplying services to meet the demands of purchasers. To argue for better resourced BME elder organisations that can meet the care needs of people with dementia is not to suggest that such services become exclusive or 'separate'. On the contrary, a majority of the organisations we interviewed had members from mixed minority ethnic groups with different faiths, customs and languages. Their common element was belonging to a 'minority'. Nor did they exclude members from the majority population. Indeed, at one weekend respite centre, the policy was for a multi-ethnic group to reflect the local population staffed by a mix of multi-ethnic workers. A Polish residential home we contacted for an interview was exclusively Polish, though this was changing through 'mixed-marriages'. The reason for exclusivity here had wholly to do with legislation after the Second World War whereby an accord was reached to 'look after the Polish servicemen and women involved in the war effort'. A Jewish residential home was also beginning to open access to non-Jewish members.

In addition to better resourcing of minority organisations, we proposed a *'satellite model'* approach to respond adequately to the development of dementia care. A 'satellite approach' entails identifying a small number of minority organisations in key inner city areas whose task would be to generate specialist knowledge and developments in dementia care. As with any new development, the 'satellite' projects would need a structure and injection of investment. The aim is to clearly help meet the indicators of well-being in persons with dementia and to act as stimuli (relevant information of the local market for purchasers) and as resource providers to a range of BME organisations.

This would enable the development of comprehensive resources, education, methods, staffing and infrastructure to be clearly focused on one aspect of elderly care – dementia – that could be utilised by many. This would help address major problems of access, appropriate care and the low knowledge base on dementia among minority communities. In turn, it would help to raise expectations of what care is possible, and where and how to obtain it.

Support from the Government

The CNEOPSA study in the UK was launched by the then Junior Minister for Health, Mr Paul Boateng MP (now Home Minister and Deputy Home Secretary) in order to:

> ... make a real and positive difference to peoples' lives (speech, March 2, 1998). There is a great deal of evidence of how people from ethnic minority communities are disadvantaged by limited access to services, which when accessed often prove not to be as effective as they might be. Despite this, many agencies continue to carry out research and to consult with local communities, without much changing on the ground. This pattern has got to stop. Even though there has been only limited material on dementia among ethnic minority older people, the publication of the impressive and authoritative CNEOPSA report today gives us sufficient information to go on to begin.

A year later, the current Minister for Health, Rt. Hon. John Hutton, in a written message in the CNEOPSA film and booklet, commented:

> The Policy Research Institute on Ageing and Ethnicity, with its European partners, is to be commended for adding an impressive tool to its flagship project, CNEOPSA in minority ethnic dementia care. Policymakers, managers, professionals and minority ethnic communities will find important messages in both the film and the booklet.

> We can all play our part in supporting the direction that the Policy Research Institute on Ageing and Ethnicity has set to help improve dementia care to minority ethnic older people. As my colleague Paul Boateng advises in the

film, care for people with dementia needs to be based on dignity and respect with full regard for their well being (CNEOPSA Project, 1999).

These are encouraging messages for two reasons. Firstly, they recognise the specific issue of dementia and BME elders. And secondly, they urge action to support the direction that PRIAE has set to develop and improve dementia care. The government has recently accepted the CNEOPSA satellite model by providing resources to work in London with a cross-section of BME elder organisations.

Mainstream Services vs. Specialist Care?

The structured pattern of care established by BME elder organisations has arisen, not from a desire to be separate, but simply to respond to growing needs and unmet care. It is our view that we should put an end to this perpetual debate *of whether mainstream or specialist care* is most appropriate as we enter the new century, for it impedes progress in responding to the known needs of elders. We have noted earlier that BME elder organisations have emerged in the absence of appropriate and effective secondary care services, and that such organisations are playing a critical role in care as well as in bridge-building with mainstream services.

We also know that in the majority society, care is characterised by diverse organisations, including faith-based organisations such as Catholic hospices, Church of Scotland services etc. We do not worry about their existence. Nor do we debate whether they should provide care or not. They simply do. So why should we be so taxed by poorly funded BME elder organisations?

As for evidence, individuals often point to the Askham et al. study (1995) which stated that: 'hardly any of the Caribbeans expressed a desire to be treated in a special way... compared with nearly half of the Asian respondents' (Askham et al., 1995: 78). The authors rightly point to the difficulty in using the term 'special' in their questionnaire. So, can we deduce from this that Asians prefer 'separate services'? Logically not, and the study does not suggest this, though we can find no evidence to support their statement 'that separation is not the majority preference' (Askham, 1995: 108), unless it is attributed to professionals. None of the questions to BME elders in the questionnaire test their preference for or attitude to 'separate services'.

Rather, all the evidence we have covered over the past twenty years shows that *it is* BME elders and their organisations who have *managed their*

own secondary care in the absence of effective care from majority organisations, mainstream and voluntary sectors. We stated in our evidence to the
Royal Commission on Long-Term Care (Patel, 1999) that:

> Given this continuity of mainstream neglect and/or indifference, we can state
> that this constitutes de facto racism. In other words, the mainstream services
> by default are structuring the segmentation of care to minority ethnic elders
> into a long-term solution. Our concern here is not that the location of services
> is in Black and Minority Ethnic (BME) elder care centres. Rather that such
> location tends to be inadequately supported, maintained and expanded. This
> makes the development of comprehensive services and ability to reach all
> sections of BME elders (disabled, frail for example) problematic (Patel,
> 1999: 258).

This is what institutional racism is about.

Our analysis of BME elder care raises a parallel with the issue of
racially motivated murders, where the message 'manage your own issues' in
the context of the public welfare system is reinforced. Since early 1997,
some 16 known or suspected racially motivated murders have occurred in
Britain. In all the cases two things are shown that apply also to the murders
prior to 1997, including the killing of Stephen Lawrence in 1993. Firstly,
there is systematic evidence of 'failure to investigate the possibility of racial
motivation, poor liaison with the family and fatal delays in collecting
evidence'. Secondly, this leads to individual families having to 'conduct
their own investigation and mount a public campaign to draw attention to
their case' (CARF no. 54, February/March, 2000). The Macpherson Report
(1999) showed that the police could not be relied upon and called on the
Home Secretary to draw up an action plan to address this issue, which has
been produced.

Age and ethnicity, as we have thus far shown, cannot be limited to a
discussion of culturally appropriate care. 'Race', racism, class and gender
are interrelated – and the debate of 'separate vs. mainstream services' can
only be justified if changes are to be made *immediately* in the mainstream
care. To debate this important issue but to fail to make the appropriate
changes in the system of care can only suggest that this group does not
warrant care or that they can wait – presumably until such time that
policymakers can agree.

The experience of BME elders suggests that they are not preoccupied
with supply or location concerns, but with having their needs effectively met
– whoever meets them. Our proposal to move on from this perpetual debate
is not because we do not see it as an important resource or as a vital

social/race-relations policy issue. We do – but in practice the debate has obfuscated pragmatic solutions to growing unmet needs. And this cannot be supported when we see increasing evidence that BME elders, whose ageing and quality of life can be made better with appropriate practical interventions – from referrals to care services – are failing to receive them.

The Present and the Future

The new Labour Government, in accordance with its manifesto commitment, set up a Royal Commission to look into the long-term care needs of older people (spanning 50 years), with a time limit to report within a year (i.e., by January 1999). Given this scope of 50 years, if we are not 'elderly' today we will most certainly be tomorrow. The Royal Commission's work and the Government's response to its recommendations in 1999 are clearly significant for *all* groups. The Royal Commission reported in Spring 1999, and it was only in Summer 2000 that the government began to respond fully to its recommendations.

The Policy Research Institute on Ageing and Ethnicity (PRIAE), which we established in July 1998 to address the fragmentation and incremental developments explained above, had been asked by the Royal Commission to produce a UK report on the perspectives of Black and minority ethnic elders and their carers. PRIAE completed this research using the seminar method (Patel, 1999). Three groups were involved: minority ethnic elders, carers and managers, focussing on four key areas. These concerned:

- *The appropriateness of current models of care*
Users and carers' experiences, views on choice and quality of current service provision in day care, residential/sheltered and nursing homes.

- *Accessing services*
The experience of carers/elders/managers in engaging and co-ordinating services with social services, health and housing.

- *Planning and paying for long-term care*
The experience and effect of means-testing and the practice of capped local budgets.

- *Reducing dependency*
What alternative models of care are being considered currently for the future?

The results of this work are highly consistent with research findings from 1990–1999. Specific recommendations are made regarding the above four themes (see the full report in Patel, 1999). However, it will suffice to say, in conclusion, that currently the BME elders show high responsiveness in looking for methods to age independently. They need urgent support to build a solid foundation in day care, sheltered living schemes, culturally sensitive professional health and social care. Furthermore, BME elders regard their organisations as the main effective supplier of care and see the future in terms of 'unity in diversity'. And at the same time, they recognise that their children, the elders of tomorrow, have similar expectations and aspirations of being treated as citizens with rights, responsibilities and the need to have dignified living and ageing free from racial discrimination.

As Sir Herman Ouseley, PRIAE's Chair and formerly the Chairman of the Commission for Racial Equality, says:

> The UK's Black and minority ethnic older people have faced the experience of old age with remarkable aplomb. They are dealing with personal challenges of ageing and struggles for racial justice on a daily basis. Many individuals from these communities have also led initiatives, which give social, cultural and spiritual support to older members and their communities (Patel and Mertens, 1999: 7).

In the millennium, the visible signs of clear demands by BME elders and organisations, together with new structures like PRIAE, to action the policy statements on ethnicity in modernising Health and Social Services give hope for future progress in elder care.

Summary: Implications for Social Work Practice and Social Work Evaluation

From the above, we can draw the conclusion that professionals can use their considerable skills and decision-making powers to make a difference in improving the ageing experience of BME elders who are a *part* of society, not *apart* from it. We emphasise that primary concern should be given to raising the profile and rewards of work with older people generally. Our experience suggests that social work training is not placing work with older people high enough among its priorities, although elder services consume a large share of local authority resources.

Regarding *service evaluation*, it is essential that BME elder care, whether in the mainstream or in the BME voluntary sector, is evaluated not simply on the basis of cultural appropriateness, but equally on the basis of age-related considerations. For BME, the latter is often overlooked; a service that is age-discriminatory but culturally relevant cannot be considered sufficient.

Regarding the *implications for professional practice*, we shall use the four themes of our report to the Royal Commission, as stated above, to identify the following:

- Access to services: *'It's the hush-hush system you know: don't know, don't hear, don't see and don't get'* (BME elder at PRIAE seminar).

Social workers occupy a range of roles from fieldwork to commissioning managers. They can address this issue in, for example, advocacy, the use of professional judgement in applying eligibility criteria and the assessment of the elder in an anti-discriminatory (antiageist and antiracist) way.

- Appropriateness of services: *'I don't understand so I don't ask'; 'if I end up in a home and have to eat English food, I'd die'* (BME elder at PRIAE seminar).

Social workers need to consider how it is possible to provide person-centred care to BME elders. Where is the distinctiveness in age and ethnicity? This may require seeking out information and assistance from BME elder organisations to purchase care as well as to be proactive to increase confidence and expectations among BME elder users that social care can improve their experience of ageing. Social work training should thus provide an understanding of BME elders' needs without assuming that their needs are being met by the family.

- Affordability and payment for care: *'Paying taxes, I'm treated as an English person; getting services, I'm treated as an Asian'* (BME elder at PRIAE seminar).

Care costs, so social workers often have to make difficult decisions on how best to manage their budgets rather rather than on how best to provide care to their service users. As BME elder care may not be readily available in the immediate locality, this may incur further costs if transport is to be provided. Culturally appropriate care often costs more because raw materials cost more. But BME elders may not be claiming their full entitlements. So this also needs to be addressed.

Social workers, thus, need to work to ensure that such considerations are met so that the material circumstances of BME elders improve as a result of their intervention. Other support services added to this would address their other needs if required.

- Dependency and Active ageing: *'We need hope not helplessness'* (BME elder at PRIAE Wales seminar).

Ill health is a major concern for all elders. Yet, our work shows that rehabilitation services, which could restore a person's independence and provide preventative support, are under-utilised by BME elders. Social workers can use their professional power, not just to assess effectively in a non-discriminatory way, but to stimulate awareness and to provide packages of care that support BME elders and their carers so that they remain independent as long as possible.

In conclusion, the guiding principle that we suggest social workers should use is the following: Professionals have sometimes conceptualised the type of care given to BME elders as based on a 'checklist approach' (Patel et al., 1998). A 'checklist approach' suggests that not only are stock questions applicable to all that fall within a particular category, but also that they form a sufficient basis on which to provide care. The approach goes something on the lines of *'X is a Black service user and all Black people therefore ...'* Such an approach suggests that the specific circumstances of the client do not matter and, inevitably, lead to a narrow stereotyped picture of the preferences and needs of a minority ethnic person.

It is also apparent from our study on dementia, cited above, that in the 'solutions' put forward by professionals, learning from other staff has proved to be of little value. This may be because certain stereotypes develop and are then passed on between staff. If professionals were to come up with a checklist based on staff-to-staff learning, it would probably reinforce stereotypical/racist thinking and practice, which we have termed 'stagnant thinking'.

For BME elders, the problems of racism, poverty, communication and inaccessible welfare services are intensified by their minority and/or migrant /refugee status. Good practice that is sensitive to the needs of minority clients means adopting an open-ended approach. Being receptive to situations rather than putting situations in a pre-designed framework is the good that we should strive for.[4]

Notes

1. This chapter was revised following the conference 'Beyond Racial Divides' held in Sweden in 1999.

2. This is why PRIAE is producing a film supported by the Home Office on citizenship to address the ageism in BME communities and among majority groups; BME elders may be seen as a dependant group (forthcoming 2000).
3. The facts suggest that they do; Asian families, for example, have higher rates of living in multigenerational families compared with White families.
4. Nevertheless, we can understand the attraction of 'checklists' as a solution to providing care for minority clients; given the current bombardment of pressure that public sector care personnel are currently experiencing, any 'new' consideration put before them will tend to be seen in its most simplistic form. In such circumstances, the 'checklist approach' to care for people with dementia from minority ethnic backgrounds clearly has an appeal. It also ties in with the current trend in competence-based training, which has been interpreted by some as favouring a 'technocratic' approach.

References

Askham, J., Henshaw, L. and Tarpey, M. (1995), *Social and Health Authority Services for Elderly People from Black and Minority Ethnic Communities*. London, HMSO.
Atkin, K. (1996), 'An opportunity for change', in W. Ahmad and K. Atkin (eds.) *'Race' and Community Care*. Milton Keynes, Open University Press.
Barnes, D. (1997), *Older People with Mental Health Problems Living Alone: Anybody's Priority?* London, Social Services Inspectorate, Department of Health.
Bhalla, A. and Blakemore, K. (1981), *Elders of the Minority Ethnic Groups*. Birmingham, AFFOR.
Brown, C. (1984), *Black and White: The Third PSI Survey*. London, Heinemann.
Brownlie, J. (1991), *A Hidden Problem? Dementia amongst Minority Ethnic Groups*. Dementia Services Development Centre, University of Stirling.
CARF (2000), *Race Investigations: The Families' Perspective*. No 54, February/March. London, Campaign Against Racism and Fascism.
CNEOPSA Project (1999), *Dementia Matters, Ethnic Concerns*. A film and a booklet. Bradford, PRIAE.
Department of Health (1989), *Caring for People*. London, HMSO.
Department of Social Security (2000), *The Changing Welfare State: Pensioner Incomes*. London, DSS.
Gaunt, D. (1998), 'Sweden', in N. Patel and H. Mertens (eds.), *Living and Ageing in Europe*. Netherlands, NIZW.
Kitwood, T. and Bredin, K. (1992), 'Towards a theory of dementia care: personhood and well-being', *Ageing and Society*, vol. 12, pp. 269–287.
Kokshoorn, E.M. (1998), *Älter werden in der Fremde,*. Hamburg, Behörde für Arbeit, Gesundheit und Soziales.
Lindesay, J., Jagger, C., Hibbett, M.J., Peet, S.M. and Moledina, F. (1997), 'Knowledge, Uptake and Availability of Health and Social Services among Asian Gujarati and White Elderly Persons', *Ethnicity and Health,* vol. 2 (1/2), pp. 59–69.
London Skills Forecasting Unit (1999), *Strength through Diversity: Ethnic Minorities in London's Economy*. London, TEC Council.
Macpherson Report (1999), *The Stephen Lawrence Enquiry*. London, HMSO.
Marshall, M. (1997), 'Introduction', in M. Marshall (ed.), *State of the Art in Dementia Care*. London, Centre for Policy on Ageing.

170   *Beyond Racial Divides*

Murray, U. and Brown, D. (1998), *They Look After Their Own, Don't They?* London, Department of Health.

National Health Service and Community Care Act 1990, London, HMSO.

Owen, D. (1996), 'Size, structure and growth of the ethnic minority populations', in D. Coleman and J. Salt (eds.), *Ethnicity in the Census*, Vol.1. London, HMSO.

Patel, N. (1990), *A 'Race' Against Time? Social Services Provision to Black Elders.* London, Runnymede Trust.

Patel, N. Mirza, N. Lindblad, P. Amstrup, K. and Samoli, O. (1998), *CNEOPSA Study: Dementia and Minority Ethnic Older People: Managing Care in the UK, Denmark and France.* Lyme Regis, Russell House Publishing Ltd.

Patel, N. and Mertens, H. (eds.) (1998), *Living and Ageing as a Minority in Europe: Profiles and Projects.* Netherlands, NIZW .

Patel, N. (1999), *Long-Term Care Perspectives of Black and Minority Ethnic Older People in Royal Commission on Long-Term Care for the Elderly.* Research Vol. 1, London, HMSO.

Pharoah, C. (1995), *Primary Health Care for Elderly People from Black and Minority Ethnic Communities.* London, HMSO.

PRIAE (1999), *'Who gets what service?' Eligibility Criteria and Fair Access: A Report to the Department of Health.* London, HMSO.

PRIAE (2000), *The Changing Face of London's Black and Minority Ethnic Elders: A Report to the City Parochial Foundation.* London, CPF.

Salt, J. (eds.) (1996), *Ethnicity in the Census*, vol.1. London, HMSO.

Warnes, T. (1996), 'The age structure and ageing of the ethnic groups', in D. Coleman and J. Salt (eds.), *Ethnicity in the Census*, vol.1. London, HMSO.

10 Lost in Public Care: The Ethnic Rights of Ethnic Minority Children

DARJA ZAVIRŠEK

Introduction

Everyone in social work practice, theory and research knows how difficult it is for social workers to advocate for children's rights from the perspective of the child. The desired principle, wish and need to work and speak from the 'child perspective' can easily lapse into speaking about adults and prioritising their rights instead of the rights of the child. This was most blatantly shown within the feminist social work perspective, which pointed out cases of domestic violence where social workers in the past, to 'protect' the rights of the adult, exposed the child to continuous psychological or even physical abuse without realising that the child's rights were being violated. In these cases the child's perspective was not taken into consideration (Walker, 1992; Mullender and Morley, 1994). This is often still the case in Central and Eastern European social work practice where a feminist social work perspective has been marginalised in favour of traditional familialistic approaches often expressed as 'better a violent parent then no parent' (Zaviršek, 1994), a practice that prioritises the family above the individual household members.

Why is it so difficult to practice a 'children's perspective', and why does it happen so often that speaking about children turns into speaking about ideologically constructed children's needs from the adult's perspective? The first answer lies in the fact that even thinking about our own childhood is most often an impossible task, because the vulnerable times of our childhood prevent many traumatic early childhood memories to appear in our consciousness. Consequently, the past becomes easily covered over with the pictures of the present and with the socially constructed ideas about our current identity. Maurice Halbwachs (1992), a sociologist conducting research on memory, believes that our past memories are always already memories that were told by the others. He calls these transmitters of memory

172   *Beyond Racial Divides*

'memory carers' who insert the memory blocs into our own memory. Family albums are the objects used to confirm the 'truth' of what is called 'my child's memory'. If a lost photograph generally means that the event did not happen, is there such a thing as a child's memory? Is it not the case that a child's memory is already also the memory of adults who are both the custodians of the memory and its gatekeepers? To make social practice even more difficult, it is obvious that children are existentially and situationally linked with parents in everyday life. Therefore, the concern of children's rights overlaps the concern of their parents and adults in general (Mullender and Morley, 1994). No wonder, then, that social work practice, while wishing to introduce the children's perspective, most often fails its own intention.

The second issue linked with ideologically constructed children's needs concerns the fact that the social work profession is not an independent enterprise but receives its mandate from the state.

This chapter focuses on social work practice with children from ethnic minorities in Slovenia belonging to the Roma and Sinti communities and children who are temporary refugees in the host country. I will claim that the process of building Slovenia as a nation-state has increased the legacy of nationalism well known from the pre-communist period, and that social work practice has been strongly influenced by everyday non-violent nationalism at the expense of ethnic minorities. Slovene social workers are nowadays trapped within a double cultural limbo: on the one hand, they are confronted with the universal difficulty of grasping a unique child perspective from an unbridgeable position of the adult persons. On the other hand, they feel challenged by cultural differences and the unique cultural experiences of children from ethnic minorities that are being incrementally subsumed under the cultural values of the dominant Slovene culture. I will claim that precisely in cases of ethnic minorities, children's rights could not be respected apart from the rights of their parents and carers, and that empowerment of ethnic minority children has to be flanked by the empowerment of the adults and carers.

Socially Constructed Conceptions of Childhood, Nationalism and Social Work Practice

Most official social work documents in Slovenia stress the role of social work practice with families and groups and emphasise the 'protection of the family', especially the 'protection of children's needs', as the primary aim of social work activities. This rather old conceptualisation of social work can be traced back to the period between the world wars when welfare was dominated by Catholic charity and to the communist period when Catholic charity was replaced by the professionalisation of social work based on a 'pathological-diagnostic causal model' of helping dysfunctional families and their children (Stritih, 1996). It is obvious that today's social work priorities do not relate to the modernising elements of the Slovene nation-state (urban lifestyle, industrialisation, globalised internationalism), nor do they follow the modern principles of individualism and rationalism. Instead they are a reflex of pre-modern notions of the family as the primal, natural bond of a homogeneous nation-state. Because social work practice always reflects and often also reproduces and fulfils the projects of the dominant discourses of the state, it is necessary to link the above-mentioned social work priorities with broader social and political discourses which, over the last eight years, have developed the idea of fearing the 'internal other' as well as the 'external others'. A vindication of the homogenous national state and the idea of a new community are always fruitful playgrounds for racist practices, as was pointed out by Renata Salecl:

> Not only does the community vindicate the racist's fears, the fears themselves vindicate the excessive commitment to the community. A simple belief in the danger of foreigners is insufficient to sustain the dread that constitutes racism; what is necessary is the knowledge that others perceive the same danger (Salecl, 1998: 122).

Nationalist rhetoric makes children a special concern of the state. Children are presented as the hope of the nation, the icon of innocence, the symbol of a happy family, of continuity and genealogy. Their socially constructed innocence also serves as a romantic personal narrative of the adults' past which is analogised with the romantic collective master narrative of the past of the nation.

This nationalist rhetoric does not embrace all children within a country, but only the desirable children who suit the homogenous idea of the nation. The children from ethnic minorities are believed to belong to those groups who always have too many children and whose fast rate of biological reproduction could threaten the dominant majority. The stronger the nationalist populism regarding the increased birth rate among members of the dominant majority, the stronger is the preventative discourse against biological reproduction of ethnic minorities, people with disabilities, single mothers or other minorities (Zaviršek, 1998).

Rener and Ule (1998) have shown that nationalism feeds on the idea of community and sentiment. Their analyses of post-communist nationalism in Central and Eastern Europe countries reveal several common core characteristics and tendencies of the dominant nationalist discourses that are based on the pre-modern construction of family, individual and community. These include: 1) The redefinition of women into mothers and wives who are supposed to ensure the biological survival and progress of the nation; 2) strong nationalist campaigns to increase the birth rate; 3) a strong campaign to ban abortion rights; 4) tendencies to increase maternity leave from one to three years with no guarantee that women can keep their jobs; 5) a tendency to keep outside the national borders everyone who does not belong to the dominant nation and to silence the ethnic minorities within the national boundaries of the state.

These social processes domesticate women on a political as well as on economic levels, and glorify children (three-years' maternity leave was proposed in Slovenia as a system for the good of children). But precisely here double standards can be observed. While nationalists praise the Slovene woman with child as a national icon, and social workers adopt more sophisticated psychological methods to help families and children, the children from ethnic minorities are either spatially segregated or pathologised. Therefore, I will claim that nationalism is one of the discourses that influence social work practice when working with refugee and Gypsy children.

Critical analysis used for understanding ideological processes in particular countries stresses that what is not expressed, written down and discussed has to be analysed in order to understand the logic and power of ideology. From this perspective it is obvious that the absence of concepts specific to social work practice with refugee children and young people as well as adults is a symptomatic moment and discloses the biased character of social work theory and practice. Refugees who came to Slovenia had to flee from places that not long ago were part of the same country. The processes of collective forgetting, which are expressed as a collective rejection of everything that comes from the Balkans, create a structural framework for everyday racism toward ethnic minorities, and this influences social work in many ways, but especially through the absence of ethnic-sensitive social work practice.

Slovenia is not alone in its demonisation of the Balkans, but it rather willingly shares a globalized view of Eastern Europe. Recently, an American social work professor used the phrase the 'balkanization of social work' in order to express his concern about the more and more fragmented, differentiated and often conflicting views of different client groups claiming their rights within social work (personal communication). He did not reflect on his own reproduction of the negative meaning attached to the word 'Balkan'.

With the revival of nationalism in Slovenia, the structural frameworks of social work practice towards minorities are also coloured with nationalism. This could be observed in the lack of culturally sensitive social work practice, in the lack of specific knowledge while working with minorities, and in the everyday ambivalence of social workers working with refugees. Refugee children are not recognised as subjects with the right to a childhood, but as atomised individuals whose most important characteristic is their 'refugee status'. The nationalist framework of social work practice appears differently between refugee children and Roma children. Eight years after the refugee children first arrived in Slovenia, most of them who did not return are still living in segregated and controlled refugee camps. Gypsy children are pathologised and sent to special schools and labelled as mentally disabled more often than are Slovene children. In both cases a spatial segregation as a way of silencing and rendering invisible children of ethnic minorities could be observed. It becomes obvious that the socially constructed idea of the desirable and blessed child is in those cases replaced by a parallel construction of children who live in public care.

Children in Refugee Camps

Since 1992 when the war in former Yugoslavia escalated, Slovenia became a host country for numerous temporary displaced persons from Croatia and especially from Bosnia and Herzegovina, most of whom were Moslems.[1] In 1993, there were approximately 70,000 children and adult refugees temporarily placed in host families across Slovenia and in so-called collective centres (refugee camps). In 1993 there were 52 collective centres across the country, with sometimes 1000 or more displaced persons living at one place. For the new Slovene state which had never experienced the refugee phenomenon, this was an overwhelming situation which many social workers addressed with personal commitment as well as with the help of volunteers of Slovene or Bosnian origins. Most of them were helping professionals to work under the, at times, unbearable conditions of overcrowded refugee camps. A young woman in her early twenties who grew up in a refugee camp where she arrived eight years ago, recalled this memory:

I was terrified when we first came here. I will never forget my feelings of horror when I saw so many people in the same room and a long laundry line occupied with washed clothes in front of the houses where we were supposed to live.

Although much has been written about the experiences of trauma among Bosnian refugee children and their need for psychosocial care (cf. Miloševic, 1993; Dervišbegovic and Hessle, 1998), there is almost no literature that conceptualises new social work practice. And yet, there is an obvious need for developing culturally sensitive social work practice. One of the studies done by psychologists and social workers has shown that of the 825 children included in the research sample and who came from Croatia, 80% experienced severe emotional trauma and 70% experienced shootings, bombings and rocket fire (Posavec, 1993: 25). The professional responses to these traumatic events most often stayed on the level of listing the traumatic symptoms and did not translate them into meaningful tools of social work education and practice capable of responding to the needs of the traumatised children.

Social workers have focused on developing short-term kindergartens in refugee camps (set up in 86% of the refugee camps; cf. Vouk-Zeleznik, 1993: 70). This has included forming different interest groups to support children's creativity, organising some experimental meetings between children from the host country and refugee children, and working on educational issues that had to be solved in order to assure the right to primary and secondary education of children and young people. Documents show that, in 1993 for instance, only 16% of the refugee camps had any free leisure-time activities for young people and only 69% organised different school activities (Vouk-Zeleznik, 1993: 70–72). At that time refugees were still not allowed to enter secondary education.[2]

One of the characteristics of these activities was the lack of continuity as all special activities (except shelter and food) depended on external sources (Western money, NGO activities) and on arbitrary state-bureaucratic decisions. After the acute period of refugee streams and especially after 1997, most of them completely disappeared.

Nevertheless, refugees did not vanish as there are today around 3500 Bosnian children and adult refugees still living in collective camps, and an unknown number of unregistered refugees, most of whom live with host families who are either relatives from mixed marriages in former Yugoslavia or friends. Even more so, when the Serb army started their campaign of 'ethnic cleansing' in Kosovo in 1999, a stream of some 7000 Kosovo-

Albanian refugees came to Slovenia, but this number rapidly sank to 3500, some 2000 of whom were accommodated with relatives living in Slovenia and the rest were placed in different refugee camps (Dzinic, 1999a). In August 1999 there were still around 3020 Kosovo-Albanians, but the numbers are rapidly changing due to their rather speedy return to their country after the severe violence of an ethnic war. Today, most of the refugees who remained in the refugee camps report experiences of apathy, social deprivation because they cannot get a job or even temporary work, and emotional deprivation because of the poor conditions and isolation in the camps (Dzinic, 1999b).

During all these years, and especially with the new arrival of refugees in 1999, social workers' strong ambivalence towards refugees in Slovenia could be observed. Social services on the one side provided some help for the children and adult refugees, but at the same time tried to get rid of them. Refugee children remained the 'internal others' who are either invisible or seen as overpowerful and therefore attacked by a well-known nationalistic slogan: 'Bosnians, go home!'

The structural framework of nationalistic social work does not exclude the fact that there have always been many committed social workers who subvert and reject the nationalist logic and have since 1992 developed a counter-practice of social work. It consists of personal efforts to understand the values and norms of the other culture, of respecting the refugees as equal human beings and in understanding the extent of loss, mourning and grief caused by the traumatic events they lived through. Many social workers learned about Moslem culture, used the user perspective, tried to advocate for the refugees and were able to develop the 'double vision' of the professional and the one who is in need of care. It becomes obvious once again that the social worker's personal commitment is often more important than the official guidelines, but this commitment often extracts a high personal price. Most of them, while being confronted with the dominant nationalist social work responses, reported a lack of professional support, burnout syndromes, personal exclusion by other workers and loss of hope that some changes within their particular organisation will soon appear.

Forgotten Children: Spatial Segregation

Children who came from Bosnia in 1992, who grew up in the refugee camps and are now usually engaged in secondary education, remained forgotten in the segregated places of refugee camps. All of them still live in refugee camps, experience everyday racism and a lack of continuity and safety regarding their future. They experience not only economic deprivation but also hidden and manifested racism. It is my claim that this is the group of children whose personal and collective memory has nearly fallen into oblivion. When they arrived they were too young to be able to articulate their traumatic memories, and today nobody asks them to recall them.

A young girl who has been living in a refugee camp since 1992 reported that in the spring of 1999 a new graffiti appeared on a wall close to the refuge camp in Maribor. It used a popular image taken from the well-known children's book 'Lassie come home' written by Eric Knight in 1938. The graffiti posed a question: 'What is the difference between a Bosnian refugee and Lassie?' The answer was: 'Lassie went home!' This racist image of a refugee being pictured with the symbol of a dog gives the message that refugees are an 'unwelcome burden' that should be lifted. The image is a powerful example of a recent hate speech against ethnic minorities in Slovenia. A dog, as a representative of a domestic space, is used as a symbol for refugees who, according to this analogy, should be domesticated (like slaves) as well as maltreated.

These, and some other ethnographic observations that I analyse below, give rise to the question: What is social work's response to the rights as well as the needs of refugee children? I claim that in most cases both are either unconsciously or deliberately ignored. The reason lies partly in the structural obstacles that social workers face (lack of money, resources, education and supervision and low salaries), and partly in the personal defence mechanisms that all too often are coloured by internalised nationalism.

One of the structural obstacles that could be observed is the fact that after a period of time the government decided not to spend money on professional social workers working at the refugee camps, so they started to employ workers on the 'public works' basis. They were most often young unemployed and poorly trained people (nurses, accountants, traders, shop assistants, and all those people who could not get any other job). One of the social workers wrote:

> At the beginning the workers in refugee camp were social workers who came from Centres for Social Work, who had knowledge and experience from professional practice; but very soon they were replaced with young unemployed people, whose experiences were very far from social work (Posavec, 1993: 47).

Vida Miloševic reported a similar situation with regard to the provision of health care for refugees:

In medical services specially organised for refugees at collective centres, usually young and inexperienced doctors are employed. They are not always able to treat the complicated psychosomatic status of their patients properly (1995: 5).

Almost seven years later when Slovenia became a host country for Kosovo-Albanian refugees, the internalised nationalist ideology was more clearly reflected also between some of the social workers:

We were told that the state wants to get rid of them and that we should push them to leave the country as soon as possible. They are made to live in bad conditions in order that they will decide to go back, soon (interview, July 1999).

It is obvious that here one of the important social work principles, to respect the right of continuity, is absent from everyday practice. Because Bosnian refugees still have the status of temporary refugees, they can be sent home at any time. Many young refugees who are today between 14 and 22 years old are horrified when they think that they might have to leave school and their friends and return to a 'home' that has nearly disappeared from their memory. A young girl who fled from Bosnia when she was 10 years old reported:

The social worker asks us once a month when will we go home. Where shall we go? Our house was burnt, we have been here for 8 years, I go to school here, we cannot be a burden to our relatives who live in Bosnia, we cannot return. We have a room here – there, we would not even have a room of our own. We know that they want us to go, they don't want us here, but I ask the social worker: 'Tell me, where shall we go, where?' This is my home now (interview, July 1999).

This statement shows not only that every person has a need to regard a place as home, which means symbolically the need to belong, but also that sometimes an institution can be perceived as home if people have no other place that could materially and symbolically maintain their identity.

While refugee children born in refugee camps and young people growing up in these places regard the camp as their home, the professionals view the camp differently – as a place where displaced persons are placed but could also be replaced depending on the needs of state institutions. For refugee children and youth, the refugee camp is a valuable place of belonging; for professionals it is just another workplace, the property of the state.

Sven Hessle (1998) defines three universal principles of child welfare today: family continuity, closeness and affirmation of the child's need to be respected as an equal human being. Young refugees, who after eight years are still living in Slovene refugee camps, often speak about their insecure future. Their lack of continuity and safety can be observed in the fact that the state might not prolong their temporary refugee status. They are regarded as a commodity that can be shuffled in different directions, as when the government decides to close a refugee camp and send the inmates to another part of the country. Children's rights are subordinated not only to the rights of the cultural majority, but also to those of their parents or other adults. Many children and young people have to leave their host country when their parents decide to return to Bosnia or to go to the West.

The commodification of bodies regarded as inferior is a part of every ethnic war; the ethnic murderers force people whom they regard as symbolically polluted bodies to move (to another part of the city so as to create a ghetto or across the border). The Serb occupation army forced Kosovo-Albanians not only to leave their homes but also to walk and move for several hours a day from one part of the country to another. The most blatant example was when the Serb army forced some hundreds of Kosovo-Albanians who had fled their homes to move in a circular direction. After a day of exhausting walking, the group of displaced people realised that they had been forced to walk in a direction that led to the same place they had left. This shows not only the humiliation of an ethnic group regarded as inferior within a multicultural society, but also a symbolic commodification of the bodies, which are seen as manipulated 'other bodies'.

Social workers, sometimes deliberately, sometimes unconsciously, display a cultural superiority in their contacts with persons from other cultures, especially towards Moslems. In late spring 1999, when most Kosovo-Albanian refugees showed ecstatic joy at waiting to be collected and returned home, most of the professionals expressed surprise that the refugees were 'so eager to return to the violent land'. Their astonishment could be explained as a symptom of cultural superiority unconsciously felt by workers coming into contact with refugees from the Balkans: 'Shouldn't they be happy that they are here; isn't life here better than back home?' (fieldwork notes, July 1999). The symptom of cultural superiority is a sign of ambivalence within the framework of public care. While on the one hand most of the professionals internalised the dominant perspective that refugees should receive modest help to either go to the West or move back to the East, on the other hand the refugees were pitied because they had to return to an uncivilised part of the world.

Social work practice in refugee camps repeats an old and well-documented contradiction: it performs care, but at the same time the children are lost in this type of state care. After years of being a refugee, this could be seen as depending on structural shortcomings: economic disadvantages (lack of resources and privacy, lack of proper living conditions compared with the average person in the country, lack of a job), social disadvantages (everyday racism, spatial segregation, internalisation of oppression, etc.) and health disadvantages (cf. McLeod and Bywaters, 1999). A young girl remarked:

> *If I had my own room like my schoolmates do I would always do my school-work. I never understand when they say they cannot learn. Here we are four to a room, but they are alone.*

It is obvious that the refugee girl recalled her traumatic experience of a long-term deprivation of proper space and privacy and that she saw herself as something 'different' from the 'others' who have the economic privileges she has been deprived of.

Furthermore, social workers often reinforce the hierarchy among the refugees themselves through the absence of multicultural learning practices. One morning upon arriving at the refugee camp we witnessed a big riot between Bosnian and Albanian children. The former complained that Albanians were not able to 'build a city', don't understand their language and don't know how to play. The Bosnian children positioned themselves as the ones who have a proper language and proper knowledge. They saw Albanian children as culturally inferior and as having less knowledge and intelligence. The arrival to the camp of Kosovo-Albanian refugees and of some Gypsy families made it possible to establish a hierarchy among the refugees themselves. The Bosnian children refused to play with the Albanian children and the latter avoided contact with Roma families, saying that they were no better than the Serbs. Where did the children's way of thinking come from? Is this not the collective narrative of their parents, which in turn consists of the old building blocks of a master memory? The master memory is full of hatred and ethnic hierarchies and is transmitted from their parents, grandparents and generations further back in the past. Therefore the children did not see themselves as children who share the same playground, but were already ethnically divided. I claim that this is an abusive memory that gets transmitted from one generation to another and which creates a collective nationalist identity as an imposed memory of an 'ethnic other'. A month and a half after their arrival, the newcomers (Kosovo-Albanians and Gypsies) are an even more culturally devalued ethnic group. They have been assigned the position formerly held by the Bosnian children who already know the language and the rules of the host country and have started to reproduce their own experiences of exclusion. The role of a social worker in this case could be to introduce the model of multicultural leaning and promote diversity.

It is obvious that in the case of refugee children, the rights of continuity, belonging, affirmation and multicultural learning are not considered the concern of social workers, even when they claim that they protect children's rights.

Pathologisation of Roma Children

There are some 8000 Roma and Sinti people (children and adults) living permanently in Slovenia. After the war in Bosnia and Kosovo, a stream of Gypsy people arrived as refugees. Some of them crossed the border illegally and it is not possible to estimate their number.

Gypsy children are usually seen as small adults for whom the common idealised conception of childhood does not apply. They are described rather as sharing the same negative attributes that are generally assigned to Gypsies: cheating, stealing, laziness and early sexual experiences. This denial of childhood often occurs in different racial discourses that infantilise the adults ('black people are like children') while withholding the Western conception of childhood from their children. One of the blatant examples was the extensive militarisation of black South African children by the Apartheid regime during the 1980s (Feldman, 1999).

In Slovenia a 12-year-old girl who was sold through a marriage contract to a Roma man became an object of social work concern. Although social workers saw more of such examples, in this case they became involved the moment the girl got pregnant and suffered physical abuse. Many professionals expressed a so-called 'cultural relativist view', according to which the cultural specificities of Gypsies have to be respected. They claimed that Roma people have a different understanding of human rights, equality and freedom, and that the abusive man in this case should be treated according to Roma laws. The idea of cultural relativism serves to cover the unconsciously produced denial of childhood of the children from this minority, expressed in words like 'they are used to that, Roma girls are actually like grown-up women'. The reality is that most often people who advocate cultural relativism are precisely the ones who on another occasion blame the ethnic minority for 'having a different understanding of human rights and values' and demand a racist policy. Then the same arguments are turned around and into a proof that Roma people are violent, rape children and therefore should not get equal citizenship rights on the level of everyday life within the society.

Another social work practice with respect to Gypsy children is their 'pathologisation'. Gypsy children are often categorised as mentally disabled whereby they are sent to 'special schools'. Slovene children with mental disabilities, on the other hand, are less often categorised as mentally disabled and are therefore allowed to attend the 'normal school'. This is a result of the implementation of the concepts of deinstitutionalisation, inclusion and normalisation, but these community-based approaches are not applied in the case of the ethnic minorities.[3] One of the social workers serving on the commission for categorising children said:

> *In our part of Slovenia we're lucky we have many Roma and Sinti children whom we can categorise as mentally disabled. If we didn't have them, we would have to close the special school* (personal communication, spring 1999).

The pathologising of ethnic minority children means in the long-term that they enter into a parallel educational system which gives them some social benefits, but deprives them from the right to proper education, a paid job, proper housing, respect within the community etc. These examples show that in order to maintain the existing institution-based mental health and disability system, ethnic minority children are (ab)used to fill the institutionalised empty space after the children from the dominant majority have been released and are treated according to the new community-based social work practices. This differentiated view shows also that not every child will benefit from recent social work changes, as there exists an underlying system of double standards that automatically excludes already deprived social groups. Mental health or disability diagnoses remain, which Mary Douglas (1994) called a 'category of accusation' when they are used as gatekeepers for ethnic minority children.

Disability diagnoses are also a strategy of rejection based on a system that organises individuals into a group that being a part of becomes a symbol for something else: Gypsy children from special schools are seen as a group symbolising danger, poverty, illness and pathology.

During the ethnic massacres in Kosovo, Gypsies were accused of being on the side of the Serbs performing the 'ethnic cleansing'. At the same time, they themselves were victims of ethnic violence, since many of them came to Slovenia as refugees expelled from their homes. Even in refugee camps they are seen both as victims and as perpetrators at the same time. In July 1999 I met a Roma family (parents and two children) in one of the refugee camps in Slovenia who had not left the room for a whole month because they were afraid that they would be violated by other Kosovo-Albanian refugees who lived in the same building. Nobody among the social workers and other professionals in the refugee camp were aware of this. This shows the level of professional ignorance as well as the lack of professional social work skills and principles toward the newcoming refugees.

Conclusions

All these examples show that the history of European anti-Islamic and anti-Gypsy resentment is deeply inscribed in social work practice itself. As evidence I observed the following characteristics of social work practice in the work with children from ethnic minorities: 1) social workers support processes that make differences invisible by referring to the concept of universal human needs; 2) they support processes that silence ethnic minorities while failing to challenge the nationalist agendas that influence social work practice; 3) they use a flexible concept of childhood; 4) they reproduce spatial segregation of children from ethnic minorities; and 5) they support the development of a pathologising framework of help in response to the children's needs.

The characteristics that mark today's dominant social work discourse and practice get support, as shown above, from a broader context of the fantasy of the nation's own power and authority. This fantasy is sustained through the formation of a community with strong boundaries that mark the existence of 'otherness'. At the same time there is a counter-discourse in social work that is not based on the idea of community and sentiment, but rather on the idea of the urban individual with a differentiated understanding of citizenship rights. This understanding takes into account the traditional concept of a citizen as a white, male, able-bodied person from the dominant culture but that a differentiated understanding of citizenship should not overlook the rights of women, children, ethnic minorities, disabled people and other minorities (Dominelli, 1995; Lorenz, 1999).

In order to respond to the needs and the rights of children from ethnic minorities, social workers have to take into consideration the following social work models:

1. *Cultural self-reflectivity and a culturally sensitive approach toward people of minority cultures.* Social workers have to understand the socially produced processes of invisibility of ethnic minorities and be more aware of the impact of structural nationalisms within a particular nation-state. Moving beyond this understanding requires a practice based on 'differentiated universalism' (Pugh and Thompson, 1999) when working with different individuals.

2. *Double advocacy and empowerment of ethnic minority children as well as their parents.* The rights of children from ethnic minorities depend on the extent of citizenship rights of their parents and other adults. The more rights parents have, the better able they are to act as advocates for their children in the sense of strengthening the children's position. In refugee camps the opposite process could be observed; namely, parents and especially mothers, who are seen as natural carers for the children, experience everyday subordination from the dominant culture, professional workers and from their husbands on whom most of those who are married are economically dependent.[4]

3. *Strengthening children's rights for continuity, safety and belonging.* Social workers working with children and young people from ethnic minorities could help them to develop individual future plans based on the principles of continuity, safety and a sense of belonging. This would also include the necessity for social workers to work to prevent removing individual young persons from where they are living, and to agitate for better resources to ensure safety and proper living conditions that would help individuals form a positive self-identity.

These social work models also demand a shift away from an 'impressionistic model' of viewing children and their experiences predominantly within a romantic 18th century ideal of childhood (Higonnet, 1998). Liz Kelly (1994) called this notion an 'impressionistic model' of childhood that is often blatant in cases of children subjected to violence. She argued that this model, while focusing on an ideal childhood, excludes many of the complex and sometimes contradictory aspects of children's experiences. This kind of impressionistic model embraces also the imagery of stories of refugee children that almost always romantically depict the host country but almost never refer critically to the experiences of childhood in the current 'home' of the collective refugee camps where the children often spend their entire childhood.

Acknowledgement

I would like to thank research assistant Katarina Gorenc for her help during the ethnographic fieldwork in the refugee camps across Slovenia in July 1999, and also Allen Feldman for intellectual support.

Notes

1. According to state regulations, in 1992 displaced persons seeking refugee status in Slovenia were not accorded the status of refugees whose rights are stipulated in the international conventions on refugee rights, but rather the status of temporary refugees. This meant that the government gave them the right to stay in Slovenia for a period of three years and provided food, shelter, basic health care and elementary school education. However, temporary refugees were not allowed to receive any kind of work allowance. After three years most of them could prolong their temporary refugee status, but until 1997 they still did not have the right to work (according to the new law from 1997 temporary refugees have the right to work 8 hours a week or 60 days a year).
2. When the refugee children arrived in 1992 the government decided to organise a parallel primary school system in the refugee camps. However, often the teachers were unqualified Bosnian nationals. Furthermore, thousands of young refugees could not enter secondary and high schools because of too few places and because they lacked financial opportunities (Miloševic, 1993). The admission of refugees to secondary schools and universities was mostly left to the decision of individual principals and staff members (ibid.). Today, all children of primary school age can now enter the general primary education system together with the majority children. The school is seen as the most important element of assimilation; however, little attention is paid to cultural differences and there are no culturally specific services that would respond to these children's needs.
3. This recent inclusionary policy is partly a result of an enormous drop in the number of elementary school children as a consequence of the declining birth rate. Schools are financially dependent on the number of children enrolled and, in order to fill their capacity, are now more keen to accept a child with learning disabilities in regular classes than there were in the past.
4. A study from 1993 made on 284 children in one of the refugee camps in Maribor, which at that time had 1200 refugees, showed that the children were cared for most often by their mothers or female relatives (85% by mothers, 11% by other female relatives and 4% by fathers). The same study showed that 7% of the refugees lived in the camp with their whole family (Posavec, 1993: 31– 34).

References

Dervišbegovic, M. and Hessle, S. (1998), *Social Work with Children under Post-War Conditions. Experiences from the Federation of Bosnia and Hercegovina.* Sarajevo, Faculty of Political Science, Dept. of Social Work, and Stockholm, Stockholm University, Dept. of Social Work.

Dominelli, L. (1995), 'Anti-Racist Perspectives in European Social Work', *International Perspectives in Social Work*, vol. 1, pp. 5–19.

Douglas, M. (1994), *Risk and Blame, Essays in Cultural Theory*. London, Routledge.

Dzinic, M. (1999a), 'Intervju s predstavnikom UNHCR v Ljubljani', *Refugee Times*, vol. 1, p. 17.

Dzinic, M. (1999b), 'Sabirni centar Celje', *Refugee Times*, vol. 2, pp. 2–3.

Feldman, A. (1999), 'Militarization of Children and Everyday Life'. Keynote speech at the conference 'Children, Culture and Violence'. Columbia University, NY. (Unpublished paper.)

Halbwachs, M. (1992), *On Collective Memory*. Chicago, University of Chicago Press.

Hessle, S. (1998), *Child Welfare and Child Protection on the Eve of the 21ˢᵗ Century. What the 20ᵗʰ Century Has Taught Us*. Stockholm, Stockholm University, Dept. of Social Work.

Higonnet, A. (1998), *Pictures of Innocence. The History and Crisis of Ideal Childhood*. New York, Thames and Hudson.

Kelly, L. (1994), 'The Interconnectedness of Domestic Violence and Child Abuse: Challenges for Research, Policy and Practice', in A. Mullender and R. Morley (eds.), *Children Living with Domestic Violence: Putting Men's Abuse of Women on the Child Care Agenda*. London, Whiting and Birch. pp. 43–56.

Lorenz, W. (1999), 'Introduction, Social Work and the State', in *International Perspectives in Social Work*. Brighton, Pavillion, pp. 9–19.

McLeod, E. and Bywaters, P. (1999), *Social Work, Health and Equality*. London, Routledge.

Milošević, V. (1993), 'The Refugees – a Challenge for Social Work', in *Social Work Education in a Changing Europe*. Torino, IASSW, European Region.

Milošević, V. (1995), 'A Model of Supervision for the Professionals in the Refugee Centres in Slovenia', *The School Field*, vol. 5 (1/2), pp. 1–17.

Mullender, A. and Morley, R. (1994), *Children Living with Domestic Violence. Putting Men's Abuse of Women on the Child Care Agenda*. London, Whiting & Birch.

Posavec, A. (1993), *Psihosocialna pomoc beguncem*. Social work research diploma, School of Social Work. Ljubljana, (unpublished work).

Pugh, R. and Thompson, N. (1999), 'Social Work, Citizenship and Constitutional Change in the UK, Social Work and the State', in *International Perspectives in Social Work*. Brighton, Pavillion, pp. 19–30.

Rener, T. and Ule, M. (1998), 'Back to the future; nationalism and gender in post-socialist societies', in R. Wilford and R.L. Miller, (eds.), *Women, Ethnicity and Nationalism. The Politics of Transition*. London, Routledge, pp. 120–132.

Salecl, R. (1998), *(Per)Versions of Love and Hate*. London, Verso.

Stritih, B. (1996), 'Pogled na socialno delo v sedanjosti za prihodnost', *Journal for Social Work*, vol. 5, pp. 385–394.

Unicef – International Child Development Centre (1997), *Children at risk in Central and Eastern Europe: Perils and Promises. Economies in Transition Studies*. Regional Monitoring Report No. 4.

Vouk-Zeleznik, J. (1993), 'Dejavnosti v zbirnih centrih, in A. Kos', J. Vouk-Zeleznik and V. Koren-Kolm (eds.), *Begunci v Sloveniji, Ljubljana*. MDDSZ. pp. 69–74.

Walker, M. (1992), *Surviving Secrets*. Buckingham, Open University Press.

Zaviršek, D. (1994), *Zenske in duševno zdravje*. Ljubljana, VŠSD.

Zaviršek, D. (1998), 'Disability as Gendered Taboo', in E. Fernandez, K. Heycox, L. Hughes and M. Wilkinson (eds.), *Women Participating in Global Change*. New South Wales, University of New South Wales, pp. 117–130.

11 Mental Health Services to Ethnic Minorities: A Global Perspective

BARBARA SOLOMON

Introduction

The demand by minority ethnic populations within national societies for equity and non-discrimination in all spheres of social and political life is a global phenomenon. Social work, like the other mental health professions, has been a target of ethnic grievance against the cultural bias perceived to suffuse its theoretical frameworks and models of practice. Some efforts are being made in ethnic minority communities to establish more culturally sensitive programs. For example, some American Indian groups in the United States (French, 1997) and Afro-Caribbean people in Britain (Wilson, 1993; Sassoon and Lindow, 1995) have developed their own culture-based mental health treatment models. However, the preponderance of ethnic minority persons with mental health problems must receive services from mainstream mental health providers. Even in "developing" nations where indigenous healers are utilized more frequently than trained professionals, the development of mental health services has meant increased access to mental health service delivery systems patterned after European and North American models.

In the United States, the *Diagnostic and Statistical Manual of Mental Disorders* (DSM) has been the primary system used to classify mental health problems. The four editions have been translated into several languages and used in many countries around the world. In the most recent edition of the manual (DSM-IV), cultural issues were incorporated to a far greater extent than in earlier editions (APA, 1994). A new section that describes cultural issues relating to several specific disorders was added. Appendices also include a glossary of the 25 most frequently encountered culture-bound syndromes in North America and an outline for the consideration of cultural issues in formulating systematic assessments of persons with mental health problems. However, there is a significant number of social work practitioners who still question the validity of assessments based on DSM-IV.

Compton and Galway (1999) have summarized the arguments against the use of the DSM-IV classification of mental disorders. The approach taken in DSM contradicts many basic tenets of social work. Important social work perspectives – systems theory emphasizing the crucial role of families, small groups, and communities; a growth and development model of human behavior; the individualization of the client; a sensitivity and commitment to multicultural diversity; the emphasis on client abilities and strengths, concerns about distributive justice; and the focus on the client empowerment for interventions – are neglected if not negated by the individual pathology-oriented DSM (p. 255).

Critics of mental health services provided to ethnic minorities in multi-ethnic societies have focused on what is perceived to be differential assessment. Reports from several countries indicate that ethnic minorities are more likely to be diagnosed as suffering from psychosis, be admitted involuntarily to hospitals, remain for longer periods in the hospital and be treated with medication rather than by counseling or social rehabilitation (Ramon, 1996: 75). The supportive evidence from empirical research is often ambiguous and controversial, not only because of methodological problems, but also because of difficulties in interpreting the data. For example, does underrepresentation among those receiving individual psychotherapy reflect selection bias or the fact that many cultural minorities consider individual psychotherapy to be inappropriate and culturally alien? Even when studies have shown that members of minority ethnic groups are more likely than members of the majority group to be characterized, individually or as a group, as "mentally ill" or "emotionally disturbed," it is not always possible to rule out reasons other than ethnic or cultural bias (Turner and Kramer, 1995: 10–13).

It has been amply demonstrated that poverty and its attendant stressors are factors contributing to a variety of social and psychological ills (Belle, 1990; Dohrenwend, Levav, Shrout, Schwartz, Naveh, Link, Skodol, and Stueve, 1992; Rieker and Jankowski, 1995). The disproportionate number of ethnic minorities among the poor in most countries is frequently presumed to account for the disproportionate number of ethnic minorities among the mentally ill. However, it has also been demonstrated that the over-representation of ethnic minorities among the poor can be attributed in large measure to economic opportunities depressed by discrimination and oppression (Galbraith, Kuh, and Thurow, 1977; Brooks, 1990: 40–66). Discrimination refers to practices based on negative attitudes toward the culture of an ethnic sub-group which place limits on participation in the economic, political or educational life of the society or which seek to force assimilation

(Berry, Poortinga, Segall, and Dasen, 1992: 299–303). Oppression has been used most often when discrimination is systematically applied throughout a society; i.e., practices are institutionalized in social policy as a means of social control (Van Wormer, 1997: 503–590). As a consequence, members of ethnic minorities are more likely to have limited access to the personal and institutional resources needed to cope with the stressors that impair social and psychological functioning. Discrimination and oppression can be considered by definition to be evidence of cultural bias as well as risk factors for mental health problems. Most importantly, poor people, ethnic minorities, and other marginalized persons in society constitute the largest proportion of persons served by the social work profession.

The focus of this chapter is on social work as a primary mental health service profession within multiethnic societies. The ethnic groups of interest are those that have settled within an industrialized or "developed" nation in which the dominant group has a different cultural orientation. The questions to be addressed are: To what extent is social work involved in the provision of mental health services in multiethnic societies? What distinguishes social work's theoretical frameworks and practice models from those of other mental health disciplines? Are these frameworks and models sensitive to the manner in which cultural biases, discrimination and oppression influence the etiology, course, and resolution of problem behavior? How can evaluative research provide information that will help to improve the effectiveness of mental health services to ethnic minorities?

The Social Worker as Mental Health Service Provider

George (1990) has defined mental health services from a broad perspective as "any and all services provided for the purpose of the identification, diagnosis and treatment of mental health problems" (p. 303). In the industrialized nations with expanding economies, "mental health problems" are broadly defined to include "problems of daily living." Treatment has referred not only to the reduction of symptomatology, but to efforts to promote a person's ability to live independently and with minimal support. For example, Bridges, Huxley, and Oliver (1994) have described the collective aims of psychiatric rehabilitation to include facilitating psychological and social adaptation to the effects of irreducible impairments and social disabilities; enabling optimal levels of self-determination and independence; and minimizing burdens on primary support systems (pp. 2–4). The more the aim of treatment includes these efforts to enhance the "fit" between persons and their social environments, the more likely it is that social workers will be seen as primary mental health care providers.

Current statistics on the numbers of mental health care providers by discipline and the number of persons served for most or even a significant number of countries are difficult to find. However, a 1993 publication of mental health data from 21 countries collected over the previous four years provides a picture of the relative positions of countries in regard to the ratio of number of persons served to number of service providers (Kemp, 1993). In many developed countries, social work appeared to be a primary mental health service provider. For example, in the United States, the professional staff of inpatient and outpatient mental health programs included more social workers than psychiatrists and psychologists combined. Mental health policy analysts in the United Kingdom, Italy, and the Netherlands also indicated that social workers provided a significant amount of the mental health services rendered in those countries to persons with mental health problems. In contrast, in most of the developing world and in some developed countries, social work was not identified as a primary mental health service provider.

In Ramon's review of mental health delivery systems in European countries, it was concluded that mental health services in almost all countries are in some state of transition as indicated by a de-emphasis on inpatient care, at least some development of a continuum of care in the community, and changing professional roles. The professional is being redefined from one who knows best to one who listens to the client, intermediates at times with other agencies and people on behalf of the client, helps to create new, informal, and flexible services if these are needed, supports the client in identifying strengths and developing abilities, including the skills required for decision making; thereby, the range of coping strategies open to the person is enlarged (Ramon, 1996: 170). This is remarkably close to the description of social work practice found in many widely used social work texts. Yet, paradoxically, this has not been accompanied by a parallel growth in the influence of social work in designing or shaping the mental health delivery system in most countries. In fact, in Britain, Fernando observed that:

> The political influence of social work as a discipline is apparently on the wane – at least in the mental health field. This is most unfortunate because this is the only discipline that has seriously attempted to address fundamental issues of race and culture in its training schemes for mental health workers (Fernando, 1995: 213).

The eroding influence of social work identified by Fernando is not uniform throughout the world. Social workers in some countries have been identified as leaders in efforts to reform mental health systems. For example, in Slovenia reformers have come mainly from the fields of social work and psychology. An example of innovation is the work of a social worker who with a psychiatrist established a new day care center – the first of its kind in Slovenia – offering a rehabilitation program to persons hospitalized for a mental illness crisis with a work-oriented program for some. Many more innovative services have been developed in the country by a small number of dedicated psychologists and social workers. However, too few psychiatrists and nurses have been engaged for the reform process, including the move to the community, to gain momentum, so the system is yet to change at its core (Ramon, 1996: 178–179).

There is some evidence that among the mental health professions social work has a larger proportion of its members who belong to underrepresented ethnic minorities (i.e., Black, Hispanic, or American Indian) than others (Manderscheid and Henderson, 1998: 218). The inclusion of cultural minorities among mental health providers has been demonstrated to have significant effects on the nature of service delivery. It has been the voices of ethnic minority group members of professional associations that has had the greatest influence on raising the consciousness of the other members of their respective professions regarding the inevitable limitations of service providers who are monocultural in societies that are not. In social work, this has led to more culturally responsive models of practice taking into account the cultural complexities encountered in multiethnic societies (Green, 1999).

Social Work Practice in Mental Health

In most mental health settings in the United States, social workers, clinical psychologists, and psychiatrists may all practice psychotherapy aimed at changing problem behavior and utilize the same theoretical orientations (e.g., psychodynamic, humanistic/existential, or behavioral) and similar practice models (e.g., cognitive/behavior therapy, client-centered therapy, or crisis intervention). However, psychotherapy constitutes a small fraction of the total array of social work functions, which include teaching and modeling life skills, collaborating with clients and their families to resolve life problems and create more supportive environments, linking and integrating agency services in the interests of the client, and developing community resources.

In psychiatry and clinical psychology, the primary concern has been symptom reduction while, in social work, the emphasis has been on positive change in social functioning or social relationships. Social workers have been accused of adopting theoretical orientations and related practice models developed in other disciplines that do not address the person-in-environment problems that the social work profession targets for change. However, disciplinary lines have blurred with the growing emphasis placed on teamwork in the planning and delivery of mental health services. Mental health teams in both hospital and community settings demonstrate a range of working relationships. On some teams, the different disciplines work together in a rigorously stratified, role-specific manner, while on other teams staff from the different disciplines work almost interchangeably (Slade, Rosen, and Shankar, 1995).

A review of social work practice literature suggests that even after consideration is given to the changing structure of mental health service delivery, including the changing working relationships among traditional service providers, there are still three dimensions along which social work may be differentiated from the others: (1) primary value orientation; (2) primary theoretical orientation; and (3) primary practice models.

Value Orientation

Social work, in its definition as a profession, has always distinguished itself on the basis of a set of core values from a philosophical tradition that is essentially democratic and humanitarian. The transcendent value is that placed on the individual; i.e., every human being is believed to have intrinsic worth, dignity, and importance (Briar and Miller, 1971). Other core values are secondary to and derive from this overarching value; e.g., the right to self-determination as stated in the profession's code of ethics in the United States: "The social worker should make every effort to foster maximum self-determination on the part of clients" (National Association of Social Workers in the United States, 1990). Another derivative value to which the profession has made strong commitment is the value placed on egalitarian social relationships, including marital relationships and gender relationships. This value is reflected in the increasing emphasis placed on reducing the power differential in the client/practitioner relationship. Still another related value is reflected in the importance placed on democratic process in the family as well as in political, economic, and social welfare institutions.

Van Wormer has reproduced in its entirety the International Code of Ethics for professional social work that was adopted by the International Federation of Social Workers (IFSW) at Sri Lanka in 1994. It describes ethical guidelines for members of 56 professional social work associations around the world. It also reflects the strong influence of Western culture and values. For example, it states that "Social workers are expected to work in full collaboration with their clients... clients are encouraged to participate as much as possible and should be informed of risks and likely benefits of proposed courses of action;" and, furthermore: "Social workers generally expect clients to take responsibility in collaboration with them for determining courses of action affecting their lives" (Van Wormer, 1997: 38–45).

The high value placed by the social work profession on the individual and on non-hierarchical egalitarian relationships, including family relationships, is perceived by some to mean that normative practice models are often inappropriately employed with ethnic group members whose cultures place the highest value on the collective – the family, the ethnic group or the nation (Ho, 1987; Rodriguez and Zayas, 1990; Green, 1999: 298–310). However, it can be argued that the profession's fundamental commitment to individual rights including the right to self-determination allows its practitioners to overcome their own ethnocentrism. For example, individuals may exercise the right to self-determination and freely choose to subordinate their desires and aspirations "for the good of the collective." In such cases, it is the function of the profession to insure that the decision is an informed one and that the person making it is truly aware of all the options as well as the costs and benefits attached to each.

Values are not always 'either-or' propositions. Although the concept of "core" values appears to be incorporated into the social work profession's value base underlying its practice, there is still evidence that values often considered to be in conflict can be held simultaneously; e.g., the value placed on the individual and the value placed on the collective. Vigilante (1983) contends that "the orchestration of individual and social forces within a value frame of reference is perhaps the most challenging test of professional (social work) skill" (Vigilante, 1983: 66). The challenge is obvious in the dictum that social workers should not impose the cultural values of the mainstream society on others. The implication is that an emphasis in an ethnic sub-group on the subordination of women's aspirations to those of the men in their families must be accepted without question. However, the value the profession places on the worth and dignity of the individual would strongly suggest that the social worker in such cases is obligated to educate both men and women in the ethnic sub-group regarding the importance it places on the opportunity for every individual to reach his or her potential as well as the perceived consequences to the individual, the family, and the society when opportunity is denied.

Theoretical Orientation

The systems perspective has been widely adopted in social work education in the United States. The fundamental assumption is that systems are mutually interacting and the nature of the interaction explains in large measure the nature of human behavior, the course of human development and the etiology of problem behavior. Its primary value is not as a theory that will generate specific practice interventions, but as a meta-theory that models relationships among systems and into which specific theories relevant to the more detailed behavior in and among systems can be fitted (Leighninger, 1977). It is particularly useful in explaining the transactions between and within ethnically diverse family systems in a multiethnic society (Greene and Frankel, 1994). Utilizing this framework, practitioners can incorporate concepts and principles from relevant theories of human growth and development such as ego psychology, cognitive/behavioral theory, existential/humanistic theory, and from sociological theories such as family systems theories, communication theories, and social group theories in order to formulate practice theory; for example, strengths-based, empowerment-oriented, task-centered, and ethnic-sensitive models of practice.

The ethnic group has been conceptualized as a system in which members "share a common ancestry, memories of a shared historical past, and a cultural focus on one or more symbolic elements such as kinship patterns, physical contiguity, religious affiliation, languages or dialect forms, nationality, phenotypical features, or any combination of these" (Schermerhorn, 1970: 12). In plural societies, relationships between members of ethnic sub-groups and mainstream individuals and organizations are relationships between two systems with different cultural orientations. The kind of ethnic identity developed by members of the minority ethnic group will be influenced by the degree of cultural overlap between the two cultures; the availability of cultural translators, mediators, and models; the amount and type of corrective feedback regarding attempts to produce normative behaviors; the compatibility of the minority individual's conceptual style with the style valued by the dominant culture; the individual's degree of bilingualism, and the degree of dissimilarity in appearance between the individual and representatives of the dominant culture (de Anda, 1984: 102). These same factors are among those identified as influencing the degree of "acculturative stress" experienced by "acculturating individuals" (Berry and Kim, 1988; Berry, 1998).

The frequent reference to a systems perspective in the literature of social work education and practice is encountered relatively infrequently in the literature of psychology and psychiatry. On the other hand, social work, as well as other mental health disciplines, has a lengthening experience with family system approaches to the treatment of mental health problems which conceptualize the family as a system but may or may not take into account its transactions with larger systems such as the ethnic group. It could be expected that a model of practice based on the latter might differ significantly from the more traditional family systems approaches. However, our theoretical frameworks in social work have typically been more useful in explaining problem behavior than in determining what to do about it. There has always been recognition that some of our understanding of what to do about problem behavior is not derived from theory but from experience or "practice wisdom."

A study was recently conducted to determine the elements that define social work expertise; its findings provide important insights about the process whereby practice wisdom is developed (Fook, Ryan, and Hawkins, 1996). Findings from the study and from the authors' review of other expertise research suggest that it is only in the early stages of skill acquisition that the professional practitioner typically relies on articulated use of formal theory (Fook, Ryan, and Hawkins, 1997). As the practitioner becomes more experienced, there is the inevitable encounter with situations "uncovered" by theory. The findings further suggest that the development of practice wisdom is essentially the development of rules uncovered by existing theoretical frameworks but found to be supported in practice. The silence of many of our theoretical frameworks on cultural variations suggest that practice wisdom may well be the source of much that we come to know about how to help the culturally-different most effectively. It is perhaps the recognition of a practice wisdom component in its knowledge base and a beginning articulation of how practice wisdom contributes to theory building that most distinguishes social work from other mental health professions.

Models of Social Work Practice

Almost since the inception of the Freudian worldview in social work education and practice, attempts have been made to differentiate the procedures of social work practice subsumed under "psychotherapy." Briar and Miller (1971) contended that the difference was political:

> ...social work has aligned itself with the psychiatric profession, but the alignment necessarily involves social casework being acknowledged as different from psychotherapy. Psychiatrists may do psychotherapy; but caseworkers do casework (Briar and Miller, 1971: 22).

Later, a Task Force on Specialization established by the professional social work organizations in the United States contended that "the fundamental zone of social work (is) where the exchange between people and the environments which impinge on them results in changes in both" (Meyer, Garber, and Williams, 1979: 2). The most recent practice literature in North America and Europe would support the view that the primary element distinguishing social work from the other mental health disciplines is the extent to which direct efforts are made collaboratively with clients and their families to manipulate the environment on the client's behalf. Although the relationship is an important element in almost all of the "talking therapies," the social work relationship has emerged as aggressively collaborative and non-hierarchical – at least in theory. It was the psychologist Carl Rogers (1957) who first described a client-centered therapy in which the therapeutic relationship was characterized as one based on warmth, empathy, and trust. This was distinguished from the distant, hierarchical relationship so characteristic of traditional psychoanalytically oriented therapy.

Social work has moved even farther in many of its practice models to emphasize the non-hierarchical collaborative nature of the relationship whereby the client is an equal partner. Many social work theoreticians have described the collaborative nature of the helping relationship in social work practice. For example, in the initial conceptualization of the empowerment perspective in social work, Solomon described empowerment-based practice as "helping the client to perceive the practitioner as peer-collaborator or partner in the problem-solving effort" (Solomon, 1976: 26). Task-centered social work has been distinguished by "its highly collaborative nature" (Tolson, Reid, and Garvin, 1994: 40). From the "strengths" perspective, the relationship is an essential component of the helping process and is characterized by mutuality, collaboration, and partnership (Kisthardt, 1997: 98).

Dominelli (1996) has described how far from reality this perception of a helping relationship based on collaboration has come in the current climate in Britain. She asserts that social work has become control-oriented and paternalistic. There has been little opportunity for users of services to make real decisions about the design and distribution of services and resources allocated to their development.

This dissonance is not uncommon in countries around the world where social work's values and practice models are frequently in conflict with mainstream values in the society where its practitioners work and live. Perhaps the most critical challenge facing the profession is how to reconcile our commitment to a helping relationship that emphasizes mutuality and collaboration when problem-solving with members of cultural groups that have traditionally viewed such relationships as *appropriately hierarchical and paternalistic.*

Implications for Evaluative Research

When the outcome sought by mental health service providers is solely symptom reduction, the effectiveness of the services can be evaluated simply by the extent to which the symptom is reduced. However, when the outcomes sought include more difficult to measure payoffs such as slowing down the rate of further deterioration or minimizing the burden on the primary support system or restoring the ability to perform particular social roles, evaluation becomes far more complex. The challenge is to develop evaluative research models that "fit" the goals of social work intervention and the nature of its helping process to the maximum extent possible. Cheetham, Fuller, McIvor, and Petch (1992) have identified the need for "methodological pluralism," a "user perspective," and "making the most of small studies." A culturally sensitive approach to evaluating the effectiveness of social work practice should incorporate all three of these approaches.

Peile (1994) asserts that it is a mistake to consider theory, practice, and research as separate entities. In reality, they are inseparable even when the practitioner is unaware that they are being intuitively connected. He suggests that the processes of research and theory are implicit in all practice and subject and researcher must negotiate measures to be used and how such measures should be applied. All research as well as practice and theory-building should involve a negotiation process (Peile, 1994: 20–21). This is much different from the usual approach to evaluation of mental health services in which the maximum involvement of clients has been the completion of client satisfaction measures upon termination. In hospital and clinic settings, the traditional patient satisfaction questionnaires usually focused on such factors as food, overall cleanliness of a facility, family travel time and promptness of the service (Sederer, Dickey, and Hermann, 1996).

In this exploration of the social work profession's core values, theoretical orientations, and practice models as applied in mental health settings, certain principles have been implied. Six principles will now be discussed which may be considered consistent with empowerment-based or strengths-based models of practice and, most importantly, when applied can serve to promote the integration of theory, research, and practice. The principles will be described as applied in the following hypothetical case:

Marva Adams, a 26 year-old, single African-American woman was referred to a mental health clinic by her family physician after the anti-anxiety medication prescribed to relieve 'nervous strain' did not seem to be working. An intake screening team reviewed the referral information in which it was reported that Ms. Adams had complained of anxiety attacks in which her heart would pound, she would break out in a cold sweat, and would be certain that she was going to pass out or die. Her first attack came soon after her parents were killed in an automobile accident when she was eleven years old. Subsequently, she had a few such attacks but they had been relatively mild until the recent death of her grandmother with whom she had lived after her parents died. Now the attacks occur daily, are more severe and make it difficult for her to work. In addition to the attacks, she is depressed and generally unhappy with her life. Within the past year, in addition to her grandmother's death, she was diagnosed with diabetes and terminated a nine year relationship with a boyfriend. Her only close relative is an aunt in another state with whom she has had little contact. She completed a two-year program in fashion design at a local community college more than five years ago but could not find employment in the fashion industry. She believes that her failure to get a job although qualified was due to the widespread racism in the fashion industry. She was hired as a receptionist in an insurance company in the African-American community where she has been employed for the past six years. She earns extra money as a seamstress for women in her neighborhood primarily from her own designs. The intake team diagnosed her problem as 'panic disorder, moderate depression.' She accepted the referral of the intake team to a clinical social worker for 'cognitive behavioral therapy.' A prescription was also given to her for Alprazolam to be taken during the first month of treatment.

Principle 1: The client or client system should have the dominant voice when setting the specific goals of intervention (Cowger, 1997; Parsons, Gutiérrez and Cox, 1998):

In their initial contacts, the social worker and Ms. Adams explored each other's worldview about such crucial issues as what constitutes 'normal' response to grief and loss and what constitutes 'satisfactory' social functioning. The social worker hoped to identify any discrepancies between their respective views of the current problem situation and how it may be resolved. The conclusion of this initial exploration was the choice of goals by Ms. Adams and the choice of theoretical orientations that fit the goals by the practitioner. Ms Adams indicated that she wanted more than anything else to

1) eliminate the anxiety attacks, but also 2) find more gratifying employment, and 3) reduce feelings of loneliness and isolation. The social worker believed that behavior and cognitive/behavior theory could provide the most useful concepts explaining the development of anxiety disorders and conditions under which they could be eliminated. Empowerment theories explaining the impact of racism and discrimination on individuals and how the effects may be reduced were also considered to be potentially useful.

More and more models of social work practice have incorporated principles of client participation in developing the goals and content of social work intervention. For several years, researchers and practitioners interested in program evaluation have been developing the concept of participatory or empowerment evaluation. Success is measured by how well people can identify their problems and work toward a consensus for resolving them (Oja and Smulyan, 1989; Brown, 1994; Van den Bergh, 1995; Fetterman, Kaftarian, and Wandersman, 1996). Empowerment evaluation has been used almost exclusively to refer to evaluation as a social action tool with community groups or groups of persons with a common problem (e.g., teenage mothers, women's support groups, etc.), and its focus is usually on process, not outcome. The concept of participatory research, however, can be generalized to the individual and family system levels as well. Success would be measured by how well individuals or families can participate in the identification of change goals and work toward goal attainment

Principle 2: The goals should be systematically recorded when set initially and whenever modified or changed (Compton and Galway, 1999: 324–330).
The systematic reporting in the case record of the client-selected goals as well as changes or additions over the course of the helping process is an important mandate for the integration of research and practice. Methods of reporting collaborative, client-directed goal-setting have been described in the mental health literature; e.g., goal attainment scaling (Kiresuk and Sherman, 1968, 1977; Seaberg and Gillespie, 1977). These data are important for purposes of both practice and evaluative research. From the practice perspective, the data document "senses" the difficulties of clients or client systems (e.g., family, support group) and can confirm any changing percep-tions of these difficulties over time. From the research perspective, any effort to determine level of "consumer" satisfaction or the relative effectiveness of alternative interventions will require an explicit statement of goals or out-comes sought (Docherty and Streeter, 1996).

Principle 3: The practitioner should clarify the relationship between the helping process in which they will be engaged and the client's goals; i.e., how the client's participation in the helping process serves to achieve the goals (Solomon, 1976: 22–27; Schon, 1983: 295–325):

In the Adams case, the practitioner explained the particular behavioral approach that would be taken to eliminate her panic attacks, including the probable number of sessions that might be required. In regard to the goal of obtaining more gratifying employment, the social worker discussed the possibility of joining an empowerment group that was currently being sponsored in the clinic. Ms. Adams was interested in what the group was formed to do and how the activities would help her find a better job. The social worker talked about the group members' interest not only in acknowledging and confirming the discrimination they had encountered but also in learning from each other as well as from invited 'witnesses' as to specific ways to 'get over.' Ms. Adams was able to ask the social worker questions about the conduct of the group.

Principle 4: The client or client system should be involved in determining how goal attainment will be assessed or measured and by whom (Kiresuk and Sherman, 1977):

The counselor discussed possible indicators of attainment of each goal with Ms. Adams, e.g., to decrease the number of panic attacks to zero; to increase the number of times she engaged in activities with one or more other persons; and to construct a design portfolio that could be shown to prospective employers. Ms. Adams and the social worker agreed upon at least one indicator for each goal including an indicator that had been suggested by Ms. Adams; i.e., 'at least one acceptable job offer during the period I am being seen in the clinic.' The social worker provided Ms. Adams with a record book for Ms. Adams to report the behaviors or activities included as indicators of goal attainment.

Principle 5: The client or client system should participate in identifying what actually happened in the intervention process and the relationship between the process and goal attainment (Maguire, 1987; Whitmore, 1991):

The social worker and Mrs. Adams agreed that in their final session, Ms. Adams would tell her history as to how she had experienced the process from the point the referral was made by her primary care physician to their joint decision that treatment should be terminated. The social worker conducted the session as an ethnographic interview. Ms. Adams' empowerment group had also used narratives in their group meetings. All of the group members were African-Americans who had experienced discrimination and bias in the workplace, in the health care system, or in the public welfare system. All had experienced intense powerlessness so that the opportunity to be heard and to have one's experiences matter was an empowering experience for almost all of them.

Germain and Gitterman (1996), McLeod (1996), Green (1999) and others have discussed working with narratives in counseling and psychotherapy where clients are asked to "tell their story" and use this narration to help the narrator and the counselor to have some sense of clients' lives and the meaning – sometimes many meanings – of their life experiences. In addition, narratives may also be used as a measurement tool; e.g., to measure the extent to which the helping process was implemented as the client had intended or achieved what the client hoped it would. The utilization of narratives as a source of data in ex post facto research designs is extremely cumbersome and costly. On the other hand, if incorporated into the practice model from the beginning, the use of narratives collected along the way as an additional source of data about the effectiveness of the process should be less problematic. Germain and Gitterman (1996) have pointed out that if at the end of a case, time is spent identifying what was helpful and what was not and why, it will be possible to generalize to practice principles. They claim: "Much of what is considered intuition in a gifted worker is actually practice expertise and wisdom, seldom raised to an explicit practice principle" (Germain and Gitterman 1996: 335).

Principle 6: The client or client system should participate in interpreting the findings (Yeich and Levine, 1992; Brown, 1994):

The members of Ms. Adams' empowerment group were extremely helpful to her in sharing the subtle and not so subtle forms of racism and discrimination that each had experienced. Their goal was to identify and implement strategies to overcome the negative impact. In comparing efforts, sharing successes and failures, Ms. Adams finally came to the conclusion that she would realize the greatest power and control over her work if she worked for herself. She made no effort then to find employment in the fashion industry, but decided to take some courses in entrepreneurship offered at a local college to understand more about how to operate her own designer boutique.

She never constructed the portfolio to show to prospective employers or moved from her receptionist job. When the social worker suggested to Ms. Adams that her goal to obtain more gratifying employment had not been attained, she disagreed. In her opinion, her receptionist job had become more gratifying since she now viewed it as a means of taking care of her basic survival needs until she could complete the tasks required to open her own business.

It is perhaps most important of all for clients to be given an opportunity to have input into the final step in which the information provided by themselves and others is analyzed for meaning. When using multiple measures, it is not uncommon to obtain findings that appear to be ambiguous or contradictory. Even a single measure may generate "inconclusive" findings. In such instances, we frequently offer our own speculations as to the reasons or alternative explanations for such findings. We do not consider that the client's speculations might be as valuable as our own.

Integrating Theory, Practice, and Evaluative Research

Over most of the twentieth century, the evaluation of the effectiveness of practice with persons with mental health problems focused on the relative effectiveness of alternative models of drug therapies, psychotherapies or combinations of both in reducing symptoms or increasing psychosocial functioning. More recently, evaluations of mental health services address multiple "outcome domains;" for example, personal fulfillment, welfare and safety, symptomatology, employability, family role functioning, or level of independence (Procter and Stiffman, 1998). Outcome domains may have differential importance for members of different cultural groups. For example, symptoms that Western cultures associate with "major depressive disorder" may not be considered abnormal at all in other cultures that do not have the word "depressed" or its equivalent in their lexicon (Manson, 1995). The service consumer or service user is surely the most reliable source of data about the manner in which they "experience" impairment. Collaboration of the practitioner and the service user may illuminate that experience to an extent that would be extremely useful in any effort to determine the effectiveness of mental health services.

In a methodologically plural approach to the evaluation of the effectiveness of the service provided to Ms. Adams in the case described above, both quantitative and qualitative data could be collected in order to answer very different kinds of evaluative questions. A content analysis of narratives from the empowerment group could be conducted to describe and conceptualize their experiences with racism and discrimination. What specific behaviors, actions, attitudes did they consider to be indicators of racism and discrimination? How were their indicators similar to or different from those indicators regularly encountered in the social work literature? What did these experiences mean at different life stages? Findings from this kind of exploration may add depth and texture to the social worker's understanding of Ms. Adams' sense of frustration and anger that became worse after the death of her grandmother. Exploration could also generate one or more hypotheses about the contribution of various kinds of institutional racism to mental health status. Quantitative data could also be collected to determine whether there was a significant reduction in the number of Ms. Adams' panic attacks over the period of treatment as compared with some baseline period prior to treatment or to determine the association between type of goal and goal attainment.

All the usual criticisms of case-studies or single-subject research designs can be made (e.g., the case is not representative of an identifiable population so that no generalizations can be made to other cases, client self-reports may be biased, or there is a possibility that positive changes could be due to some variable other than the social work intervention). However, Cheetham et al. (1992) have made the point that the value of small studies is enhanced by the systematic review and synthesis of findings. For example, meta-analysis is a technique that allows the cumulative results of large numbers of many small studies to be analyzed, and is considered to be particularly appropriate for social work research in which small studies generally proliferate. The potential of this technique often cannot be realized because of the common failure of reports of small studies to describe their samples, methods, and findings in sufficient detail (Cheetham et al., 1992: 144). The routine integration of theory, research and practice within and across multiple practice settings could provide quite large samples in methodologically appropriate studies of the effectiveness of practice.

There are critical questions that will still need to be addressed. To what extent are opportunities for the integration of practice and research limited in the implementation of traditional research models which mandate random assignment or the collection of data that may not be immediately relevant to the problem-solving work? If research and practice are integrated, what kind of protocol is required in order to assure the client's informed consent to participate? If "life stories" become regularly obtained on audio tape or even videotape, how will issues of confidentiality be handled? These issues are complex but the commitment of the profession to social work practice as a collaborative enterprise with the persons served means that these questions cannot be ignored and must be resolved.

Conclusions

This chapter has explored the nature and function of social work as a mental health provider in multiethnic, industrialized nations. The following conclusions can be drawn:

- Mental health problems in industrialized nations have been broadly defined to include almost any behavior that fails to meet the requirements of social adaptation and acceptability.

- The slippery notion of what constitutes a mental health problem provides opportunities for those in power to define it in their own best interest and to the extreme disadvantage of the powerless who are likely to be disproportionately members of ethnic minority groups.

- Despite considerable overlap in the functioning of the professional disciplines in mental health, social work can be distinguished by its commitment to core values including commitment to the rights and welfare of the individual and its derivative values of egalitarianism, commitment to social systems as an overarching theoretical perspective, and commitment to practice models that are collaborative and non-hierarchical.

- This period of transition in the structuring of mental health services in most countries with more community-based mental health services and more multidisciplinary mental health teams provides an opportunity for an even greater involvement of the social work profession which functions primarily at the interface between persons and their environments.

- The effectiveness of social work practice in general and with members of ethnic minority groups in particular can be determined most definitively by the integration of theory, practice, and evaluative research with maximum client involvement.

- Social work's historical mission, relatively long-term development of theoretical frameworks for practice with ethnic minorities, increasing engagement in both qualitative and quantitative research related to that practice suggest that the profession can make a significant contribution, to the training not only of its own practitioners in cross-cultural practice but of other mental health professionals as well.

References

APA, American Psychiatric Association (1994), *Diagnostic and Statistical Manual of Mental Disorders*. Washington, D.C., APA.

Belle, D. (1990), 'Poverty and Women's Mental Health,' *American Psychologist,* vol. 45 (3), pp. 385–389.

Berry, J.W. (1998), 'Acculturative Stress,' in P.M. Organista, K.M. Chun, and G. Marin (eds.), *Readings in Ethnic Psychology*. New York, Routledge, pp. 117–122.

Berry, J.W., Poortinga, Y.H., Segall, M.H., and Dasen, P.R. (1992), *Cross-cultural Psychology: Research and Applications*. Cambridge, Cambridge University Press.

Berry, J.W. and Kim, U. (1988), 'Acculturation and Mental Health,' in P.R. Dasen, J.W. Berry, and N. Sartorius (eds.), *Cross-cultural Psychology and Health: Towards Applications*. London, Sage, pp. 207–236.

Briar, S. and Miller, H. (1971), *Problems and Issues in Social Casework.* New York, Columbia University Press.

Bridges, K., Huxley, P., and Oliver, J. (1994), 'Psychiatric Rehabilitation: Redefined for the 1990s,' *The International Journal of Social Psychology*, vol. 40 (1), pp. 1–16.

Brooks, R.L. (1990), *Rethinking the American Race Problem.* Berkeley, CA, University of California Press.

Brown, P.A. (1994), 'Participatory Research: A New Paradigm For Social Work,' in L. Gutiérrez and P. Nurius (eds.), *Education and Research for Empowerment Practice*. Seattle, Washington Center For Policy and Practice Research, University of Washington, pp. 291–302.

Cheetham, J., Fuller, R., McIvor, G., and Petch, A. (1992), *Evaluating Social Work Effectiveness.* Buckingham, Open University Press.

Compton, B.R. and Galway, B. (1999), *Social Work Processes*, 6th ed. Pacific Grove, Brooks/Cole.

Cowger, C. (1997), 'Assessing Client's Strengths: Assessment for Client Empowerment,' in D. Saleebey (ed.), *The Strengths Perspective in Social Work Practice*, 2nd ed. New York, Longman, pp. 59–73.

de Anda, D. (1984), 'Bicultural Socialization: Factors Affecting the Minority Experience,' *Social Work*, vol. 29 (2), pp. 101–107.

Docherty, J.P. and Streeter, M.J. (1996) 'Measuring Outcomes,' in L.I. Sederer and B. Dickey (eds.), *Outcomes Assessment in Clinical Practice.* Baltimore, Md., Williams and Williams, pp. 8–18.

Dohrenwend, B.P., Levav, I., Shrout, P.E., Schwartz, S., Naveh, G., Link, B.G., Skodol A.E. and Stueve, A. (1992), 'Socioeconomic Status and Psychiatric Disorder: The Causation-Selection Issue,' *Science,* vol. 255, pp. 946–952.

Dominelli, L. (1996), 'Deprofessionalizing Social Work: Anti-Oppressive Practice, Competencies and Postmodernism,' *British Journal of Social Work*, vol. 26 (2), pp. 153–175.

Fernando, S. (1995), 'The Way Forward,' in S. Fernando (ed.), *Mental Health in a Multi-Ethnic Society*. London, Routledge, pp. 193–216.

Fetterman, D.M., Kaftarian, S.J., and Wandersman, A. (eds.) (1996), *Empowerment Evaluation: Knowledge and Tools for Self-Assessment and Accountability.* Thousand Oaks, CA, Sage.

Fook, J., Ryan, M., and Hawkins, L. (1996), 'Expertise in Social Work Practice: An Exploratory Study,' *Canadian Social Work Review,* vol. 13 (1), pp. 7–22.

Fook, J., Ryan, M. and Hawkins, L. (1997). 'Towards a Theory of Social Work Expertise,' *British Journal of Social Work,* vol. 27 (6), pp. 399–417.

French L.M. (1997), *Counseling American Indians.* Lanham, Md. University Press of America.

Galbraith, J.K, Kuh, E. and Thurow, L.C. (1977), 'Toward Greater Minority Employment,' in J. Rothman (ed.), *Issues in Race and Ethnic Relations: Theory Research and Action.* Itasca, Ill., F.E. Peacock.

George, L.K (1990), 'Definition, Classification and Measurement of Mental Health Services,' in C.A. Taube, D. Mechanic, and A.A. Hohmann (eds.), *New Directions For Mental Health Services.* New York, Hemisphere, pp. 303–319.

Germain, C.B. and Gitterman, A. (1996), *The Life Model of Social Work Practice.* New York, Columbia University Press.

Green, J. (1999), *Cultural Awareness in the Human Services: A Multi-Ethnic Approach,* 3rd ed. Boston, Allyn and Bacon.

Greene, R.R. and Frankel K. (1994), 'A Systems Approach: Addressing Diverse Family Forms,' in R.R. Greene (ed.), *Human Behavior Theory: A Diversity Framework.* New York, Aldine de Gruyter.

Ho, Man Keung (1987), *Family Therapy With Ethnic Minorities.* Newbury Park, CA, Sage.

Kemp, D.R. (ed.) (1993), *International Handbook on Mental Health Policy.* Westport, CT, Greenwood Press.

Kiresuk, T.J. and Sherman, R.E. (1968), 'Goal Attainment Scaling: A General Method for Evaluating Comprehensive Community Mental Health Programs,' *Community Mental Health Journal,* vol. 4 (6), pp. 443–453.

Kiresuk, T.J. and Sherman, R.E. (1977), 'A Reply To The Critique of Goal Attainment Scaling,' *Social Work Research and Abstracts,* vol. 13 (2), pp. 9–11.

Kisthardt, W. (1997), 'The Strengths Model of Case Management: Principles and Helping Functions,' in D. Saleebey (ed.), *The Strengths Perspective in Social Work Practice,* 2nd ed. New York, Longman, pp. 97–113.

Leighninger, R.D. (1977), 'Systems Theory and Social Work: A Re-examination,' *Journal of Education for Social Work,* vol. 13 (3), pp. 44–49.

Maguire, P. (1987), *Doing Participatory Research: A Feminist Approach.* Amherst, University of Massachusetts.

Manderschied, R.W. and Henderson, M.J. (1998), *Mental Health, United States, 1998.* Rockville, Md., U.S. Department of Health and Human Services, Center for Mental Health Services.

Manson, S.M. (1995), 'Culture and Depression,' *Psychiatric Clinics of North America,* vol. 18, pp. 487–501.

McLeod, J. (1996), 'Working with Narratives,' in R. Bayne, L. Horton, and L. Bimrose (eds.), *New Directions in Counseling.* London, Routledge.

Meyer, C.H., Garber, R., and Willliams, C.W. (1979), *Specialization in the Social Work Profession.* Council on Social Work Education, Commission on Educational Planning. (Mimeograph.)

National Association of Social Workers, (1990), *Code of Ethics.* Washington, D.C., NASW.

Oja, S.N. and Smulyan, I.L. (eds.) (1989), *Collaborative Action Research*. Philadelphia, Palmer.

Parsons, R.J., Gutiérrez, L.M., and Cox, E.O. (1998), 'A Model For Empowerment Practice,' in L.M. Gutiérrez, R.J. Parsons, and E.O. Cox (eds.), *Empowerment in Social Work Practice: A Source Book*. Pacific Grove, Brooks/Cole.

Peile, C. (1994), 'Theory, Practice, Research: Casual Acquaintances or a Seamless Whole?' *Australian Social Work*, vol. 47 (2), pp. 17–23.

Procter, E.K. and Stiffman, A.R. (1998), in J.B.W. Williams and K. Ell (eds.), *Advances in Mental Health Research: Implications for Practice*. Washington, D.C., NASW, pp. 259–286.

Ramon, S. (1996), *Mental Health in Europe: Beginnings, Ends and Rediscoveries*. New York, St. Martin's Press.

Rieker, P.P. and Jankowski M.K (1995), 'Sexism and Women's Psychological Status,' in C.V. Willie, P.P. Rieker, B.M. Kramer, and B.S. Brown (eds.), *Mental Health, Racism and Sexism*. Pittsburgh, University of Pittsburgh Press, pp. 27–50.

Rodriguez, O., and Zayas, L.H. (1990), 'Hispanic Adolescents and Anti-social Behavior: Sociocultural Factors and Treatment Implications,' in A.R. Stiffman and L. Davis (eds.), *Ethnic Issues in Adolescent Mental Health*. Newbury Park, CA, Sage.

Rogers, C.R. (1957), 'The Necessary and Sufficient Conditions of Therapeutic Personality Change,' *Journal of Consulting and Clinical Psychology*, vol. 21, pp. 95–103.

Sassoon, M. and Lindow, V. (1995), 'Consulting and Empowering Black Mental Health System Users,' in S. Fernando (ed.), *Mental Health In a Multi-Ethnic Society*. London, Routledge.

Schermerhorn, T. (1970), *Comparative Ethnic Relations: A Framework for Theory and Research*. New York, Random House.

Schon, D.A. (1983), *The Reflexive Practitioner*. New York, Basic Books.

Seaberg, J.F. and Gillespie, D.F. (1977), 'Goal Attainment Scaling: A Critique,' *Social Work Research and Abstracts*, vol. 13 (2), pp. 4–9.

Sederer, L.I., Dickey, B. and Hermann, R. (1996), 'The Imperative of Outcomes Assessment in Psychiatry,' in L.I. Sederer and B. Dickey (eds.), *Outcomes Assessment in Clinical Practice*. Baltimore, Md., Williams and Williams, pp. 1–7.

Slade, M., Rosen, A., and Shankar, R. (1995), 'Multi-disciplinary Mental Health Teams,'*International Journal of Social Psychology*, vol. 41 (3), pp. 180–89.

Solomon, B.B. (1976), *Black Empowerment: Social Work in Oppressed Communities*. New York, Columbia University Press.

Tolson, E.R., Reid, W.J., and Garvin, C.D. (1994), *Generalist Practice: A Task-Centered Approach*. New York, Columbia University Press.

Turner, C.B. and Kramer, B.M. (1995), 'Connections Between Racism and Mental Health,' in C.V. Willie, P.P. Rieker, B.M. Kramer, and B.S. Brown (eds.), *Mental Health, Racism and Sexism*. Pittsburgh, University of Pittsburgh Press, pp. 3–25.

Van den Bergh, N. (ed.) (1995), *Feminist Practice in the 21st Century*. Washington, D.C., National Association of Social Workers.

Van Wormer, K. (1997), *Social Welfare: A World View*. Chicago, Nelson-Hall.

Vigilante, J. (1983), 'Professional Values,' in A. Rosenblatt and D. Waldfogel (eds.), *Handbook of Clinical Social Work*. San Francisco, Jossey-Bass.

Whitmore. E. (1991), 'Evaluation and Empowerment: It's the Process That Counts,' *Networking Bulletin*, vol. 2 (2), pp. 1–7.

Williams, J.B.W. (1998), 'Classification and Diagnostic Assessment,' in J.B.W. Williams and K. Ell (eds.), *Advances in Mental Health Research: Implications for Practice.* Washington, D.C., NASW, pp. 25–48.

Wilson, M. (1993), *Mental Health and Britain's Black Communities.* London, King's Fund.

Yeich, S. and Levine R. (1992), 'Participatory Research's Contributions to Conceptualization of Empowerment,' *Journal of Applied Social Psychology*, vol. 22, pp. 1894–1908.

PART IV:

RECLAIMING HERITAGES THROUGH SOCIAL WORK PRACTICE

12 Making Circles: Renewing First Nations Ways of Helping

GORD BRUYERE

Introduction

Ella Deloria (1944) said that 'All peoples who live communally must first find some way to get along together harmoniously and with a measure of decency and order. And that way, by whatever rules and controls it is achieved is, for any people, the scheme of life that works'. I would like to share with you my own thoughts and feelings about a particular aspect of the Anishnabe 'scheme of life' and explore one application related to social work practice. In sharing my personal understanding, I will attempt to speak predominantly from my own experience and acknowledge that I am engaged in learning, as we all are, and what I know today I will hopefully know better tomorrow. My intention is not only to share my personal understanding but also to promote further exploration about how other schemes of life may similarly help human beings address the problems we all face.

This chapter describes a selected set of First Nations teachings known as the Medicine Wheel which symbolise the relationship between a particular First Nations people, the Anishnabe, and the world around them. These teachings have been used to inform a multiplicity of cultural practices since time immemorial. The 'scheme of life that worked' which characterised the diverse nations of peoples of Turtle Island, and the day-to-day practice of the Medicine Wheel teachings were interrupted by the colonisation experience in Canada. First Nations peoples are in the process of renewing the cultural practices that make them distinct peoples. One contemporary application of Medicine Wheel teachings, based on an ancient ceremony described as 'the Circle', is explained as one example of how that renewal is unfolding. Lastly, I will offer an alternative conception of racism as a spiritual force and explore concomitant ways by which to address it.

The Windigo

In trying to find a way to begin to tell you what I know about racism and
how we may move beyond racial divides, I will share this story (Windigo,
1993):

*To begin, I am Anishnabe. It is a name that a people have given themselves,
and in accordance with the purpose of naming, 'Anishnabe' means more to
these people than its literal interpretations which are 'the good people', 'the
real people', 'human beings'. Since our creation, Anishnabe people have
lived with the land that cradles 'gitchi-gaming', those Great Lakes in
Ontario, Canada and the mid-western United States.*

*Anishnabe people still talk about the Windigo. The Windigo have
existed in actual physical form as huge misshapen giants with an appearance so horrible that it would take away the breath of human beings and
cause plants to wither and die. Mothers would admonish their children to
stay close to home and to obey family members or the Windigo would get
them.*

*Besides their ghastly visage, something else caused the people to fear
them. You see, the Windigo were once human beings who lived among us as
family and who contributed to our society as much as any other person or
clan. Yet through the consequence of some agony endured, those human
beings were made to eat the flesh of other human beings. Sometimes it was
overwhelming hunger brought on by the harshest of winters that caused this
to happen. In other instances, people were told through the force of their
dreams that they were supposed to commit this act. It was a rare occurrence
but it was one that was sure to bring fear to the people. It is said that the
cannibalistic act was caused when the Windigo spirit invaded a human
being and that you could identify persons inhabited by the Windigo spirit by
the vacant, hollow look in their eyes and by the sickly translucence of their
flesh. At times people would be so desperate that they would use the most
extreme measures to rid themselves of the threat of a Windigo. Yet, other
than killing a Windigo, there were means by which our medicine people,
healers and most learned elder, could rid a human being of that Windigo
spirit. Those means involved the will of the entire community and was a
most delicate spiritual, ceremonial matter.*

A Scheme of Life That Works

Anishnabe people and the many diverse indigenous nations of Turtle Island or North America have always had fecund, complex ways of organising their societies and continue to greater and lesser degrees to practice those ways. In the story of the Windigo, I alluded to ceremonial ways of addressing an extreme social situation. While I am unable to discuss the remedies for that particular situation because of my own limited understanding and the special focus of this chapter, I would like to turn our attention to one specific way, one specific scheme, if you will.

Since at the present time I am engaged in my own practice as a teacher, I want to discuss this aspect of our scheme of life in relation to the contemporary context of social work education.

The Circle as Symbol

Earlier, I rooted the location of Anishnabe people in a particular territory. It is my understanding that our philosophies, values and beliefs – our scheme of life – are particular to that territory. It is the land herself that teaches us how to live with all of Creation, including other human beings. So it makes sense that the mechanisms that guide our relationships be predicated on what we see around us.

Here I will use the term 'Medicine Wheel' to refer to the set of teachings that are encapsulated in this symbol, and later I will use the term 'Circle' to depict the application of these teachings. I should point out that medicine wheels are actual stone formations created by the Plains peoples, and that the term Medicine Wheel has come to be used in a contemporary sense as a kind of pan-indigenous rubric to identify sets of similar teachings that have unique histories among a wide variety of First Nations peoples. The historical origins of Medicine Wheel teachings and of the Circle are virtually impossible to pinpoint because their ceremonial and customary usage arose and predominately continues to arise out of oral traditions. To be blunt, it is not so important to distinguish their historical origins as it is to understand that they are intrinsic to many First Nations societies (and indeed, to many indigenous societies globally). It is safe to say that these teachings have been discretely elucidated by elders and teachers within our societies and are also simply reinforced through conscious and unconscious personal relationships in the world around us. I should also state that not all First Nations peoples make use of the symbol of the circle or ascribe to

Medicine Wheel teachings. Medicine Wheel teachings also reflect how diverse cultures evolve and grow by adapting and adopting aspects of other cultures.

Many of the peoples indigenous to Turtle Island do make use of the symbol of the Circle. It has been described as the Circle of Life (Windigo, 1993) or the Sacred Hoop (Allen, 1986; Black Elk, 1932) or the Medicine Wheel (Bopp, Bopp, Brown and Lane Jr., 1984; Buswa and Shawana, 1993). The Circle as symbol is witnessed concretely within the elements of the natural world. Birds' nests, the trunks of trees, the sun and moon and the unobliterated view of the horizon show the Circle. The representation of life as a cycle is a truth in relation to the passing of seasons, the ebb and flow of tides, the phases of the moon and a human lifetime. The Circle has no beginning and no end unless one is arbitrarily imposed and so it represents wholeness or completeness and 'includes a way of living that emphasises responsibilities, values and ethics that ensure achieving balance and harmony' (Longclaws, 1994). Thus we conceive of the Circle as natural law.

Medicine Wheel teachings locate us upon the earth and place us in relation to all of Creation. Wherever we are is the centre of the Wheel. From where we sit or stand we can look out to four cardinal directions. The East is where the sun rises and symbolises beginnings, births or rebirths, the start of a day, the coming of light, warmth or awareness. The East reminds us of the start of every day that could be our last or our first; so whatever the case, we better be present and make the most of it. The South is the direction where the sun sits highest and strongest in the sky, representing growth and fullness. The West, where the sun sets, helps us to acknowledge the darkness, the unknown. The North, being the fourth direction, brings us to completion or resolution and is the place where wisdom begins. When we place ourselves at the centre of the Four Directions, we are reminded that we are but one piece of Creation and, since we are at the centre of Creation at the present time, that we also have a place within all of Creation.

As part of all of Creation, we are taught that human beings and everything else is made up of Four Elements – Earth, Air, Water and Fire. In acknowledging the universality of these elements, we can understand that we are not any more or less than any other part of Creation and that we are not ever separated from Creation. We are in relationship with Creation.

Those four elements come to us in many guises, and part of the shifting face of Creation is the Four Seasons. Where Anishnabe people live there are four distinct faces to Creation. Each season comes with its particular feel and purpose. Of course, Spring is the time where we see many living beings take part in the sacred ritual of change, of birth, rebirth and renewal. Summer is the season of warmth, rapid growth and activity. Autumn is the time of harvesting and preparation. Winter is the time of decay, of incubation and hibernation. The earth undergoes great change from one season to the next and reminds us that the essence of Creation is change and that life occurs in cycles, that things happen in their own time and in their own way.

In turning our attention to human beings, the Medicine Wheel teaches us that there are four kinds of human beings, Red, Yellow, Black and White. I was once told a story about how the human beings were lowered to the Earth by the Creator. You see, the Creator had placed all of Creation and had covered the Earth with all kinds of living beings. Yet, the Creator thought the Earth needed another kind of being to bring all of Creation together, to serve as custodians for the rest of Creation. The Creator would seek balance, as always, by making those custodians the weakest of all living beings, dependent upon the rest of Creation in order to survive. So the Creator took some Earth, mixed in some Water, blew Air into it and placed it all into a Fire. Four times the Creator did this and each time the Creator lowered those Four Races to Earth, setting them off in different directions.

Often the Medicine Wheel will be drawn divided into four sections. This can be misleading in that the Medicine Wheel and the Circle are not meant to imply division, nor are they meant to categorically relegate all human beings to four distinct kinds. The Four Races concept illustrates that difference is part of life and that we all belong to make up the whole.

Each of the Four Races has respective responsibilities for the Four Elements. The Red people are responsible for Earth, the Yellow people are responsible for Air, the Black people are responsible for Water, and the White people are responsible for Fire. While it may connote otherwise, this teaching is designed to show that all human beings have a role to play in custodianship of the Earth.

From the Medicine Wheel we are taught that human beings are comprised of physical, mental, emotional and spiritual aspects (Bopp et al., 1984). The development of a human's potential is dependent upon an intentional nurturing of the Four Aspects. Personal health consists of a conscious balance of these Four Aspects. The means by which an individual strives for this balance and enactment of potential is the volition or will.

The individual is not the only manner of acknowledging human relationships with the rest of Creation. There are Four Faces of Human Identity – Individual, Family, Community and Nation. The rights and responsibilities of these Four Faces of Human Identity are interdependent and mutually reinforcing, and reflect the primacy of kinship and relationship for Anishnabe and other First Nations peoples. You can see that when individuals enact their own potential through volition, they contribute to the strengthening of the other Faces of Human Identity and, since there is an interdependence, individual development is not intended to occur in isolation or purely for the benefit of the self.

Human beings enacting their potential go through Four Stages of Life – Infancy, Youth, Adulthood and Elderhood. These stages of life have parallels with the Four Seasons. When we place ourselves at the centre of the Medicine Wheel, these Four Stages of Life indicate that within the life of an individual, family, community or nations there are opportunities to include all members of that society.

The wisdom-making process itself can also be conceptualised as having four components (Native Child and Family Services of Toronto, 1990). It begins at the vision stage where we recognise a learning opportunity and make the choice to begin. We may also have some idea what it is we wish to learn. Time is the second component of the learning process, as it takes time to experience or relate to the people or situations as they exist. It takes time for the third component of the wisdom-making process to become apparent: the third component of learning is Knowledge. Knowledge is the development of awareness, skills and understanding within ourselves individually and collectively. The fourth component is Action and it results from behaviour enacted in relation to the other three components of the wisdom-making process. These four components are interdependent and reflect the primacy of relationships within the Medicine Wheel teachings. It also shows that human beings learn in accordance with natural law.

A crucial concept within the Medicine Wheel concerns the Four Sacred Medicines – Tobacco, Cedar, Sage and Sweetgrass (Benton-Banai, 1988; Buswa and Shawana, 1993). These are by no means the only plants that are used for medicinal purposes by First Nations people, but they are the four that are common to many of our ceremonies and everyday life, particularly among the Anishnabe.

There are many other teachings that come from the Medicine Wheel. I have only outlined certain concepts that are crucial to help to create a good way of being together.

A Broken Circle

At the present time, First Nations peoples in Canada are initiating an incredible cultural, social and political resurgence. This resurgence is incredible for a number of reasons. Most notably, First Nations peoples have been subjected to systematic, purposeful policies and practices carried out by all levels of the Canadian governments. These policies and practices have been wholly founded and perpetuated on the misbegotten assumption that the colonisers – initially and most influential from European nations – were superior to First Nations people. That misbegotten belief, in concert with a worldview that saw the world as a supply of resources waiting exploitation for profit, allowed for the construction of the First Nations of Turtle Island as a racial group. According to this spurious, cruel worldview, the interests of First Nations peoples were thus minimised, ignored or disparaged, allowing for the socio-economic marginalisation and dislocation from their lands and schemes of life. This current resurgence is also incredible because, through colonisation, First Nations peoples have retained a sense of identity, some connection to ancestral lands and varying degrees of affinity with the tenets of traditional cultures.

The cultural resurgence of which I am speaking is being played out in differing conceptions and arrangements for self-government within the Canadian polity. Those arrangements for self-government include responsibility for the design, implementation, monitoring and, increasingly, financing of social programs and services to deal with the poignant ramifications of colonisation. The effects of the contradictory and long-standing policies of assimilation and social isolation, from my perspective, constitute ritual abuse of a people, genocidal actions, and I am tempted to recount them here. However, there are many other sources that do so, the most comprehensive of which is *The Final Report of the Royal Commission on Aboriginal Peoples* (1996).

Besides detailing the deplorable social conditions that many First Nations peoples face, the Royal Commission on Aboriginal Peoples has also documented the ways in which First Nations peoples are addressing those social conditions, one of which is the Circle.

Mending the Circle

The Circle is not only a symbol but also a ceremony which may be held for various purposes. First Nations organisations and the people working within them are renewing very old traditions like the Circle. Child welfare agencies may call them 'Family Conferences', the Canadian justice system may call them 'Sentencing Circles', and addiction treatment centres may simply call them 'Healing Circles'. These approaches are being instituted by indigenous nations that have extensive traditional foundations within their cultures for such uses and other nations are adapting and adopting Circles based upon similar cultural precepts unique to those cultures. These approaches are being instituted with varying degrees of accord with the different levels of Canadian governments.

The use of Circles is being reaffirmed not only in First Nations organisations and institutions. There are those of us who are trying to bring our scheme of life that works to places that have seldom seen those ways in action. The application that I wish to discuss is a Teaching and Learning Circle. I use this approach in virtually all teaching situations that I facilitate where I am engaged in exploring the impact of colonisation and issues of racism in Canadian society, particularly as it relates to First Nations peoples.

The primary basis for regulating our collective behaviour is the Medicine Wheel teachings as I have outlined them above. As I noted earlier, there are many layers to these teachings, but I apply them selectively for our purposes. I also share other cultural teachings that help to guide our learning.

People are seated in a circle facing each other, and I prefer that barriers such as tables or textbooks are removed from in front of people. Within a circle, you cannot tell who is first or last, and there is no physical separation between student and teacher. There are different ways of facilitating the opportunity for each participant to have his or her say. Often a sacred object will be passed – a feather, 'talking stick' or stone – that signifies that whoever holds the sacred object has the sole right to speak without interruption at that time, sharing as much or as little as the person wishes.

When I am inviting students to learn in Circle, I advise them that learning is not just a mental exercise, but is also a physical, emotional and spiritual undertaking. I suggest that if they are too uncomfortable with this notion, then perhaps they are not ready to learn in this way. Many students in my classes have no problem relating to the first two aspects, but are more hesitant to acknowledge the emotional and spiritual aspects of self. Many others are enthusiastic to engage themselves in other than a purely intellectual or mental sense.

Once students make the choice to participate in the class, then the Four Sacred Medicines are introduced such that they may be used in a purification ceremony. Again, I offer this ceremony to students as part of my personal identity and should be inseparable from the work I hope to do, which, in this case, is to facilitate some learning. Most students have entered my classes with an explicit purpose to learn how to better work with Aboriginal peoples or to develop some understanding of an Aboriginal worldview and so are open to beginning each session with this ceremony and are willing to be respectful of its sacredness. I share what I know about the ceremony, the Four Medicines and the Sacred Objects that are present to help people to be respectful.

In laying the foundation for working in Circle, I ask students to consider that 'the head has no answers and the heart has no questions' and invite them to learn by speaking from the heart rather than simply from the mind. Students are also asked to consider that, when speaking, 'there are hard words and soft words' and that there are ways to share a wide variety of opinions and experiences (about delicate issues such as racism, sexism, homophobia, colonisation) and still nurture a safe learning environment. We are also challenged to conceive of ourselves as part of Creation and that human beings are custodians of Creation. Our responsibility to Creation means that we are responsible to each other and to the kind of learning environment we create, that our Circle is a microcosm of the kind of world we want to see for our children. People come to their own understanding about what is meant by these things and make their choice to participate or not.

Throughout my own social work education I found that the terms 'listening' and 'respect' were discussed in practice-related courses. We all have a conception of what these terms mean. Yet, in no academic course of which I am aware have 'listening' and 'respect' been considered so integral to learning as they are within Anishnabe culture and within working in Circle. People are reminded that to feel safe to speak from their hearts, we need to feel we are listened to and respected. I ask people to listen to others and respect others as they themselves desire. Agreement to allow only one speaker at a time, he or she who is holding the stone or feather, means that people spend much more time listening than they do talking. This gives people the opportunity to simultaneously attend to their own internal processes and they can listen knowing that they will have an opportunity to speak if they wish. They are learning about themselves, how they learn, as much as they are learning from other students. They also are learning to find their own voices and to trust in what they know, that what they say will be heard and valued.

One other means to create respect is the idea that we are all teachers and learners. I acknowledge that I have power over students in my responsibility for evaluation and this is specifically a factor when students submit work for evaluation. The trick is to minimise that 'power-over' during our discussions in Circle. In my opinion, that requires the facilitator to take some risk to share personal feelings and experiences and not simply be a talking head. I also acknowledge that I am no expert on anything and that we all have thoughts and feelings that we can share. Even though readings may have been assigned and I may take an active role in imparting information, it is impossible to predict where the discussion will go when so many people speak about what concerns them at the present time. What is said may not appear to relate in a direct, linear fashion, but what every person says contributes to collective knowledge and wisdom, and each one may take something different (or what they are ready to take) as knowledge. If we all tried to mimic one another and reach the same conclusions, that would be boring. Circle is an excellent place to acknowledge that we are all capable of manifestations of genius (Pelletier, 1972) and to open ourselves to learning from one another in an equitable manner.

Learning in this manner proceeds according to the willingness of participants to engage themselves since 'learning is considered a personal journey towards wholeness, determined by the individual's own pace of development' (Hart, 1996). Working in Circle, in my experience, may initially be intimidating because people do not have faith in the process and the classroom dynamics, reinforced throughout a lifetime of institutionalised education, are not deconstructed instantaneously. I remember incidents where I had explained the process and outlined my own personal belief in its benefits, when students asked, 'Yeah, but how do we confront someone we disagree with?' I did not provide any kind of answer in those situations as that seemed to be part of learning from a perspective that does not place central value upon confrontation or competition.

Many students have spoken about how the learning is not simply related to content but to process as well. Circle takes on a life of its own. It becomes an organic expression of the lived history of all participants, energised by their volitional belonging in the present, fulfilled in the living out of their individual futures. I often wonder what kind of sharing and learning people could do if their lives were not bound by the institutional structures of where I practice.

Racism as a Spritual Force

I choose to work in Circle because I want to affirm my identity as an Anishnabe person and I want to teach others that our scheme of life is relevant and equal to the schemes of life of other peoples. Working in this way allows me to bring in the spiritual aspect of my self, my family and my nation to how I conduct myself on a daily basis.

What is the approach to this next leg of our history? A noted Aboriginal author and activist, Lee Maracle, recently sat among a small group of Aboriginal social work students at the University of Victoria and asked this question. I found her question and our collective answers to be a suitable guide to my approach here in that I was encouraged to consider racism as a spiritual force.

The worldview of Anishnabe people leads us to accept that all of Creation is imbued with spirit, that the world is alive and is one of our relatives. I have wondered if a conceptual parallel to racism existed in our historical Anishnabe society. I was forced to admit that my own belief that First Nations people are no better or worse than other human beings led me to a logical place of discomfort. I have no doubt that Anishnabe and other First Nations peoples have internalised the colonisers' conception of racism and that it is alive and well. So I looked to our traditions to see if I could find a way to understand and engage this contemporary racist society.

In *The Wretched of the Earth,* Franz Fanon (1963) analysed the decolonialisation process and found that what began in violence must end in violence. Elsewhere I have described how First Nations peoples have largely not reacted against the colonisation process with outward expressions of violence towards the rest of Canadian society, but that we have turned that violence inward upon ourselves (Bruyere, 1999). The ways in which First Nations peoples, and indeed Canadian people in general, have internalised racism leads me in my heart and mind to view racism as an act of cannibalism. That was my purpose in sharing my story about the Windigo. As hyperbolic as it may be, I wanted to find something within the brand of consciousness that makes me Anishnabe that will allow me to face racism from a place of power, an individual and collective power that is not destructive or exploitative. It is important in the ongoing renewal of our scheme of life that we not only utilise the tools that help us to identify the problem, but also find the means to create solutions. I personally may not be able to perform the ceremonies that Anishnabe ancestors would to deal with the Windigo spirit that afflicted human beings. Yet, I can personally take responsibility for working in Circle and describing a scheme of life that works in order to, in some small way, move human beings beyond racial divides.

To maintain our own balance, eradicating racism must follow natural law. By this I mean a number of things. The Medicine Wheel can be a guide.

The Four Directions and the Four Elements illuminate a sense of connection and interdependence, an invitation to responsibility that emphasises relationship, equality, mutuality and respect. The Four Seasons, while they are distinct faces of Creation, connote gradual change that can be virtually imperceptible until we step back a bit and see the changes over time. This may help us to persist and yet be flexible. Changes in the seasons suggest that some things are simply beyond human control, inscrutable, and yet are also necessary. We may learn how to address racism as a spiritual force with the understanding that everything happens in its own time and in its own way. Thus, eradicating racism should, at times at least, involve the exercise of patience and the considered recognition of a fertile situation when dealing with it within ourselves and with others.

In relation to the Four Aspects of human beings, potential is enacted volitionally. Thus, anti-racist work is an act of creation, an act of will to seek balance. Since we are always in relation, anti-racism begins with ourselves and moves outward and back to involve the Four Faces of Human Identity. The Earth is strong and yet the balance is delicate. So it is when teaching and learning with other human beings. We must be strong and gentle with ourselves and with others. Fertile situations that create change, we must recognise, occur throughout our lifetime and must involve people throughout the Four Stages of Life to stem the ongoing spread of that cannibal spirit. Viewing racism as a spiritual force means that we have to confront the ways in which our own spirits are malnourished by the lifestyles we live that allow us to unconsciously and cavalierly use more of the Earth's sustaining forces than we need to live.

Working to move beyond racial divides, of course, means creating a vision, allowing time for that vision to unfold and for knowledge to be built and shared, and to act accordingly. Taking into account the Medicine Wheel means working in a life-affirming, creative way. Change in human beings comes from working with the good, the affirmative, in people. Enacting affirmative aspects creates affirmative change, creates balance, allowing us to remain balanced within ourselves as we work.

It can mean creating an understanding of the relationship human beings have with all of Creation and that we are custodians of Creation in a way that no other living beings are custodians. When we begin to see the world through a Medicine Wheel, and when we begin to move within the Circle of Creation, 'the spiritual and the commonplace are one' (Fire and Erdoes, 1978), everything becomes sacred. When that recognition happens, life itself becomes a ceremonial process that is constantly unfolding, and we are consciously and inevitably participating in the ongoing change.

Interweaving Circles

Is this participation, this renewal, limited to the Anishnabe nation or only to First Nations peoples in Canada? Is this way of relating to life and to the world limited to one particular kind of people? My belief is that what makes these teachings resonate within human beings from diverse ethnic and cultural backgrounds is that all human societies have indigenous roots and the teachings of the Medicine Wheel may parallel the root teachings of many past, present and future human societies. Diverse human beings relate to these teachings because they are *human* teachings, not merely teachings for a particular ethnic group. It would be a mistake to presume that Medicine Wheel teachings are simply categorical in their conception or in who may use them. Medicine Wheel teachings are meant to be universal in conceptualising diversity simply by virtue of incorporating non-human life into the Circle and by conceiving that *everything* is a living being, including supposedly inanimate things like stones, winds, rivers or volcanoes (Soydan and Williams, 1998).

As such, the Circle, which flows from these teachings, can peacefully co-exist with other circles, with other human ways of envisioning equitable relationships. As with most theoretical frameworks or paradigms, it presumes the good will of those who are determined to make use of it.

Conclusion

In some ways I have tried to share a particular way of being in the world, one that is intimately bound with my identity as an Anishnabe, a First Nations person. I have attempted to share the root teachings that have led me to practice helping as a social worker and teacher. These roles have led me to try to reaffirm particular cultural, ethnic precepts that may help me, First Nations peoples and other human beings to move beyond racial divides as equal, conscious participants.

When I consider racism as a manifestation of Windigo, the cannibal spirit, perhaps it is as Fanon says, that what begins in violence must end in violence. However, I have a difficult time reconciling that possibility with what I feel to be the responsibility for the custodianship of the Earth. We are here to do something good for Creation and thus, meeting destruction with destruction, exploitation with exploitation, seems futile, damaging and enervating. Yet, meeting force with force, spiritual force with spiritual force, conceiving of it in that way, makes more sense to my way of being in the world. Given the history of the relationship between the indigenous nations of Turtle Island and the colonising peoples, it may be too easy to forget that Anishnabe people and others are still here, and that despite the racist policies and practices designed to eradicate us as an ethnic and racial group, we continue to assert the right to retain, reaffirm and renew our schemes of life to again make them work for us. Considered assistance in the decay that leads to renewal – in individuals, communities, societies, the Earth herself – will bear fruit in a garden our children can faithfully inherit. Our roles as custodians of Creation, including human beings, will have been fulfilled in our unique, yet mutual and interdependent ways. We will all have a place.

References

Allen, P.G. (1986), *The Sacred Hoop: Recovering the Feminine in American Indian Traditions*. Boston, Beacon Press.

Benton-Banai, E. (1988), *The Mishomis Book*. Minneapolis, The Red School House.

Black Elk (1932), *Black Elk Speaks: Being the Life Story of a Holy Man of the Oglala Sioux as Told to John G. Neihardt*. New York, W. Morrow.

Bopp, J., Bopp, M., Brown L. and Lane Jr., P. (1984), *The Sacred Tree*. Lethbridge, Four Worlds Development Press.

Bruyere, G. (1999), 'The decolonization wheel: an Aboriginal perspective on social work practice with Aboriginal peoples', in R. Delaney, K. Brownlee and M. Sellick (eds.), *Social Work with Rural and Northern Communities*. Thunder Bay, Centre for Northern Studies.

Buswa, E. and Shawana, J. (1993), *Nishnabe bimaadziwin kinoomaadwin: Teachings of the Medicine Wheel*. Manitoulin Island, Ojibwe Cultural Foundation and Nda-Gkenjge Gaming.

Deloria, E. (1944), *Speaking of Indians*. Lincoln, University of Nebraska Press.

Fanon, F. (1963), *The Wretched of the Earth*. New York, Grove Press, Inc.

Fire, J. and Erdoes, R. (1972). *Lame Deer, Seeker of Visions*. New York, Simon and Schuster.

Hart, M. (1996), 'Sharing circles: utilizing traditional practise methods for teaching, helping, and supporting', in D. West and S. O'Meara (eds.), *From Our Eyes: Learning from Indigenous Peoples*. Toronto, Garamond Press.

Longclaws, L. (1994), 'Social work and the medicine wheel framework', in B.R. Compton and B. Galway (eds.), *Social Work Processes*. 5th ed. Toronto, McGraw-Hill.

Native Child and Family Services of Toronto, (1990), *Native Family Well-Being in Urban*

Settings: A Culture Based Child and Family Services Model. Toronto, Native Child and Family Services of Toronto.

Pelletier, W. (1972), 'Dumb Indian,' in R. Osborne, (ed.), *Who Is the Chairman of This Meeting?* Toronto, Neewin Publishing Company, pp. 1–10.

Royal Commission on Aboriginal Peoples (1996), *The Final Report of the Royal Commission on Aboriginal Peoples*. Ottawa, Canada Communications Group.

Soydan, H. and Williams, C. (1998), 'Exploring Concepts', in C. Williams, H. Soydan and M. Johnson (eds.), *Social Work and Minorities: European Perspectives*. London, Routledge, pp. 3–35.

Windigo, J. (1993), Personal conversation. Thunder Bay, Ontario.

13 A Maori Social Work Construct

WAERETI TAIT-ROLLESTON

SHARON PEHI-BARLOW

As Maori peoples in Aotearoa/New Zealand, our struggle has been a long and arduous one across years of resisting colonialism to reclaim our identity, lands and original ways of ensuring the well-being of our people. This reclamation had to be consistent with the philosophical premises of a Maori worldview; Maori knowledge creation and transmission processes; values specific to a Maori vision of social reality; and Maori beliefs in the interconnectedness of the individual, the family, kinship systems, the physical environment and 'te ao wairua' (the spiritual realm). Maori perspectives of society firmly embed the individual in his/her family, community, and world system according to sets of beliefs that traverse the intellectual, emotional, physical and spiritual domains. In other words, Maori practices and relationships are based on a holistic view of the person as part of a wider community to which he or she is tied across time and space.

This chapter is written by two authors, who whilst sharing a common identity as Maori women, are also distinct in that we belong to different tribes. In this we reflect the plurality of the Maori peoples, bound together in a common heritage. Thus, the chapter consists of two parts, each written by one of us to reflect our own particular tribal place in Maori society. Part I is written primarily by Waereti Tait-Rolleston. It offers a conceptual frame work that places the Maori child in Maori society within tribal structures and a complex set of ritualised relationships that govern behaviour. Part II, written by Sharon Pehi-Barlow, locates the development of Maori social work in the relationship between the tribal space, the physical environment and non-Maori peoples.

Overall, the chapter provides a framework that enables Maori peoples to develop models of practice appropriate to us; that is, those that are responsive to our specific needs as indigenous peoples, overcome the deleterious impact of colonialism and racism on our well-being, and promote a positive and comprehensive approach to development that is consistent with Maori beliefs and practices – a model of practice relevant to contemporary Maori society. This model provides an example of indigenous peoples regaining control of our own lives and our own voices that have been 'silenced' by the damage that racism and colonialism have wrought on Maori psyches, Maori relationships and Maori access to social goods, services and resources.

Social work as a profession purports to address people's well-being. In practice, however, Pakeha (European based) social work has not served the needs of Maori peoples. The *Puao-te-ata-tu (Daybreak) Report* of the Ministerial Advisory Committee on a Maori Perspective for the Department of Social Welfare was published in 1986 after widespread consultation with Maori about the care of Maori children by the state. It found that:

> At the heart of the issue was a profound misunderstanding or ignorance of the place of the child in Maori society and its relationship with whanau (extended family), hapu (sub-tribe), iwi (tribe) structures (*Puao-te-ata-tu (Daybreak) Report,* 1986: 7).

Significant changes to policies and practices of government agencies were recommended in the Report. However, it quite clearly stated that these changes would be: '... to no avail unless that community in turn picks up the challenges and significantly strengthens its tribal networks' *(Puao-te-ata-tu (Daybreak) Report,* 1986: 7).

Consequently, as Maori practitioners we have had to undo a legacy of damage, while at the same time carve out a space in which Maori peoples can celebrate our own being and respond to Maori needs in ways consistent with our views of the world.

Many of the Maori concepts we use do not translate directly into English, and in keeping with reclaiming and using our own voices, as authors of this chapter, we have chosen to use Maori terminology to convey the preciseness of meanings that reflect our position. For those readers who do not speak or read Maori, the key terms are the following:

whakapapa (genealogy)	whenua (land)
whanaungatanga (kith & kinship ties)	whanau (family)
maatua (parents)	tamariki (children)
kuia/ koroua (grandparents)	mokopuna (grandchildren)
iwi (tribe)	hapu (sub-tribe)
tupuna (ancestors)	Kaumatua (elders)
waka (canoe)	te ao Maori (the Maori world)
te ao Wairua (the spiritual realm)	koha kii (gift of words)

Ngai Tuhoe, Te Arawa, Te Atihaunui-a-Paparangi (names of our tribes)
Mataiawhea (name of our new hapu taken from a common ancestor)
Pakeha (people of European descent or colonisers)
Puao-te-Ata-tu (Daybreak) Report, Ministerial Advisory Committee on Maori
Perspectives for the Department of Social Welfare

Rituals that acknowledge the connections between one generation of Maori and another, between Maori peoples and non-Maori peoples, are an important part of the relationship-building process and integral to Maori culture. This chapter is written in a way that respects those beliefs, and we refer to some of the key ones below. The written word, therefore, must reflect a process of teaching that is consistent with the oral traditions on which Maori culture is based.

PART I: *He Koha Kii: na kui ma, na koro ma* – A Gift of Words from Our Ancestors as a Knowledge Base for Social Work in Aotearoa: A Maori Social Work Construct

This section focuses on the conceptual framework that informs the Maori worldview and locates the Maori child in a whakapapa (genealogy) that descends from the gods. It also examines the place of traditional beliefs and organisational systems and their relevance for contemporary Maori society. Furthermore, it offers an 'insider's' perspective of the complex sets of relationships around the Maori child that social workers in Aotearoa need to confront in order to successfully re-establish tamariki (children) within their whanau (family) structures. In short, it provides the theoretical under-pinnings of a Maori social work construct that is comprehensive and responsive, of which the family group conference as a process has been adapted for use in countries other than Aotearoa/New Zealand as a result of the *Puao-te-ata-tu (Daybreak) Report* of 1986. Children are central to Maori relationships as they link the different generations, provide continuity from one to the other and the eldest mokopuna (grandchildren) are the repository of our own 'knowledge economy' handed down from our kuia and koroua (grandparents). Those who work with children are expected to be mindful of their status and respect their being as such. For children are considered precious charges with significance beyond the whanau (family) into which they are born.

The greetings that follow show respect for past, present and future generations of Maori peoples. They are also relevant to non-Maori peoples who are asked to show respect for Maori culture as part of the interaction which allows a cross-cultural exchange to take place with dignity.

Mihi (Greetings)

He Koha Kii

E ta e taku mokopuna
Te mana whakaheke o oku tupuna
He wa poto noa koe i waenga
I te wa kua hipa i te wa kei te tu mai
No reira kia tere te whakarata i to ngakau
ki nga ahuatanga a tou nei ao ...

Whaia te matauranga o tou nei Ao
Kainga rawahia, hai kinaki i to kai tuturu,
ko tou kai tuturu ko te matauranga o ou Tupuna

Me aro koe ki te ha o te tangata
E hika mahia o mahi kia rite tona
ki to whenua kia tika ai ko to taumata ko te rangi e ...

Ehara noa he koha kii na taku kuia
tenei te tangi kia koutou e . . .

(na Hori Tahurioterangi Tait)

My beloved grandchild
Inheritor from my ancestors
You are but a moment between two
Eternities, the past and the future
So hasten and come to terms with
the circumstances of your time . . .

Seek the knowledge of your time.
Consume it as an appetiser, for your true course,
that being the wisdom of your ancestors
Pay heed to the dignity of people.
May your deeds be as wide as the earth
to justify your place in the sky ...

A gift of words indeed, grandmother
I weep for you all ...

Links between the Past, Present and Future

The *Puao-te-ata-tu (Daybreak) Report* of the Ministerial Advisory Committee on a Maori Perspective for the Department of Social Welfare was published in 1986. This was a momentous event that took place after years of Maori people organising for changes in a welfare regime that had failed to meet Maori needs and respect Maori rights to be a self-determining and sovereign peoples under the provisions of the Treaty of Waitangi (See Appendix), signed in 1840 between the British Crown and Maori peoples.

The *Puao-te-ata-tu (Daybreak) Report* stands internationally as a unique illustration of indigenous social science research. It collected the views of New Zealand's Maori peoples concerning the care of tamariki (children) under the aegis of the whanau (family). The Committee was chaired by the distinguished kaumatua (elder), John Te Rangianiwaniwa Rangihau of the Ngai Tuhoe people. Like the tupuna (ancestors) who had gone before, he heard the voices of the iwi (tribes) as they resounded on marae (sacred ancestral houses). Their koha kii (gift of words) hang suspended in time, held forever in the heke (rafters) of the 34 whare tupuna (tribal meeting places). We need only sit within these hallowed spaces to feel the power of and compassion in their words.

The *Puao-te-ata-tu Report* led to the passage of the Children, Young Persons and their Families Act in 1989. Under this legislation Maori processes of working with whanau were legitimated as a national framework

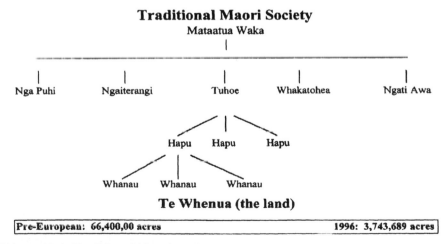

Figure 13.1. Traditional Maori society.

for social work intervention for both Maori and non-Maori peoples living in Aotearoa/New Zealand. This Act is now the focus of international attention and has been central to the popularisation of the family group conference model of working with families in countries such as the United Kingdom, Canada and Sweden (Dalley, 1998; Dominelli, 1999).

The challenge before Maori peoples and those interested in facilitating the use of indigenous models of practice in other settings is captured in the following koha kii:

> He pukenga wai, ka puta te rakau
> He pukenga tangata, ka putu te korero
> Ko ta tatau, ko te tiki atu i nga Totara
> nga korero, ka whakamahia

> Felled trees are left by the surge of the floodwaters,
> Gifts of words are left by 'surging tides of people'.
> Ours is to select the Totara[1] of those gifts and make
> them work for our circumstances, and for our time.

The 'oral accounts' of our people, together with the cultural templates or indigenous knowledge and metaphors of learning of iwi, hapu, and most of all whanau, are what we as Maori peoples must use as navigational points to move 'Beyond Racial Divides'.

According to our ancestors, puao-te-ata-tu is a division of time. It is that brief period, that pause, just before and leading up to the sudden brightness of daybreak. For us as Maori it is timely that we rekindle and recapture the 'mauri' (the 'life force' principle) handed down through the generations, 'mai ra ano'.

It is our tamariki (children) and mokopuna (grandchildren), who will carry us into the future. Their rightful place in Maori society must be secured by us, their maatua (parents), by their kuia and koroua (grand-parents), their whanau, hapu and iwi. Metaphorically speaking, it is timely that we revisit the practice wisdoms, the 'koha kii' of our ancestors, secure our cultural position, harness our collective strength and move beyond racial divides into the new Millenium.

Te Ao Maori (Maori world) is where I return to replenish my soul, rejuvenate my spirit and rekindle my kith and kinship ties. It is, therefore, with deep respect and humility that I share with you in this chapter aspects of my culture. I invite you, albeit for a brief moment, into my world to share with you if you will let me, 'snapshots' of whanau (family), hapu (sub-tribe) and iwi (tribe) relationships and the values, beliefs and customs upon which these structures are based.

Celestial and Terrestrial Knowledge

Maori society emphasises the relationship between Ranginui (Skyfather) and Papatuanuku (Earthmother) as the basis of social relationships. Ranginui and Papatuanuku chose to dwell in close proximity to one another, such was their bond to their children and their love for one another. In their desire to remain together, however, Ranginui and Papatuanuku denied their children knowledge of, and the ability to traverse, the outer limits of the universe beyond their control. Instead, their children were cocooned in relative darkness between their parents. The children plotted to separate their parents. They held the first hui (family group conference), and successfully separated their parents. Consequently, light came into the world (Cairns and Tait-Rolleston, 1998).

The children of Ranginui and Papatuanuku, unlike their more humble parents, adopted more 'god-like' mantels of authority. Some of these children were: Tane-Mahuta (God of the forests and birds); Tumatauenga (God of war/ human pursuits); Tangaroa (God of the seas); Tawhirimatea (God of the winds); Haumiatiketike (God of uncultivated foods).

The personification of the elements of the universe established the framework for binding relationships between humankind and their environment. This framework underpins the cultural value base and practices of contemporary Maori society and is depicted in Table 1. According to Durie (1998: 22):

> In this sense ... Maori gave some priority to the principles which underlie sustainable management and the needs of future generations.

Table 13.1. Nga Atua Maori: Guardians of the Environment.

Atua	Domain	Resource Interests
Tangaroa	seas and waters	fisheries and fish
Rongomataane	kumara	cultivated crops
Haumiatiketike	fern roots	bush undergrowth
Tane Mahuta	forests	trees and birds
Tawhirimatea	the elements	wind, rain
Tumatauenga	humankind	human exploitation

Source: Durie, M. (1998), *Te Mana, Te Kawanatanga – The Politics of Maori Self-Determination*, p. 22.

Tangata noa – Humankind

It was Tane Mahuta who searched for the uha, the female element necessary to create humankind. He found instead the uha of plant life. And by joining the male element of himself to this female element, he gave growth to plant life on earth. The uha to create humankind was hidden in Kurawaka, the pubic area of Papatuanuku. Tane Mahuta, with assistance from celestial beings, formed Hine-ahu-one, the first female made from clay at Kurawaka. Hine-titama, the Dawn Maiden, their first-born later became the wife of Tane. Upon discovery that her husband was also her father, Hine-titama left the world of light and became Hine-nui-te Po, Goddess of Death (Grace, 1984).

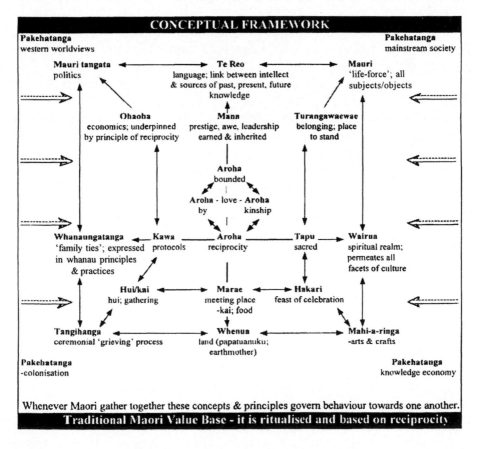

Figure 13.2. Traditional Maori value base.

The traditional Maori system based on decentralised tribal authonomy and the organic solidarity of kinship, consisted of four organisational levels, all linked to a greater or lesser degree by a common ancestor or event. For the Maori of Aotearoa, the waka (canoe) formed the largest socio-political unit, consisting of a group of tribes whose ancestors reached Aotearoa/New Zealand in the same canoe. No co-operative form of government, however, existed among them. Members of a tribe or iwi, on the other hand, were linked by descent from a common ancestor who was on one of the canoes and whose name they took. Tribal feeling was strong and each tribe formed an independent, self-sufficient set of groups under the leadership of the Ariki.

Tribes were divided into a smaller organisation, the hapu (sub-tribe). They took the name of a common ancestor and established a marae as its operations base comprising two major buildings – the wharekai (dining room) and wharenui, (meeting house). Although hapu readily joined other hapu in times of war or ceremonial occasions, each hapu was responsible for its own government, autonomy was fundamental (*Puao-te-ata-tu Report*, 1986: 58–59).

Rituals of Encounter

It is at this point in our journey that we pause to examine some of the 'sacred rituals of encounter' that take place on the marae, and in so doing revisit the story of Ranginui and Papatuanuku.

From our most ancient histories our tribes have mixed, divided, migrated and formed fresh relationships with each other (*Puao-te-Ata-tu Report*, 1986: 59). Inter-tribal and inter-hapu battles were won and lost, new territories were gained through conquest. The maintenance of boundaries presented challenges for those hapu on the tribal boundary lines. Whenever conflict occurred between these units, creative and long-lasting solutions were sought. Let me give you an example. The 'holders' of this story live in Waikaremoana, which is the southern most boundary of the Ngai Tuhoe people and was shared by my whanaunga (relative), Jenny Takuta-Moses, of Ngai Tuhoe, Kahungungu and Ruapani descent. Te Tatau Pounamu – The Jade Door, was created between the two tribal territories of Kahungunu and Tuhoe as a 'corridor of safety' between tribal boundaries and secured through the marriage of two mountains. To this day the right of peaceful passage from one tribal territory to another is remembered.

Te Nohotahi o te iwi Maori, te iwi Pakeha i roto o Aotearoa i te wa nei:
Conceptual framework of the Traditional Maori Value Base System

We as Maori peoples in Aotearoa/New Zealand are faced everyday with the
struggle to maintain our own traditional value base systems of organisation;
reclaim and regenerate our own 'knowledge economy' that was forced
underground by the Tohunga (cultural 'expert') Suppression Act (1907),
whilst also maintaining pakehatanga systems (those of the coloniser) in
order to access '…all the rights and privileges of British subjects' (Article 3,
Treaty of Waitangi, 1840. See Appendix).

Conceptual Framework

Pakehatanga	Western worldviews, mainstream society
Te Reo	Language – the link between the intellect and sources of past, present and future knowledge
Mauri	In the Maori world one is confronted with the idea that all subjects, all objects have mauri or life-force
Wairua	The spiritual realm of Maori culture
Io Matua Kore,	The supreme being occupies the uppermost layer of the divine order
Wairua	Permeates through all facets of the culture
Mahi-a-ringa	Arts and Crafts
Whenua	Land, Papatuanuku (Earthmother); also the placenta, the afterbirth of a child. Without whenua, humanity is lost
Tangihanga	The ceremonial grieving process
Whanaungatanga	Founded in 'family ties' as expressed in the principles and practices of whanau
Tangata Mauri	Politics
Mana	Prestige, awe, leadership – earned and inherited
Turangawaewae	Belonging – a place to stand
Hakari	Feast of celebration
Marae	An area designated by hapu as their meeting place
Hui	A gathering; meeting
Kai	Food
Kawa	Protocol
Ohaoha	Economics underpinned by the principle of reciprocity
Aroha	A love bound by reciprocity, kinship

The following diagrammatic representation of traditional Maori value
base systems was developed by John Te Rangianiwaniwa Rangihau over a

period of 25 years. Whenever Maori gather together to celebrate kinship, to mourn, to plan and make decisions, the following concepts and principles govern their behaviour towards one another. They are ritualised, they are based on reciprocity and they are central to understanding the worldview and relationships that underpin Maori work practices.

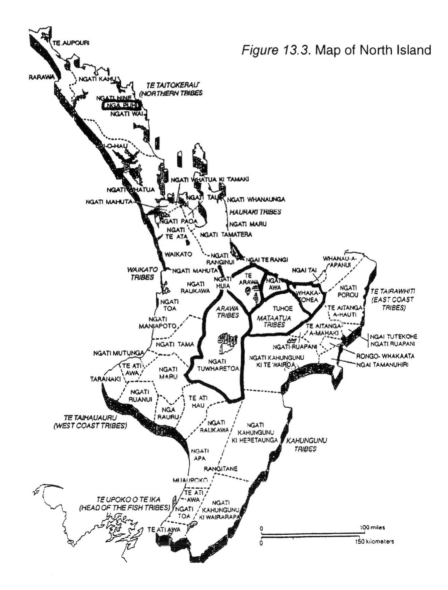

Figure 13.3. Map of North Island

Creation of a New Hapu

The division and blending of our tribes are what Maori tradition is all about. These are processes, however, that can only be controlled from within Maoridom, responding to Maori needs on a Maori timetable (*Puao-te-ata-tu Report*, 1986: 59).

The *whanau* or extended family is the final level of social organisation and is the cornerstone of Maori society. As the *Puao-te-ata-tu Report* states:

> The basic unit of Maori society was the extended family or whanau. Children, grandchildren and great-grandchildren with their spouses, made up the whanau, which was responsible for making the basic day-to-day decisions on the basis of kinship *(Puao-te-ata-tu Report,* 1986: 59).

This is my (Waereti Tait-Rolleston's) whanau. We belong to the Te Arawa and Mataatua waka. We span two tribal territories of Te Arawa and Tuhoe iwi. And although the creation of Mataiawhea hapu is in progress, we do belong to several hapu of both Te Arawa and Tuhoe. The Tait whanau is my immediate nuclear family. We have undertaken a whakapapa-based (genealogy) applied research pilot project over the last 12 months to determine our social, economic and cultural position with the view to implementing growth strategies proposed by our whanau over a decade ago.

There are currently four generations living today (paternal side) comprising nine autonomous whanau units with 75 first cousins, 254 grandchildren and 122 great grandchildren. Almost 50 percent are 18 years of age or over; collectively, we number 453 people. As we are forming a new hapu, we have taken the name Mataiawhea, a common ancestor back five generations (Mataiawhea Database, 1999).

I am one of nineteen children. Seven of my siblings were adopted through whakapapa (genealogical links) to other whanau and hapu of my tribal people, Ngai Tuhoe iwi. This process of adoption is known as whangai, where 'the child is not the child of birth parents, but of the family, and the family was not a nuclear unit in space, but an integral part of a tribal whole...' (*Puao-te-ata-tu Report*, 1986: 59).

The implementation of whakapapa-based processes in relation to the Maori child are flexible to ensure a relatively smooth re-entry into the child's birth whanau. The kinship links between whanau and hapu are renewed and sustained through this 'fluid' arrangement.

My father and his teina (younger brother) and tuahine (sisters) were raised in the traditional framework of the whanau. They shared the same understanding of tikanga (value base) and they observed the principles in accordance with customary leadership. That is to say, their elder brother (my father) was tuakana and they expected to represent their issues and concerns at hapu and iwi levels. A key matter that surfaced for them twenty years ago was that of projected growth of their whanau and the need to strategically plan for that growth.

Plans included the securing of whenua (land) where they could establish a papakainga (settlement) as the first stage toward the creation of a new hapu. Approval in principle was granted them by elders from one of their hapu as guardians of the whenua. The land inherited from their father was proposed as a resource to assist the development. We, their children, also agreed in principle to the concept. Legislation[2] concerning land tenure, drawn out processes and the complex procedures associated with Maori land prevented the implementation of these plans. It was only in 1993 that legislation in the form of the Te Ture Whenua Act was introduced to enable Maori whanau to establish papakainga (settlements) such as those proposed by our parents 20 years ago. The Act was enacted to halt the further alienation of Maori land, so it has not restored the pre-colonial lands held by the Maori peoples. With regard to the Mataiawhea, it does mean, however, that a projected potential asset-base in land with a collective value of over one million dollars is potentially available for development. But, as the 'snapshot' of ownership in Table 2 below indicates, the land is 'tied up' in legislation and multiple ownership and cannot currently be used for Mataiawhea developmental purposes.

Table 13.2. 'Snapshot' of Mataiawhea Land Database.

Name of Block	Total No. Shares	$Value per Full Share	No. of Owners	$Value of Total Block	$Value of Mataiawhea Shares
Okere 1C3A7	15.26165	$1,638.09	294	$25,000	$4,965.38
Waiteti 2A1B2A5	5.5	$16,000.00	89	$88,000	$20,000.00
" 2 sec 1B4B2	446.56666	$765.84	501	$342,000	$1,723.12
Rotohokahoka F5	248.18886	$282.04	1116	$70,000	$44.06
Pukeroa Oruawhata	997.38740	$21,973.00	2833	$24,000,000	$302,541.62
Mangorewa Kaharoa	301.15	$189.27	179	$57,000	$709.76
Paengaroa South 5	753.66667	$1,745.17	438	$1,130,000	$66,927.26

The task of realising our parents' dream of reclaiming our lands and laying the basis for future growth now falls to us. It is our turn to implement the strategies that our parents proposed so that our tamariki (children) and mokopuna (grandchildren) have a turangawaewae (place to stand). The maintenance of whanaungatanga through land utilisation based on tikanga handed down by our tupuna (ancestors) and physical and spiritual reconnection to the land is at the heart of our project. Durie (1998) writes:

> Whanaungatanga is a process by which whanau are empowered and depends on active leadership, an economic base, effective communication, the creation of new resources and facilities to meet the changing needs of whanau, and legislation that is compatible with whanau values and aspirations (Durie, 1998: 10).

Moreover, we need to ensure that this is anchored firmly inside the framework of the whanau, hapu and iwi structures. This is a duty that we owe to past, present and future generations. It will also establish a base from which Maori social workers can begin to work with their peoples in ways that are respectful of their traditions and respond to their specific needs.

Final Remarks to PART I

I thank you for your invitation to partake of your world by writing a chapter for this book. I see it as an honour and a privilege. I hope I have been able to reciprocate that honour and privilege by sharing part of my world with you and inviting you to think about a worldview that has evolved over aeons of time, right back to the myriad of gods. For it establishes the framework for practice that I have attempted to encapsulate in these pages and ask you to consider. This framework for practice is collective, comprehensive, inclusive, interconnected and responsive to the needs of whanau. Its features are pivotal to ensuring Maori self-determination in the rebuilding of Maori communities which have been undermined by dominant taken-for-granted worldviews that have profoundly misunderstood the place of the Maori child within their own culture (Cairns, Tait-Rolleston, Kereopa, Niania, and Fulcher, 1998).

The need for cultural responsiveness and a comprehensive approach to the social and economic needs of Maori peoples has never been greater. This point was emphasised in the last keynote address offered by the eminent Maori Elder and social worker, John Te Rangianiwaniwa Rangihau, to a conference of New Zealand social worker educators. He said:

> *It may not be too long before it is realised by professional groups that intervention vis-à-vis social problems may not be limited solely to social*

strategies. It will need to depend on an amalgam of cultural and economic remedies. Maori people have long held the view that 'people development' is synonymous with 'economic development'. If you align that viewpoint with people inseparable from their culture, then you have a recipe that takes us out of 'welfare' and into 'development' and the new negotiated order of 'empowered communities' (Rangihau, 1987: 26).

The Maori worldview is capable of offering guidance in the conduct of social relations not only amongst Maori peoples, but also between Maori and non-Maori peoples. For it contains within it principles to guide relationships between one individual and all other peoples, plants, creatures and phenomena in the universe. The key to the interaction between them is that of being accorded the respect and dignity that belongs to all who base their behaviour on relationships of reciprocity and interdependence. The next section reflects more specifically on some of the issues raised by these interconnections.

PART II: Maori Conceptualisation: A Theoretical Framework for Social Work

This section focuses on the relationship between the peoples from a particular tribal group and the physical environment that is associated with them as the basis of a social system that ensures their well-being. In the process of considering this, the deleterious effects of colonialism and racism on indigenous tribal structures are described. Lastly, it argues that Maori social work can only develop effectively in a context that challenges existing oppressive structures and returns to its roots.

Mihi (Greeting)

Tena Koutou, Tena Koutou, Tena Koutou Katoa

Mihi ana tuatahi ka lhoa nga mano
Matua tama wairua tapu me nga anahera pono me te mangai ae
Mihi ana tua rua ki nga

Waima te marae
Ngapuhinui tonu
Rahiri te tangata
Sonny Pehi toku matua

Ruapehu te Maunga
Whanganui te awa

Ati hau nui a Paparangi ta iwi
Pikotuku te tangata
Ki ta taha o toku whaia
Te mataara tana ingoa

Kaui Maunga

E rere kuamai
Te awanui mai te Kauai maunga
Ki tangaroa
Ko au te awa
Ko te awa ko au

The river flows from the mountain to the sea.
I am the river and the river is me.

Greetings to the people of this land, the tangata whenua,
the people of the land.

Greetings, greetings, greetings. To those from New Zealand
Greetings to you from the Land of the long White Cloud.

Greetings

Setting the Scene

Through this written work, I (Sharon Pehi-Barlow) enable you to have a glimpse through the keyhole of the Maori world, so as to share with you our hopes and aspirations for a world free of racism.

The river flows from the mountain to the sea
I am the river and the river is me.

This saying is a traditional form of identification for my people. I recognise the mountain, river and major ancestral chiefs with whom I have a direct genealogical connection. These connections have been recognised for thousands of years by members of my tribe, Ati hau nui a Paparangi.

This whakatauki or proverb reinforces my place in Aotearoa/New Zealand and the world and the universe. It informs the listener about my tribe and the relationship that I have with the natural elements that surround the Whanganui River, the mountain Ruapehu and the lands associated with both. Those belonging to the river tribe Ati hau nui a Paparangi have used this whakatauki for thousands of years to the present day. The Whanganui River has always reflected, and continues to reflect, the social, economic and psychological well-being of the river tribes. The Whanganui River has for thousands of years given life-sustaining support to the people who have dwelt on her river banks. The awa or river remains today the wellspring, the nurturer, the provider.

This concept, extended by Maori theory, proposes that everything animate and inanimate possesses a mauri or life-essence or life-principle. Each has a spiritual existence that compliments the physical state. Further, any damage to this physical state will inevitably have an impact on the wider mauri or life-force including that of humankind. Today, the river struggles with the effects of man-induced pollution, lowered water levels affected by dams and, until recently, sewage disposal.

Embedded within the capitalist economic system is a refusal to acknowledge the life-giving nature of the river, and a political system that does not recognise or understand the necessity of maintaining a relationship of reciprocity between the river and humankind. Despite being denied the right to participate in the decision-making processes of this system, Maori peoples have struggled to regain a place consistent with their beliefs.

Tribal knowledge, values and beliefs have been subsumed by the dominant culture beneath the persistent truth-bearing flag which heralds the new, better, and superior way. As a result of colonialism and racism, our customary guardianship role over the river, our land, children and way of life have diminished over time. So too, local wisdom has been abandoned along with local tribal narratives containing philosophical concepts and records of the tribal customs, history and traditions. Yet, alongside language, these form the foundation of my culture, and I suggest, any culture.

As the well-being of the iwi is reliant on the relationship with the river, the welfare of the people and the river has declined during the last 150 years. By the mechanism of colonisation, any rights to the use of the river and the associated resources were forcibly removed from the control of the tribes.

Also, a series of legislative fiats, government policies, church endorsed activities, tourist initiatives and recreational fishing endeavours have directly contributed to the changing relationship between the indigenous peoples and their physical environment. Yet, in seeking to assert their rights as they affirmed them, the river tribes have resisted all these measures.

During the mid-1930s to 1950s, a major urban drift by Maori peoples made a significant contribution to the deterioration in the relationship between tribal members and the river. As contact between the river and the people of Ati hau nui a Paparangi collapsed, so did the affinity between the river and the tribe.

The onslaught on their rights and affinities has been unremitting. Maori peoples have struggled to regain these rights for many years, but with limited success. One of the more recent attempts to impose dominant norms over Maori peoples occurred in March 1999, when Doug Grahame, MP, openly declared the position of the New Zealand government. This was to insist that Maori peoples could not hope to regain guardianship over the rivers as the state intended to reinforce its claim of ownership and control over all rivers and waterways in Aotearoa, including that of the Whanganui. This position is a complete negation of the Treaty of Waitangi of 1840 which guaranteed to Maori tribes and signatories the right to manage these resources.

This issue highlights the dilemmas that confront us as a people. The lack of reciprocity between the Maori and the Pakeha (colonising Europeans and their descendants) poignantly reflects the present position of the tribes that belong to the river and their relationship with the state.

I have guardianship responsibilities to the river, the land and our children. This is a role I share with other tribal members. This role bears both rights and responsibilities. Each time I repeat the proverb, 'I am the river and the river is me', the implicit social contract that exists between the river, the land and our children is made explicit. I am compelled to heed the call to protect it and ensure its future viability.

The struggle for liberation by the people of this land, therefore, is our only option for the future. The drive for liberation has taken a number of forms. Specific to the tribes associated with the Whanganui area has been the strategic, though sometimes sporadic, occupation of tracts of land that have been illegally alienated and severed from those tribes that formerly held them.

Social Work Theory

Maori social work theory is a developing field that draws on our own beliefs about the world. It critiques and questions some of the basic assumptions within western paradigms, especially the notion of the individual as an autonomous being unrelated to others and without responsibilities towards them.

In Maori social work, theory and frameworks for practice emerge from conceptualisations based on humankind's relationship with the physical environment and the universe as well as their relationships with each other. Concepts of balance, reciprocity, genealogy, the tribe or extended family are central to this paradigm and directly affects notions of human justice, social justice and the law and what they mean to Maori peoples. Maori visions of reality in terms of practice and customs are based on the belief that each action affects the balance of the whanau, hapu, iwi, indeed, the cosmos. Working with this paradigm enables the Maori practitioner to move beyond the boundaries and constraints of current Pakeha practice frameworks to explore new ways of providing social work services to Maori peoples.

The Maori paradigm of social work has been overwhelmed with the materialism of the western paradigm which has isolated it from its spiritual roots. The clash of cultures that occurs for Maori practitioners on a daily basis as one culture encounters another in social work interactions, raises the questions of what are the consequences when paradigms for practice collide and who bears them?

The western paradigm, with its confidence about truth, religion, social theory, child protection and law, sets itself above other views of the world, and by implication invalidates other people's truths. These are then relegated to myth, legends, superstitious fairytales and quaint explanations. Yet, Maori stories about our origins are not myths and fantastic artifacts of make-believe. They are a way of life. The dominant society, in denying the authenticity of other systems of knowledge and theory, seeks to deliver fatal blows to other cultures and their long-term sustainability.

Maori practitioners are asked to move between two worlds – their own and that of the Pakeha. Several questions become pressing: How would it be possible for them to see the same world that others do? How do two people dialogue with each other across differences? The notion of law and social justice from a western paradigm maintains a focus on proof of innocence or guilt and punishment. To work, these concepts draw on particular assumptions about the nature of human beings, thought, language and the way we perceive the world. They do not often endorse the principles, values and customs on which Maori peoples build their lives. Nonetheless, Maori social workers are required to bridge the two spheres to survive in the alien world of the Pakeha and to reclaim and sustain the Maori world.

I have been born into a society steeped in a particular language, thoughts, worldview and ways of thinking. From this experience, I recognise that different paradigms exist. However, I know that it is not possible to understand another culture by observation and analysis alone. In reaching out to others different from me, I must at the least suspend judgement when faced with something I do not understand. It would increase reciprocity across cultural divides if Pakeha social workers could return the compliment and not rate negatively Maori worldviews and practices. They currently have little basis from which to assess these in a fair and just manner.

I would assert that western-oriented practitioners are now faced with this challenge: How can they free themselves from the fixed rigidities of response that they endorse in social work relationships with clients from other cultures? In Aotearoa/New Zealand, this is obviously linked to Pakeha social workers' failure to respond appropriately to the needs of Maori clients. Seeing and thinking about society and reality is a largely unconscious act that draws on taken-for-granted assumptions. In bicultural contexts like the one that formally exists in Aotearoa/New Zealand, some of these beliefs can become embedded in both worldviews so that they become culturally shared.

As I reflect on the theme, *Beyond Racial Divides: Ethnicities in Social Work Practice,* weaving together the elements of culture, identity and practice, finding answers to the following question seems critical to gaining any real understanding of the issues that are being confronted: How have history and the external political, social and economic forces that prevail in this country shaped Maori understandings of the world and Maori peoples' place in it? The current imperative Maori peoples face is dual-faceted. Racism is one aspect. The other is that we Maori peoples are challenged by the overriding concern of reclaiming our heritage and re-orienting our energies toward the revival and re-institution of our lost languages, cultural customs and practices. The debate surrounding racism in Aotearoa/New Zealand is a challenge that must be borne by those who perpetuate this racism – the colonists, the dominant persons who often refuse to acknowledge their racist actions. Confronting the influence of personal and institutional racism forms the daily reality of Maori practitioners. Eliminating racism should be affirmed as a matter of routine in the lives of the Pakeha social workers.

Education: A Site for Struggle

Maori peoples consider education as an important transmitter of cultural values and have organised to ensure that the social work curriculum reflects theirs. The Whanganui Regional Community Polytechnic is situated in the middle of the small rural city of Whanganui, located within the traditional tribal area of Ati hau nui a Paparangi. The Polytechnic has become the site of Maori educational practices.

The Polytechnic offers a two-year Diploma in Social Work. Over the last five or six years, the aims and objectives of this programme have been directly influenced by the local Maori community within which it is situated. During this time, there has been a clear policy to seek to employ Tangata Whenua or people linked by birthright to the local tribes associated with the Whanganui River. This policy has shaped and encouraged the development of an indigenous social work theoretical framework. This framework promotes the development of whanau (or extended family), hapu (the sub-tribe) and/or iwi (the tribe). Of particular importance in this framework is the place of the child, politically, economically and socially.

The use of observation and experiential methods are highly favoured as methods of teaching and learning by Maori peoples. Reflexivity and looking for wider connections is also part of our commitment. Local tribal elders mentor social work students, practitioners and tutors who understand that practice springs from a framework embedded in reciprocal relationships that exist between humankind and the natural environment. As a result of these endeavours in Whanganui, the development of indigenous models of social work within a Maori or iwi social service intervention framework is gaining ground. As we evaluate the curriculum, particularly the content and delivery of these programmes over time, we will be in a better position to contribute to the discussions of more ethnically relevant models for social work at the global level.

Recently, a number of social work institutions in Aotearoa, who dared to introduce innovative indigenous methods of teaching or advance a Maori paradigm for social work, have been accused of racism in the form of excluding Pakeha people. Closure of schools that have supported the teaching of Maori paradigms of social work has been one outcome, and threatened closure hangs over others. Openly challenging the dominant culture and suggesting the existence and validity of another paradigm is a risky business. Yet, whether we like it or not, that is the situation in which Maori social workers have to practice. Moreover, dealing with these issues consumes energies which could be better used in serving the needs of the Maori peoples.

Conclusions

Reclaiming the birthright of indigenous peoples in Aotearoa/New Zealand has been a difficult process involving suffering, pain, anger, reconciliation – and joy when success has been achieved. Social work education and practice have been integrally bound up in the process of both the attempt to sub-ordinate Maori peoples to Pakeha regimes and our resistance to this. That we are able to write about our challenges to oppression and reaffirm our heritage is a tribute to the resilience and creativity of Maori generations past, present and future. Under our control, Maori social work has an important role to play in facilitating our growth in a society that moves 'beyond racial divides'.

Notes

1. Totara refers to a native tree of Aotearoa that grows to immense heights and girth. Renowned rangatira or chiefs are often referred to metaphorically at their death as 'kua hinga te totara' – the great totara has fallen.
2. 1852   New Zealand Constitution Act (enacted in Great Britain) – provided for maintenance of tribal districts in which Maori customary laws and practices would prevail; same rights/privileges as British subjects => reality – imperial policies not applied at the frontier (NZ).
   1862   Native Lands Act.
   1864-1909 'Te Kooti tango whenua' – 'the land-taking court' (the term coined by a Crown agent, Biggs, in 1867) was established as an effective government agency instrumental to the alienation of Maori land from 66,400,000 acres in 1840 to 3,743,689 acres in 1996.
   1864   Public Works Act – compensation for the expropriation of Maori land.
   1886   Treaty, a 'legal nullity' – court ruling by Judge Pendergast; precedent established and maintained for almost 100 years.
   1900   Maori Councils Act – some local autonomy; some legal power over land => special conditions, restricted gains.
   1900   Native Lands Administration Act – tribal councils – marked decrease in sale of land => repealed in 1905.

References and Bibliography

Bradley, J. (1995), 'Before You Tango with Our Whanau You Better Know What Makes Us Tick: An Indigenous Approach to Social Work', *Social Work Review*, vol. VII (1), pp. 27–29.

Bradley, J. (1997), 'Iwi and Cultural Social Services Policy: The State's Best Kept Secret', *Te Komako – Social Work Review*, vol. VIII (1), pp. 3–5.

Bradley, R. (1997), 'Puao-te-ata-tu: "he manako te koura i kore ai"' (The Paradigm Shift Fusing Fiscal Responsibility and Tino Rangatiratanga in the New Millennium), *Te Komako – Social Work Review*, vol. VIII (1), pp. 18–19.

Cairns, T. (1991), 'Whangai – Caring for a Child', in G. Maxwell, I. Hassall and J. Robertson (eds.), *Toward a Child and Family Policy for New Zealand*. Wellington, Office of the Commissioner for Children.

Cairns, T., Tait-Rolleston, W., Kereopa, H., Niania, P. and Fulcher, L. (1998), 'Nga Parikarangaranga o Puao-te-ata-tu' (Towards a Culturally Responsive Education And Training for Social Workers in New Zealand), *Canadian Social Work Review*.

Casson, S. and George, C. (1995), *Culture Change for Total Quality*. London, Pitman Publishing.

Cheyne, C., O'Brien, M. and Belgrave, M. (1997), *Social Policy in Aotearoa New Zealand*. Oxford University Press.

Coates, K. and McHugh, P. (1998), *Living Relationships: Kokiri Ngatahi: The Treaty of Waitangi in the New Millenium*. Commentaries by M. Durie, D. Caygill, R. Maaka, B. Mansfield, A. Mahuika, W.H. Oliver, G. Rudland, M. Wilson and J. Williams. Victoria University of Wellington, Victoria University Press.

Dalley, B. (1998), *Family Matters: Child Welfare in Twentieth-Century New Zealand*. Auckland, University Press.

Dominelli, L. (1997), 'Educating Social Workers in a Changing Cultural Context: Social Work under Globalisation', *Social Work Review*, vol. IX (4), pp. 3–8.

Dominelli, L. (1999), *Anti-Racist Social Work*, 2nd edition. Macmillan.

Dreadon, E. (1997), 'Matua whakapai tou Marae, ka whakapai ai I te Marae o te tangata: First set in order your own Marae before you clean another', *Te Komako – Social Work Review*, vol. VIII (1), pp. 6–8.

Durie, M. (1997), *Whaiora: Maori Health*. Oxford University Press.

Durie, M. (1998), *Te Mana, Te Kawanatanga: Politics of Maori Self-Determination*. Oxford University Press.

Durst, D. (1992), 'The Road to Poverty Is Paved with Good Intentions: Social Interventions and Indigenous Peoples', *International Social Work*, vol. 35 (2), pp. 191–202.

Ely, P. and Denney, D. (1987), *Social Work in a Multi-Racial Society*. Aldershot, Hants, Gower.

Fleras, A. and Elliot, J. (1992), *The Nations Within: Aboriginal-State Relations in Canada, the USA and New Zealand*. Toronto, Oxford Press.

Fook, J. (1996), *The Reflective Researcher – Social Workers Theories of Practice Research*. Allen & Unwin.

Friere, P. (1970), *Pedagogy of the Oppressed*. New York, The Seabury Press.

Friere, P. (1990), 'A Critical Understanding of Social Work', *Journal of Progressive Human Services*, vol. 1 (1), pp. 1–12.

Fulcher, L. (1988), *The Worker, the Work Group and the Organisational Task: Corporate Restructuring and the Social Services in New Zealand*. Wellington, Victoria University Press.

Fulcher, L. and Ainsworth, F. (1994), 'Child Welfare Abandoned? Ideology and the Economics of Contemporary Service Reform in New Zealand', *Social Work Review*, vol. VI (5), pp. 1–18.

Fulcher, L. (1997), 'Changing Care in a Changing World: The Old and New Worlds', *Social Work Review*, vol. VII (1&2), pp. 20–26.

Grace, P. (text) and Kahukiwa, R. (illus.) (1984), *Wahine Toa: Women of Maori Myth*. Auckland, William Collins, p. 222.

Harris, P. and Twiname, L. (1998), *First Knights: An Investigation of the New Zealand Business Roundtable*. New Zealand, Howling At The Moon Publishing Ltd.

Hudson, J., Morris, A., Maxwell, G.M. and Galloway, B. (eds.) (1996), *Family Group Conferences: Perspectives on Policy and Practice*. Annandale, NSW, Federation Press.

Hudson, W. and Nurius, P. (eds.) (1994*)*, *Controversial Issues in Social Work Research: Debates in Social Work Research*. Sydney, Allyn and Bacon/ Paramount Publishers.

Ihimaera, W. (ed.) (1998), *Growing Up Maori*. New Zealand, Tandem Press.

Irwin, K. (1994), 'Maori Research Processes and Methods: An Exploration and Discussion', *Sites*, vol. 28 (Autumn), pp. 25–43.

Kahn, V.S. (1982), 'The Role of the Culture of Dominance in Structuring the Experience of Ethnic Minorities', in C. Husband (ed.), *Race in Britain*. London, Hutchinson.

Kelsey, J. (1997), *The New Zealand Experiment: A world model for structural adjustment?* Auckland: Auckland University Press.

Leigh, J.W. (1998), *Communicating for Cultural Competence*. Sydney, Allan and Bacon.

Mataiawhea (1999), *Mataiawhea Database* (unpublished).

Mason, K. (1992), *Review of the Children, Young Persons and Their Families Act, 1989: Report of the Ministerial Review Team to the Minister of Social Welfare*. Wellington, Department of Social Welfare.

Maxwell, G. and Morris, A. (1993), *Families, Victims and Culture: Youth Justice in New Zealand*. Wellington, Social Policy Agency and Institute of Criminology, Victoria University of Wellington.

McCreary, J.R. (1994), 'Keynote Address to the 1964 Conference of the New Zealand Association of Social Workers, *Social Work Review*, vol. VI (4), pp. 4–6.

Ministerial Advisory Committee (1986), *Puao-te-ata-tu (Daybreak) Report*. Ministerial Advisory Committee on a Maori Perspective for the Department of Social Welfare (includes appendix). Wellington, Government Printer.

Moses, J. (1999), (Oral source.) *'Whakapapa from the Creation: Ngai Tuhoe'* Murphy, T. (1997), *Te Pumaomao: An Awakening to Rediscover and Celebrate MANA MAORI*. Indigenous Rights Conference, Rotorua. Workshop material.

Parata, N. Te Kairangahau (1991), *For the sake of decent shelter ...* . Ministry of Maori Women's Affairs Housing Research Project Report. Wellington, NZ.

Pere, R.T. (1997 reprint), *Te wheke: A Celebration of Infinite Wisdom*. Wellington, Ako Global Learning NZ Ltd.

Pere, R.T. (1992), *Ako: Concepts and Learning in the Maori Tradition*. Paper No 17. Department of Sociology, Hamilton, University of Waikato.

Rangihau, J. (1981), 'Being Maori', in M. King (ed.), *To Ao Hurihuri: The World Moves On*. Auckland, Longman Paul.

Rangihau, J. (1987), *Beyond Crisis*. Keynote Address to the First New Zealand Conference on Social Work Education. Christchurch, Rehua Marae, University of Canterbury, Department of Social Work.

Rei, T. (1993), *Maori Women and the Vote*. Wellington, Huia Publishers.

Rountree, K. (1995), *Writing for Success – A Practical Guide for New Zealand Students*. Longman Paul Ltd.

Salmond, A. (1975), *Hui: A Study of Maori Ceremonial Gatherings*. New Zealand, Reed Publishing.

Saville-Smith, K. and James, B. (1989), *Gender, Culture and Power*. Oxford University Press.

Schaef, A.W. (1995), *Native Wisdom for White Minds*. Sydney, Random House.

Smith, L. (1993), 'Maori Education – A Reassertion', in W. Ihimaera (ed), *Te Ao Marama: Regaining Aotearoa – Maori Writers Speak Out*. Auckland, Reed.

Tait-Rolleston, W., Cairns, T., Fulcher, L., Kereopa, H. and Niania, P. (1997), 'He Koha Kii – na kui ma, na koro ma: A Gift of Words from Our Ancestors', *Social Work Review*, vol. IX (4), pp. 30–36.

Tapiata, W.W. and Ruiwhiu, L. (1995), 'He Korerorero', *Social Work Review*, vol. VII (1), pp. 31–35.

Te Pumanawa Hauora (ed.) (1998), *Te Oru Rangahau*. Massey University, Maori Research & Development Conference, 7–9 July.

Te Whaiti, P., McCarthy, M. And Durie, A. (eds.) (1997), *Mai I Rangiatea: Maori Well-Being and Development*. Auckland University Press/Bridget Williams Books.

Vercoe, A. (1998), *Educating Jake: Pathways to Empowerment*. Palmerston North, NZ, Dunmore Press.

Walker, H. (1995), 'Where Is *Puao-te-Ata-tu* and the Department of Social Welfare?' *Social Work Review*, vol. VII (1), pp. 12–16.

Walker, R. (1990), *Ka Whawhai Tonu Matou: Struggle without End*. Penguin Books.

Wilcox, R., Smith, D., Moore, J., Hewitt, A., Allan, G., Walker, H., Ropata, M., Monu and Featherstone, T. (1991), *Family Decision-making, Family Group Conferences – Practitioner's Views*. Lower Hutt, NZ, Practitioners Publishing.

APPENDIX

The Treaty of Waitangi

Te Tiriti o Waitangi
(Articles only)

Ko te Tuatahi
Ko nga Rangatira o te Wakaminenga me nga Rangatira katoa hoki ki hai i uru ki taua wakaminenga ka tuku rawa atu ki te Kuini o Ingarani ake tonu atu – te Kawanatanga katoa o o ratou whenua.

Ko te Tuarua
Ko Te Kuini o Ingarani ka wakarite ka wakaae ki nga Rangatira ki nga hapu – ki nga tangata katoa o Nu Tirani te tino rangatiratanga o o ratou wenua o ratou kainga me o ratou taonga katoa. Otiia ko nga Rangatira o te Wakaminenga me nga Rangatira katoa atu ka tuku ki te Kuini te hokonga o era wahi wenua e pai ai te tangata nona te wenua – ki te ritenga o te utu e wakaritea ai e ratou ko te kai hoko e meatia nei e te Kuini hei kai hoko mona.

Ko te Tuatoru
Hei wakaritenga mai hoki tenei mo te wakaaetanga ki te Kawanatanga o te Kuini – ka tiakina e te Kuini o Ingarani nga tangata Maori katoa o Niu Tireni ka tukua ki a ratou nga tikanga katoa rite tahi ki ana mea ki nga tangata o Ingarani.

The Treaty of Waitangi
(English – original translation)

Article One
The Chiefs of the Confederation of the United Tribes of New Zealand and the separate and independent Chiefs who have not become members of the Confederation cede to Her Majesty the Queen of England absolutely and without reservation all the rights and powers of Sovereignty which the said Confederation or Individual Chiefs respectively exercise or possess, or may be supposed to exercise or to possess, over their respective territories as the sole Sovereigns thereof.

Article Two
Her Majesty the Queen of England confirms and guarantees to the Chiefs and Tribes of New Zealand and to the respective families and individuals thereof the full, exclusive and undisturbed possession of their Lands and Estates, Forests, Fisheries and other properties which they may collectively or individually possess so long as it is their wish and desire to retain the same in their possession; but the Chiefs of the United Tribes and the Individual Chiefs yield to Her Majesty the exclusive right of preemption over such lands as the proprietors thereof may be disposed to alienate at such prices as may be agreed upon between the respective Proprietors and persons appointed by Her Majesty to treat with them in that behalf.

Article Three
In consideration thereof Her Majesty the Queen of England extends to the Natives of New Zealand Her royal protection and imparts to them all the rights and privileges of British Subjects.

14 Appropriateness of Social Work Practice with Communities of African Origin

ASHER JOHN-BAPTISTE

Introduction

In attempting to move beyond racial divides, it is not enough to simply reduce issues of 'culture' to matters relative to or synonymous with 'fluidity' or 'hybridity'. There are deep structural aspects of culture that communities of African origin[1] experience as fundamental to the living of their lives. The linking of structural aspects of culture to highly contentious notions of 'essentialism' does little to offer an explanation that encourages understanding, acceptance or inclusion. Further, it serves to undermine perceptions of helping which in themselves are fundamental to the success of healing processes – to which the profession of social work is so closely related.

In the West, the power to name and define a people, and to then define their reality and have that 'people' accept that definition of reality as if it were their own, holds a fundamental place in the nature of human relationships between white people and those defined as 'cultural others'. Added to this is the position whereby the labels we choose for ourselves and the labels we use to refer to those 'other' than ourselves are loaded with meaning and are influenced by the frame of reference within which an individual places them or uses them (Martin and Mitchel-Martin, 1999).

However, there seems to be a misconception in social work that the process of helping remains free from cultural bias in terms of theoretical givens and their translation into service delivery; in terms of how social work theory and practice inform the 'nature' of a social worker; and how both can influence practice perceptions of the service receiver. Further, in the rush to eliminate anything but basic and tangible references to cultural specificity (e.g., language, skin and hair care and religion), social work has

257

invested its future in the belief that representations of hybridity better explain the current picture of culture as it informs elements of social work practice and expectations of practitioners and 'clients'.

Uniforming the influence of culture as a determinant in the lives and needs of 'clients' would also go a long way towards the prediction of social work need and resources, in a social work climate of increasing special-isation, resource scarcity and downsizing.

The importance of culture cannot be underestimated, reflected in the ongoing academic and intellectual struggle presently taking place between so-called 'essentialist' and 'non-essentialist' positions. To ascribe any particular essence or foundational positioning to aspects of 'Black'[2] culture is deemed essentialist – or rather, an attempt to force 'multicultural' peoples into inflexible cultural 'givens'. Conversely, the importance of taking a non-essentialist position on culture is equated with the significance of ensuring that culture remains the fluid phenomenon that it is – neither bound by rigid categorical 'givens', nor the boundaries of foundational positions that aim to speak against the realities of multiple cultural positionings which better reflect the experience and movement of culture today.

So why the subtle yet determined social work interest in culture? I would argue that with culture comes the important aspect of agency – and that if we can predict the scope of agency likely to be present in the social work field, it then becomes much easier to direct power, predict resource implications and practice determinants and to predict practice outcomes. And a controlled social work service is a happy social work service.

But in the midst of that control the question is: Can social work incor-porate the expectations of African-origined communities in terms of the need to deliver a service that recognises their right to self-definition and self-determination and the relative connection of both to definitions of need?

In a bid to further the debate on this issue, my own research interest has focused on whether the role and place of culture in the delivery of a social work service to communities of African origin has an effective role in the way in which a social work service will be perceived and taken up by that community. My research is linked to the practice outcomes of a local authority community social work service which I run specifically (but not exclusively) for communities of African origin. 'Users' of the service have made it quite clear that their reasons for doing so were influenced by the possibility that they would not have to pretend to be anyone other than themselves in order to seek help; and that help could be sought when they wanted rather than when crisis had set in, removing elements like choice and control from their hands.

Further examination of the research results revealed the importance of the role of culture as a determinant for 'users' in terms of the choice to use or not use the community social work service.

My intention here is to explore two converse positions on culture that have featured in my research findings, as well as to explore some of the issues that underpin the debate with regard to the role and place of culture in the delivery of a social work service to communities of African origin.

Setting the Scene – Essentialism vs. Non-Essentialism

The culture debate locates itself within two positions in relation to African-origined communities. The position traditionally seen as Eurocentric views culture in a non-essentialist way, identifying itself with the importance of influences such as hybridity and fluidity as being foundational in the structural content of culture. An alternative position is that of African-Centredness which is seen as traditionally viewing aspects of culture in an essentialist way, seeing culture as being transgenerational in nature and substantive in its contribution to and influence in the lives of African-origined people.

For those defined (Eurocentrically) as 'essentialist' in their representation of culture, African-Centred thinking is seen as the essentialist representation of a number of cultures specific to communities of African origin.

For advocates of African-Centred thinking, however, culture is seen as reflecting and representing the identity of a people and as the glue that unifies and orders experience in such a way as to allow its members to experience a sense of organisation, consistency and system (Ani, 1994). Ani uses the definition of Wade Nobles (1991) who further identifies culture as a process that gives people a general design for living and patterns for interpreting reality. Its 'aspects', he says, are ideology, ethos and worldview; its 'factors' are ontology, cosmology and axiology; and its 'manifestations' consist of behaviour, values and attitudes (Nobles, 1991: 4).

Culture, Ani (1994) says, orientates its members around conceptions of reality via its worldview. It gives its members group identification, creating a sense of collective cultural identity and building on shared historical experiences. It orders the life of members via prescriptive authority. Members share in the creation of values formed through shared experiences, representing the values systematically as a set of ideas and single coherent statements. Culture provides the basis for the creation of shared symbols and meanings, making culture the primary creative force of collective consciousness and the constructor of national consciousness. She adds, further, that culture is the instrument that makes co-operation a natural phenomenon, stressing the importance of worldview in culture as functional in presenting a perceived order to its members by supplying definitions of reality that they can use to meaningfully organise their experiences and surroundings. The deep structure and logic of culture, she states, '... has a most powerful influence on the shape of the culture and the thought patterns of its members...', and concludes that:

> Culture 'teaches' its 'logic' and worldview to the ordinary participants who then assimilate it, assume it, and push it beneath the surface, from where it influences their collective behaviour and responses (Ani, 1994: 4).

Similarly, Sesh Am Neter (1995) focuses on culture as being constituted through systematic group-generated and group-orientated behaviour, not created by individuals, but rather the sum total of all groups of people with shared histographies which house a way of viewing the world and the realities with which the world presents them. The understanding of culture, he states, provides a means of comprehending the total sum of a historically linked people's philosophy, behaviour, ideas and artefacts.

Scheurich and Young (1997) concur with the work of the above authors with one slight distinction in that they prefer the term 'civilisational ideology' rather than 'culture' as being representative of the creative element in people's lives. Civilisational ideology, they state, underpins ideological formation from both a historical and present-day position through to the setting down of future predictions and expectations. It is, they say, a fundamental ideology, functioning at a level that encompasses the deepest, most primary assumptions about the nature of reality ... the ways of knowing that reality (and) morality and values – in short, presumptions about the real, the true and the good (Scheurich and Young, 1997: 6).

It is therefore true to say, argues Azibo (1996a), that cultural responses will speak to the distinct 'peoplehood' of a people rather than to cultural indicators based on the types of superficial communities represented in the current geopolitical definitions of community. Cultures can be represented as culturally specific paradigms that speak to the cultural reality of a people and the right therefore of a people to be interpreted from that cultural standpoint – particularly since African cultures have survived transgenerationally in enough form to be clearly visible as having replicated themselves in various 'Diasporic' standpoints and cultures of African origin (Azibo, 1996a; Daly, Jennings, Beckett and Leashore, 1995).

One such 'Diasporic' standpoint is the African-Centred paradigm. Its exponents argue that it is the primary academic, practical and conceptual framework upon which any meaningful study of the cultural background and the cultural reality of African people should be grounded. It is unapologetic in its primary relevance to people of African origin (i.e., African-African, African-Caribbean, African-American, Black-British, West Indian-American etc., cf. Schiele, 1990), its primary focal points being those of cultural specificity and consciousness-raising based on traditional African communal systems of interrelatedness and collectivity (Ekwe-Ekwe and Nzegwu, 1994). Its intention is to establish a firm footing upon which the re-establishment of African principles of group self-determination and self-representation are firmly rooted in African cultural, psychological and con-ceptual strengths (Addae, 1996; Ani, 1994; Asante, 1980, 1990; Azibo, 1996b; Jacques-Garvey, 1986; James Myers, 1991; Nobles, 1991; Schiele, 1990; Wonkeryor, 1995).

Seen as the modern-day conceptualist of African-Centred thinking and practice, Molefi Kete Asante (1980, 1990)) argued that to be African-Centred was to place Africans and African interests at the centre of any approach to problem solving because of its reflection of African principles of interrelatedness and of the importance of 'feeling', 'knowing' and 'act-ing' as indicators of human phenomena. African-Centred thinking and prac-tice carries within it a strong locational aspect which posits what African-Centredness is expected to do, as a way of understanding what it means. In effect, the African (or recipient) becomes the helper and the helped simultaneously.

Kambon (1996) defines the African-Centred paradigm as a) ... the con-struction of African social reality from the framework of the history, culture and philosophy of African civilisation; b) it recognises and articulates the basic continuity of the African worldview throughout the diverse African populations around the globe; c) it recognises and articulates the basic distinctness and interdependence of the African worldview (relative to any other, such as the European worldview); and d) it projects the African spiritual thrust as the centre of African social realities (Kambom, 1996: 75).

Semmes (1981) in much the same way sees the African-Centred para-digm as being primarily concerned with the culturally based, appropriate analysis of the life experiences, adaptive responses and creative struggles of people of African origin. And in summing, up Akbar (1976, 1994) sees the

African-Centred worldview as the functional representative of the inter-connectivity of African people with all things that make up the universe – their nature of 'beingness'. The African is viewed as the holding and serving vessel through which the African worldview can be realised and actualised – with the firm belief that the separation of people from their nature of 'being-ness' is to interrupt their 'flow', their 'rhythm' and their 'swerve', thereby making them a-rhythmic and a-functional (Maxime, 1993).

However, to view culture in this way has led to its labelling as 'essentialist', illogical and unworkable in terms of generating answers to today's reality of multiple cultures, identities and localities. Concerns have been raised about the way in which culture has become romanticised, and, in action, serves to misrepresent the demands and aspirations of oppressed groups by essentialising aspects of their lives.

Arguments Opposing Essentialism in Favour of Hybridity

Much of the concern has centred on the essentialist nature that some aspects of the field seem to see as accompanying discussions on culture. Essentialism is referred to as being the essential aspects of culture or civili-sation, which are held up as having transcended time and space in relation to their continuing presence and relevance to a particular 'group' of people.

Earlier writers such as E. Hall (1981) initially registered confusion on the above issues, arguing as he did against the importance given to Western definitions of culture seen as having been forged upon stressing the impor-tance of linear, sequential and step patterns of identifying the self. This type of patterning, Hall stressed, has led Western man to enshrine discussions and definitions of culture in systems of logic which have wrongly come to be synonymous with truth. However, simultaneous to decrying Western logical and fragmentary experiences as incomplete in their ability to ac-curately reflect cultural truth, he concedes that culture is non-essentialist in nature.

Webner (1996) leaves no such ambiguities in stating his position, arguing that:

> Essentialism serves to impute a fundamental basic, absolutely necessary con-structive quality to a person, social category, ethnic group, religious com-munity, or nation. It is to post falsely a timeless continuity, a discreteness or boundedness in space and organic unity. It is to imply an internal sameness and external difference or otherness ... to any form of analysis which may be said

> to obscure the relational aspects of group culture or identity and to valorise instead and subject on itself, as autonomous and separate, as if such a subject could be demarcated out of context, unrelated to an external other or discursive purpose (Webner, 1996: 228).

Simply put, the feeling is that essentialism serves to disguise and distort reality and is given agency via the process of representation whilst simultaneously muting the voices of oppressed people.

Stuart Hall (1991) concurs with Webner's concerns, adding that such narrow approaches to viewing culture did little more than emphasise structured representations of culture which could only achieve their positive by viewing the 'other' through the narrow eye of the negative.

Later, writing in 1996, Stuart Hall would go on to ground innately defined descriptions of culture firmly in the field of essentialism. He defines culture as fluid in nature; thereby, it is not representative of that part of the self that remains intact and stable at its core. That culture could not be represented as that which remained unchanged and identical across time, or as a representation of our collective or true self, forced to take refuge within our superficial or artificially imposed self in order to protect some common shared history or ancestry which it supposedly represents and which protected would guarantee an unchanging 'oneness' or a cultural unity. Instead, he posits a definition of culture that is strategic and positional, which:

> ...accepts that identities are never unified (but are instead) increasingly fragmented and fractured; never singular but multiply constructed across different, often intersecting and antagonistic, discourses, practices and positions. They are subject to radical historicization, and are constantly in the process of change and transformation (Webner, 1996: 4).

Solomos (1996) likens arguments of cultural specificity to notions of race purity. He argues that holding on to such notions rather than moving towards positions of hybridity is problematic in terms of their representativeness of the kinds of positions with which the 'far right' have come to be preoccupied. His argument rests on the principle that race is not a scientific category, but rather a socially constructed medium through which non-essentialist categories of 'Black' and 'White' have come to be, via historical and political struggles over their meanings. Instead, concepts such as race and ethnicity should be seen as representations of difference informed by relations of power and sites of power which lead to groups experiencing themselves as the dominators and the dominated.

Mercer (1994), in a similar vein to Solomos (1996), also bemoans the rise of essentialist aspects of cultural and identity specificity. Mercer associates the rise of such positions with the influence of the positions of the 1980s emerging Black communities which appeared to focus on resistance and antagonism cushioned on an emerging Black politic – all of which centred on a discussion about race. The author argues against the rigidity with which Black people increasingly define their experiences, and states that this leads to the notion of fixed hierarchies of oppression. This, then, prompts oppressed groups to fight for the status of first victim – leading to an overall undermining of their struggles against discrimination, and a failure to recognise commonalties between struggles as being linked to difference rather than to essentialism. Resolutely in the camp of hybridity, he sees it as providing for the possibility and necessity of creating new cultures with new social actors and new political agendas as opposed to essentialist notions of culture, which he regards as brittle responses shaped in similar veins to English nationalism and various other forms of religious and cultural fundamentalism.

Gilroy, contributing further in his 1993 work, *The Black Atlantic*, argues that modern-day representations of 'Africanisms' are not so problematic in relation to the question of whether or not they survived intact in one form or another, but that their modern-day representations are restrictive and so far removed from their original or traditional state as to render them ineffectual as a means to figure the inescapability and legitimate value of mutation, hybridity and intermixture, en route to better theories of racism and of black political culture than those so far offered by cultural absolutists of various phenotypical hues (Gilroy, 1993: 223).

And as if to try and conciliate between essentialist and non-essentialist positions, Greenburg (1998) asks us to consider whether the notion of cultural hybridity is able to offer a co-terminus refuge of sorts between the positions of essentialism and non-essentialism. Hybridity, he argues, could be representative of some vague and undetermined place occupied by people who inhabit both cultural realities but are forced to live in the interface between the two.

Giddens (1991) suggests that it is little wonder we have ended up in this dichotomous situation, given the role of modernity in contrast to post-modernity in contributing to the development of social individuality in finite forms alongside other distinct social forms, which because of their positions with regard to self-definition, have come to find themselves occupying marginalised positions. Simultaneously, modernity is accused of reflecting all that is essential and, therefore, indisputable about the superiority of the West (Nederveen Pieterse, 1994).

Rattansi (1994), alternatively, attributes the intrinsic suspicion of essentialist notions of culture and origin to the postmodernist corrosion of cultural essences in favour of 'de-essentializing' and 'decentring' positions as valuable deconstructive standpoints on race, culture and ethnicity. Rattansi claims that '... there are no unambiguous, water-tight definitions to be had of ethnicity, racism and the myriad terms in-between' (Rattansi, 1994: 53) – positions that he considers reflect the decadence with which modernity positions have traditionally become linked. Rattansi's views resonate with the stance of Modood (1998), whose view is that positions of modernity have become largely responsible for the decadence with which the 'Atlantico-centric' model of Black–White relations has come to essent-ialise positions of race relations in the Western world. Modood challenges the existence of binding processes in relation to the term 'Black' as able to represent the vast range of cultural experiences of the multitude of groups confined within its limiting 'modern' boundary. His position is one of seeing modernity as representing fixed, rigid and essential notions of culture and identity; whilst his preference is for postmodernity which, he argues, is representative of fluidity and diversity. Here, identity becomes global, mobile, changing and limitless.

Essentialism or Non-Essentialism – Relative or Reactionary?

The strength of feeling surrounding the essentialist – non-essentialist debate leaves readers in no doubt about the dichotomous nature of the discussion they are expected to straddle in order to get an overview of the key positions at stake.

Clearly, in the writings of Blaut (1993), Cambridge (1996), Hilliard (1978, 1991), Joseph, Reddy and Searle-Chatterjee (1990), Ngugi (1993) and Sivanandan (1998), there is strong opposition to the way in which the fluidity-hybridity debate has sought to control media, academic and social opinion, and the way in which race has become an abstraction no longer lodged in a history and process of struggle and transformation – emphasised if anything by the way in which terms like 'Black' or 'racism' borne out of struggle have been so easily replaced by a preoccupation with language surrounding the racialisation process. In effect, racism has become no longer what is done to people; rather, it is reduced to the position of a discourse.

Oftentimes, because of the sharpness of the attack against the place of Africa in relation to its primacy, history and value to other cultures, we find that dialogue on Africa in relation to other worlds tends to take on a reactionary stance. The result is to make Africa a 'world' that can only be grasped as being of value in relation to other worlds (Soyinka, 1990). Attempts are then made to suffocate anything that is said to represent the 'African-ness' of African people. This has been the reaction to the African-Centred paradigm – as a representation of cultural specificity.

Yet, non-essentialist positions give little recognition to the possibility that people of African origin are clear about their reasons for projecting certain aspects of their culture for strategic and other purposes. I have made earlier references to positions that emphasise the importance of the right of a people to be situated in their own paradigmatic reality as a means of being able to project their reality. But, clearly, positions of fluidity and hybridity seek to define the 'good' and acceptable aspects of culture for people of African origin (e.g., sport, music, food and dance), with little regard to the possibility that people of African origin might have differing opinions on how they wish to be seen and are prepared to pursue those opinions through strategic applications of culture. The purpose of such action would be to project a means of reclaiming the right to self-definition and self-determination as well as to begin the process of reclaiming and relocating the power of 'terms of reference-setting' back in the hands of people of African descent.

Seeing themselves as modern-day 'bendy-toys', communities of African origin might well argue that they have given all there is to give and see absolutely nothing wrong with holding on to aspects of their cultures that they see as fundamental to the living and expression of their lives. From this position, is it really beyond the scope of imagination to see that people of African origin have human agency enough to be able to create the kind of identity, cultural depth and external response that speaks to their particular spiritual and human needs?

What is not so easily rationalised, however, is why Eurocentrism, as the powerful cultural statement that it is, should feel so threatened by positions of cultural specificity which I would argue that, unlike hybridity, do not refer to specificity as an absolute representation of all that culture is. Rather, the stress on specificity is in relation to the importance of recognising the transgenerational value of culture and the likely consequences of applying universalist cultural judgements in the face of the increased likelihood of transubstantive error.[3] The answer could lie in some of the criticisms of the African-Centred paradigm that have come from supporters of paradigms like 'Black Perspectives' who believe that African-Centredness has set itself up to compete with Eurocentrism at the expense of paradigms that are more readily accepted as routes to unifying perspective, policy, theory practice and understanding of 'group' differences. Writers such as Marable (1993) and D'Souza (1995) have little time for paradigms like African-Centredness, which they classify as 'race based' in nature, defining them as limited because of their projections of reactionism and their symbolic representation of a presumed cultural homogeneity which they find conceptually limiting.

The perceived threat could also be that of challenging too close to the Eurocentric worldview on 'beingness', which is founded on an acceptance of the domination of man over nature (Kambon, 1996); the force by which European culture and people are projected as the centre of the universe (Ani, 1994); the primary cultural force responsible for diffusing culture to all other people (Blaut, 1993); and as a system of domination which sustains itself by creating and projecting truth in its own image (Hilliard, 1991).

But in all of this it seems the point has been fudged – that we should really be talking about two types of culture – threatening and non-threatening. It is okay for people of African origin as the Eurocentrically defined 'cultural other' to have culture as long as it does not make any demands that stand outside dominant Eurocentric culture. Indeed, the fluidity-hybridity position would support the idea that people of African origin no longer need to make reference to 'who we are' or 'where we came from' – the emphasis would instead be on 'what we might become'. However, a cultural reference absent in a past or present positional statement focusing merely on potential runs in direct contradiction to many cultures of African origin where past, present and potential operate simultaneously and at all times (Ngugi, 1993).

This past, present and potential position is linked to the transgenerational nature of some aspects of culture to which the non-essentialist debate does a great disservice by taking up polarity positions which emphasise the cultural choice as being either 'roots' or 'routes' (i.e., subject or object). Choose the former and we are relegated to 'fantasy' status – the latter and we will be invited to sit at the 'postmodern' cultural negotiating table.

In addition to this, little care is taken to ensure that Eurocentric notions of support or objection to positions of race purity are not seen as representative of 'cultural other' or culturally essentialist positions. Authors like Gilroy (1993), Hall (1996), Mercer (1994) and Solomos (1996) do much to attach culturally essentialist positions to the race purity debate in a bid to emphasise the threat to society should race-purist positions on culture prevail. So, in the case of the race-purity debate, the subjective-objective choice to be made is supported by the threat of being regarded as a race purist should we choose cultural representations so defined as essentialist.

And let us be clear here: there is no support for those who would posit cultural specificity as a diversion for activating beliefs in the right to translate power into a tool of hatred and murder of the cultural other. Having said that, however, it is accepted that the African-Centred paradigm often presents itself as having difficulty talking about the benefits of African-Centred thinking without focusing on the disadvantages of Eurocentric thought and practice; and that this reality can appear as a window of opportunity to those who are intent on smearing the intentions of African-Centredness.

However, the African-Centred paradigm is clear in its purpose of speaking for people of African origin in the belief that the need to have control of the definition of African reality is crucial to and for African people. African-Centredness, and in particular its use of characteristics such as culture and language, assists in the redefinition and reconceptualisation of African experiences, providing for a firm and relative footing upon which to actively advance African interests, as well as wrestling African experiences out of the ideological domain of Eurocentrism.

Aspects of culture are defined at 'life's negotiating table', of that there can be no dispute, nor of the consequence, which is the acceptance of an aspect of culture that is constantly fluid.[4] The dispute arises in the views that postulate and attempt to define for others that the whole of culture must be fluid, 'or else'.

The African-Centred paradigm as a proponent of aspects of cultural specificity, again, stands in stark contrast to Eurocentrically protected positions of fluidity and hybridity – with its position of not seeking to speak for other peoples and other cultures. And the African-Centred paradigm has no quarrel with what seems to be a clearly marked position in Eurocentrism, which suggests that in order for us to have a positive attitude to culture, the precondition of self-denial as a facilitator of radical political attitudes must be in existence (Soyinka, 1990). Where the two part company, however, is at the refusal of Eurocentrism to recognise the ability of the 'cultural other' to assemble behaviours, symbols, customs, motifs, moods and icons into a single comprehensive affirming presence – preferring instead to define African-Centred positioning as a type of cultural nationalism. At the same time, however, Eurocentrism assumes a universalised existence and status of its traditional concepts in relation to all areas of human engagement, and in all countries and all cultures (Silavwe, 1995).

In the struggle over culture as a means of interpreting identity, hybridity adds a certain degree of romanticism and actualisation to the idea of people being 'fluid' in nature. However, the continued human and social positioning (or rather dispositioning) of people of African origin belies this utopian view of the world. It does sweeten the imagination to see the future in a hybrid and fluid context, as long as we do not look at this future through 'rose-coloured cataracts' that blind us from seeing the realities of Euro-centric institutionalised failures to deal with wealth and power-sharing issues. But as long as we continue to reduce issues of wealth and power to discourses on representation, those defined as the 'cultural other' will continue to see hybridity positions as an attempt to remove aspects of the power base from groups so defined.

Implications for Social Work Practice

Exponents of African-Centred thinking and practice would argue that there are aspects of culture which reflect norms of conduct and identity crucial to the lives of people of African decent, and which are not easily dismissed by judgements as to whether they reflect hybridity or ambivalence.

One major area of concern is the assumption often made in social work that people of African origin see, internalise experiences and externalise need in the same way as other racially distinct groups and also in the same way as the dominant community – belying the existence of differing deep structures of cultural thought and practice, and aspects of culture that are transgenerational in nature; and the possibility (I believe, reality) that words and actions can stand for different things in the speakers' or hearers' thoughts and emotions.

Yet, social work, in attempting to practice against backdrops of social inequality and injustice (perceived or real), introduces the question of cross-cultural indicators and influences in the process of cultural interpretations, assessments and interventions – as well as the role these may play in the 'social-working' process. It also raises the importance of the social work setting and its ability to see culture as influencing the interpretation of one's environment in all its representations.

In addition to this, however, there is a need for social work to look at the concern that assumptions informed by culture may be made with regard to the interpretation of behaviour, and the influence of those interpretations on practice outcomes.

Indeed, Joseph et al. (1990) state that the idea of horizontally consistent, unifying stages in cognitive development is now being challenged, as is the belief that aspects of interpersonal behaviour are informed by the same causal processes cross-culturally, thereby carrying the same cultural meaning in different contexts.

This belief also extends to the view that concepts of 'meaning' developed in the West and of importance to Western societies can be universally applied in cross-culturally comparative situations. Such assumptions suggest and actively practice the measurement and judgement of all people from the same cultural standpoint with social work academic and practice power bases; and tenet houses suggesting that there is nothing specific, fixed or absolute in any culture that should be of any significance in deciding priorities and predicting outcomes (Banks, 1997; Ellison-Williams and Ellison, 1996).

Now of course, if social work prides itself on rigidly supporting practice-positional statements that emphasise a flexibility in practice, founded on the importance of managing cultural diversity via a focus on hybridity as the prevailing cultural statement – then somewhere, somehow, 'clients' of African origin will end up trapped, and some will be totally lost in the gulf between who and what they actually are and what they are expected to be or present as, if they expect to get a social work service. Such a situation points to the issue of the labelling of phenomena, which to some extent is a function of and is influenced by the implicit assumptions of the culture that holds the power to label and interpret (Turner, 1991).

Silavwe (1995) adds that, given the purpose of social work as a facilitator of social functioning and at times the supportive lead into the effectiveness of other social institutions, cultural specificity holds a key place in reflecting that people and their social institutions rely on aspects of specificity 'not so much in their outer aspect, or their objective form, as they do psychologically, that is to say, in their meaning and value for those who participate in them and make them vital and dynamic social forces' (Silavwe, 1995: 72). Silavwe concludes that cultural differences in social institutions must therefore equate to differences in social work theory and practice – informed by the foundational characteristics of social organisation from which people make sense of their experiences. The work of Azibo (1996a, 1996b) and James Myers (1998) further strengthens the requirement of social work to take into account both the deep structural levels of culture responsible for holding cultural philosophical assumptions and the surface structures of culture which are subject to relatively rapid change – when looking at an appropriate social work service for people of African origin.

In view of the importance of culture, Eurocentric social work knowledge and practice bases could never be seen as having universal application in explaining human behaviour in all peoples and in every culture. And despite its cleavage to positions of hybridity and fluidity, social work can only be seen to have limited success in its ability to reach and relate to the needs of people and communities of African origin. This is because it presents itself to such communities as expecting them to bring into the consulting room only those most scant and peripheral of cultural givens – which in themselves are so well rehearsed by anti-discriminatory social work practice as to have little bearing on the emphasis of practice intervention.

One example in point is the belief that the requirements of people of African origin who came from the Caribbean can be fully considered because they speak English as a first language. Yet, it is not unusual for African (Caribbean) social workers to find themselves being asked to interpret on behalf of social workers and welfare officers who cannot understand, for example, the language spoken by Dominican or St. Lucian elders. On meeting such 'clients', I have often found that they can speak perfect English – and so my obvious question is why the service was unable to understand them; or similarly, why they felt they would not be understood. The most common reply was that there were no similar words in English that captured the true essence and meaning of what was felt or experienced by the 'client', and every time they tried to use the nearest English equivalent they found that it did not really mean the same thing; or that part of the meaning or what they were feeling was lost during the translation process. The elders also felt that it was just assumed that they spoke or would prefer to speak English.

This leads us to suppose that the translation of need and pain from one cultural life and expression to the Eurocentric culture which, in effec, will be the culture of need assessment and interpretation, inevitably means that something will be lost between. This would be to the detriment of people of African origin who would lose their originating ground and the strengths associated with their natural forms of expression.

The importance of language as a salient aspect of cultural specificity should not be underestimated, argue Ani (1994) and Addae (1995, 1996), who state that language is an important vehicle for imparting culture and defining reality. They argue strongly for the recognition of the importance of languages used by people of African origin in the belief that languages espouse in real terms the actuality of African-origined human experience because they are infused by strengths of the culture, making language one of the most important determinants of the African experience.

So what of a social work profession that chooses to take none of the above indicators on board? Both Graham (1999) and Saleebey (1994) contend that just such a profession is in operation today, representing nothing short of a culturally sympathetic practice that ends up inherently promoting existing social work interventions by appealing for remedies, changes in behaviour, outcomes and assimilations which inevitably amount to support for the collective interests of the dominant culture. No culture has a monopoly on truth, yet existing paradigmatic social work models in themselves represent a subtle form of cultural oppression in that their universalistic projection serves to maintain the legitimacy of Eurocentric hegemonic social work theory and practice, to the exclusion of even the thought that other theories could exist.

Further, there seems little in current social work practice to suggest that social work seeks to take on board the importance of cultural specificities as functional aspects that might correlate to the onset or manifestation of distress and need. In their work, Ellison-Williams and Ellison (1996) highlight studies on social work practice where social workers indicated that they did not need to ask about cultural appropriateness to effectively provide services, and if they did ask, were unsure how to weigh the responses in relation to their practice intervention methods. Positions such as this are typical of present-day anti-discriminatory practice models that take a reactive stance to theory and practice of discriminatory practice in social work, taking as their core starting point Eurocentric models, values and measurements of social well-being. Such models do not recognise the need for support, understanding or nurturing of emotional, spiritual and developmental needs as a core component in social work practice with 'cultural other' groups (Graham, 1999). Forte (1999) is clear that in order to be effective, social work and its practitioners should be able to communicate with clients from various cultures, having taken time to become 'variedly-cultured'; that is, having invested in becoming aware of as many forms of cultural communication as possible in order to relate to as many cultural maps as possible. After all, it is possible for social workers to learn that differences between white groups and people of African origin may be better explained by an awareness of and sensitivity to cultural barriers that seem to emphasise a negative interpretation of difference rather than being open to the possibility that differences may be better explained by differences in worldview (Daly et al., 1995).

What seems clear from the above contributions is that social work faces an uphill struggle if it continues to nail its theory and practice methods to the masts of absolute cultural hybridity whilst simultaneously dismissing the importance of aspects of cultural specificity as speaking for particular aspects of African need. Yes, social work needs to begin to develop theory and practice models for dealing with the issues raised above. But the profession has yet to enter into concrete discussions with communities of African origin (or Asian origin for that matter) in order to discuss how they intend to develop around issues that they know little if anything about, particularly when the ground has been so influenced by the supposed successes that could be won by 'managing' diversity rather than working with it. Indeed, it would come as no surprise to see social work completely ignore the primary cultural statement of African-origined people, which is that 'we proceed as we perceive'. Instead, what is likely to be valued is the determination of social work to remain completely separate from and objective in the face of what may be seen as external 'alien' influences – regardless of the consequences.

What remains clear is that without the proper positioning of 'place' in the inquiry process, investigative and outcome-specific procedures can never be said to truly represent successful social work inquiry into the 'needs' of people of African origin.

Moving Beyond Racial Divides in Social Work – Conclusions

Eileen Younghusband's (1978) seminal texts, *Social Work in Britain 1950–1975* (vols. 1 and 2, 1978), written on the back of the Beveridge (1942) and Seebohm (1968) reports, were for many years the leading texts relied upon to inform the social work practice environment of the time with regard to the social work services' expectations of the newly arrived 'immigrants'. Her work highlights a clear anticipation that communities of African origin should and would learn to fit in with existing service provision, and principally not give birth to an expectation of different or separate provision; and that the general objective should be to treat them the same way as other citizens are treated (Deakin, 1970).

In view of this, there was a definite policy position that advocated the disregarding of any specificity that might inform 'Black' need, in favour of a position that stood on the expectation that African-origined communities would have to adapt their modes of transmitting needs if they were ever to be in a position to access social work services (Hiro,1978; Humphrey and John, 1971).

This positional assertion would later become known as the 'colour-blind' or 'assimilationist' position, which firmly located itself in the belief in the same service content, mode and method of delivery for all, irrespective of 'race' or cultural difference (Cheetham, 1972; Griffith, Henderson, Usbourne and Wood, 1960; Kent, 1972; McCulloch and Smith, 1974).

I begin at this point because in many ways the views that cemented the political, theoretical and practice position of early social work have not changed, despite the publication of the Barclay Report (1982) which described social services responses as 'patchy, piecemeal and lacking in strategy' (p. 84), advocating instead that social work should maintain an open and creative social work mind as the best tool for creating appropriate practice for 'Black' communities.

What has changed is the language in which it is couched. Then it was called colour-blind or assimilationist; now it is called cultural fluidity or hybridity. And in all the efforts to give the impression that things have changed for the better, one thing remains rooted and unchanged – the 'modus operandi'. Yes, the arguments relating to the acceptance of difference have moved on to see the importance of 'Black' people needing to retain their cultures for reasons that can be important only to them. But, the power to demand or set the terms of that acceptance and anything which may ensue with regard to need or service has remained firmly in the hands of the culturally dominant. So, in effect we end up with a situation which says that aspects of African-origined (or Asian-origined) culture may be of importance to the respective communities, but Eurocentric values will decide what if any weight will be given to their place in the interpretation or translation of need into appropriate service delivery modes. We are left, then, with a service that not only operates 'colour-blind' but also 'culture-coloured'. That social work should then be in a state of ideological turmoil with regard to culture should not be in dispute.

Indeed, in the British government's priority areas through which services like social work are expected to tackle issues such as social exclusion and welfare, matters relating to the importance of developing a vehicle capable of working with 'felt' need take little, if any, priority at all. Furthermore, the route to social justice for people of African origin has been identified as being through employment (Statham, Balloch and Beresford, 1998) – a highly contentious path that continues to remain marked as one of the most litigious areas in relation to racial and cultural exclusion, and differences in treatment on the grounds of race and culture.

Where then do people of African origin find their place in this increasingly clinicised and specialised area? Daly et al. (1995) argue that in the face of such concerns, social workers need to develop theoretical and practice knowledge and understanding of traditional values and beliefs held by people of African origin in order to gain a full appreciation of factors which may affect well-being, and in order to ensure the use of appropriate intervention methods aimed at identifying and supporting coping mechanisms that enhance individual, family and community functioning.

The importance of creating social work theories and practice methods that are bias-free cannot be underestimated against a backdrop of African-origined people interpreting a world from one dimension whilst receiving a service that is fixed and determined in its provisions by another, and more dominant, dimension. The issue of the culture of 'otherness' then, in relation to service, would be seen as being of peripheral importance, and translated into care it would not be unusual to see culture being viewed as an inconvenience.

Clearly, practitioners cannot bring into their practice what they do 'not know' or value. And in terms of moving 'beyond racial divides', value does not necessarily have to mean supporting or agreeing or disagreeing with positions that espouse aspects of cultural specificity. Rather, it is about ensuring that such positions have a fundamental (i.e., in terms of agency and resources) 'place' in the rules governing the application of theory to practice – a failure of which could lead to the charge of social work trying to predict practice resources and outcomes by controlling the influence of culture.

Social work can no longer cleave to the impotent position of multiculturalism as meaning that the diversity of cultures could be better managed and imposed upon by the dominant culture. It is simply not acceptable to negotiate towards a position of cultural diversity based on the hybrid position of 'all different – all equal' as this would assume little more than the acceptance of a cultural diversity charged with reflecting the hybrid nature of a unitary (dominant) culture. Such a principle, Deland (1997) argues, if assigned the power of right, would create inner (i.e., host culture) contradictions which would invariably lead to cultural hostility and conflict. We would undoubtedly be confronted with a situation where discourse would set about reframing inequality as differences in culture, whilst hybridity would become the means to avoid debating the failures of the race equality agenda.

Social work needs to consider what its intentions are to the people it claims to service. If social work is not about making people authors, actors and agents in their own destiny – what is it about? If it is about this, what and where is the blueprint for bringing it into being? Clearly, that blueprint must focus on the increased importance of working across the 'specialisms' of service provision and professional boundaries. But the blueprint for moving 'beyond racial divides' has to contain plans for social work to undergo a theoretical, practical and paradigmatic shift that does not feel threatened by the content and possibilities proclaimed by positional statements which focus on aspects of cultural specificity. Rather, it should see such a shift as an opportunity to take on board the creative and transformatory qualities grounded in the cultural statements of other authenticities besides the Eurocentric cultural statement.

On a practical level, social work can begin by accepting the practice importance of 'Black' practitioners, not just in a visible context as if somehow more 'Black' practitioners automatically rectifies the ills of the service. It must also accept that for 'Black' practitioners to have the kind of effect expected, they must be properly resourced and enjoy endorsement and support at local and national government levels appropriate to underpinning the creation of institutional and strategic change.

Social work practitioners need to develop skills in recognising, respecting and accepting what Martin and Mitchell-Martin (1995) refer to as 'diverse cultural and lifestyle groups' and their relationship to the social institutions of dominant society. There needs to be a move towards the kind of practice development that supports a professional move towards organising and supporting Black communities to become agents of change in the determination of their own life chances. Social work is one of the few professions gifted with the opportunity to operate on individual, group, community and societal levels. As such, its practitioners must address delivery issues that fail to respond to the need to explore the importance of the experiences of African-origined people in relation to how problems are viewed, what kinds of helpers are preferred, what methods are viewed as helpful and what goals and outcomes are viewed as ideal (Martin and Mitchel-Martin, 1995). The emphasis must be on operationalising and systematising African experiences to make social work functional in a relative way, and certainly the African-Centred paradigm in representing the cultural values of African-origined people, when applied to social work, represents a theoretical base upon which new and appropriate models of practice can be developed. It also presents as the best and most appropriate theory to replace such old and tired models of practice as ethnic-sensitive, minority-ethnic and anti-oppressive practice models, which make a mere apology for suggesting a move to new practice models. Jerome Schiele makes no apologies in his suggestion that it is the survival presence and role of traditional African cultural vestiges that determine the unsuitability of Eurocentric methods in favour of African-Centred methods as a vehicle of explanation for behaviour and ethos. He surmises that 'The Afrocentric paradigm maintains that the personalization of the professional relationship and reciprocity within professional relationships are essential components of the helping or healing process' (Schiele, 1990: 291).

'Beyond racial divides' must incorporate the potential for broadening practice possibilities to include interventions based on aspects of cultural specificity that assist in the understanding of definitions of social well-being and distress. It must literally mean that the power bases charged with the responsibility of defining worth and valueless aspects of peoplehood must be instructed to examine the root influences of their positional statements in order to avoid 'generalising out' a whole range of culturally specific people who simply will not fit in. Simply put:

> The African-centred worldview challenges social work to expand its philosophical and intellectual base to embrace humanity; to release the domination of the Eurocentric worldview over the psyche of African peoples, and open the way for the transformation, creativity and unlimited potential that is embedded within authenticity (Graham, 1999: 253).

Failure to do so will see unfounded accusations of essentialism and absolute ideals of hybridity make sweeping generalisations about whole cultures and communities without any accountability or information as to what is being labelled. Such a position totally discounts the experiences of people for whom historical culture is real and living.

Notes

1. For the purpose of this contribution, unless otherwise stated, I am referring particularly to people of African origin/African descent people; i.e., African-Ghanaian, African-Dominican, African-Ethiopian, African-Jamaican, etc.
2. 'Black' spelt with a capital B came into popular usage in the seventies. Black continues to be used as a unifying term to represent recognition of the politicisation of the accompanying experiences of being and belonging to racially distinct communities.

3. Transubstantive error is defined as '...where the meanings, beliefs, values and behaviours of one culture are erroneously compared, evaluated and interpreted by the values of another culture...' (Banks, 1997: 32). For a more in-depth discussion, refer to Azibo's chapters in D. Azibo (ed.) (1996), *African Psychology*, New Jersey, Africa World Press.
4. See James Myers (1991, 1998) for discussions on 'surface culture' and 'deep structural culture' as representative of the two levels of culture.

References

Addae, K. (1995), *The Maafa and Beyond*. Colombia, Kujichagulia Press.
Addae, K. (1996), *Reality Revolution: Return to the Way*. Colombia, Kujichagulia Press.
Akbar, N. (1976), 'Rhythmic patterns in African personality', in L.M. King, V.J. Dixon and W.W. Nobles (eds.), *African Philosophy: Assumption Paradigms for Research on Black Persons*. Los Angeles, Fanon R & D Centre, pp. 176–189.
Akbar, N. (1994), *The Community of Self*. Tallahassee, Florida, Mind Productions Pub.
Ani, M. (1994), *Yurugu: An African-Centred Critique of European Thought and Behaviour*. New Jersey, Africa World Press.
Asante, M.K. (1980), *Afrocentricity*. New Jersey, Africa World Press.
Asante, M.K. (1990), *The Afrocentric Idea*. Philadelphia, Temple University Press.
Azibo, D. (1996a), 'African psychology in historical perspective and related commentary', in D. Azibo (ed.), *African Psychology*. New Jersey, Africa World Press.
Azibo, D. (1996b), 'Personality, clinical and social psychological research on Blacks: Appropriate and inappropriate research Frameworks', in D. Azibo (ed.), *African Psychology*. New Jersey, Africa World Press.
Banks, N.J. (1997), 'Social Workers' Perceptions of 'Racial' Difference', *Social Services Research*, vol.1, University of Birmingham.
Barclay, P. (1982), *Social Workers, Their Roles and Tasks*. London, Bedford Square Press.
Beveridge, W. (1942), *Social Insurance and Allied Services: Cmnd Doc. 6404*. London, HMSO.
Blaut, J.M. (1993), *The Colonizer's Model of the World*. London, The Gifford Press.
Cambridge, A. (1996), 'The beauty of valuing black cultures', in V. Amrit-Talia and C. Knowles (eds.), *Resituating Identities: The Politics of Race, Ethnicity and Culture*. Ontario/NY, Broadview Press.
Cheetham, J. (1972), 'Immigrants, social work and the community', in J. Triseliotis (ed.), *Social Work with Coloured Immigrants and Their Children*. Oxford, Oxford University Press.
D'Souza, D. (1995), *The End of Racism: Principles for a Multiracial Society*. New York, The Free Press.
Daly, A., Jennings, J., Beckett, J.O. and Leashore, B.R. (1995), 'Effective coping strategies of African Americans', *Social Work*, vol. 40 (2), pp 240–246.
Deakin, N. (1970), *Colour Citizenship and British Society*, 2nd ed. London, Panther Books.
Deland, M. (1997), 'The cultural racism of Sweden', *Race & Class*, vol. 39 (1).
Ekwe-Ekwe, H. Nzegwu, F. (1994), *Operationalising Afrocentrism*. Reading, International Institute for Black Research.
Ellison-Williams, E. and Ellison, F. (1996), 'Culturally informed social work practice with American Indian clients: Guidelines for non-Indian social workers', *Social Work*, vol. 41 (2), pp. 147–151.

Forte, J. (1999), 'Culture: the tool kit metaphor and multicultural social work', *Families in Society*, vol. 80 (1), pp. 51–62.

Giddens, A. (1991), *Modernity and Self-Identity*. Cambridge, Polity Press.

Gilroy, P. (1993), *The Black Atlantic*. London, Verso.

Graham, M. (1999), 'The African-Centred Worldview: Developing a Paradigm in Social Work', *British Journal of Social Work*, vol. 29 (4), pp. 251–276.

Greenburg, S. (ed.) (1998), *Hate Thy Neighbour: The Dividing Lines of Race of Culture*. London, Camden Press.

Griffith, J.A.G., Henderson, J., Usbourne, M. and Wood, D. (1960), *Coloured Immigrants in Britain*. Oxford, Oxford University Press.

Hall, E. (1981), *Beyond Culture*. New York, Doubleday.

Hall, S. (1991), 'The local and the global: Globalization and Ethnicity', in A. King (ed.), *Culture, Globalization and the World System*. London, Macmillan.

Hall, S. (1996), 'Introduction: Who needs "Identity"', in S. Hall and P. du Gray (eds.), *Questions of Cultural Identity*. London, Sage.

Hilliard, A.G. (1978), *Free Your Mind, Return to the Source. The African Origin of Civilisation and European Scientific Colonialism*. Notes and outline for presentation.

Hilliard, A.G. (1991), 'Afrocentrism in a multicultural society', *American Visions*, August, pp. 23.

Hiro, D. (1978), 'Racism in Social work', *Social Work Today*, 29th November.

Humphrey, D. and John, G. (1971), *Because They're Black*. London, Penguin.

James Myers, L. (1991), 'Expanding the psychology of knowledge optimally: The Importance of Worldview Revisited', in R.L. Jones (ed.), *Black Psychology*. California, Cobb & Henry.

James Myers, L. (1998), 'The deep structure of culture: relevance of traditional African culture in contemporary life', in J.D. Hamlet (ed.), *Afrocentric Visions*. Thousand Oaks, CA, Sage.

Jaques-Garvey, A. (1986), *The Philosophy and Opinions of Marcus Garvey*. Massachusetts, The Majority Press.

Joseph, G.G., Reddy, V. and Searle-Chatterjee, M. (1990), 'Eurocentrism in the social sciences', *Race & Class*, vol. 31 (4), pp. 1–26.

Kambon, K.K.K. (1996), 'The Africentric paradigm and African-American psychological liberation', in D. Azibo (ed.), *African Psychology*, New Jersey, Africa World Press.

Kent, B. (1972), 'The social workers cultural patterns', in J. Treseliotis (ed.), *Social Work with Immigrants and Their Families*. Oxford, Oxford University Press.

Marable, M. (1993), 'Beyond racial identity politics: Towards a Liberation Theory for Multicultural Democracy', *Race and Class*, vol. 35 (1), pp. 113–130.

Martin, E. and Mitchel-Martin, J. (1995), *Social Work and the Black Experience*. Washington D.C., Nasw.

Martin, E. and Mitchel-Martin, J. (1999), 'What Do White People Want to Be Called? A Study of Self-Labels for White Americans', in T. Nakayama and J. Martin (eds.), *Whiteness: The Communication of Social Identity*. London, Sage Publications.

Maxime, J. (1993), *Positive "Nurturance" of the Black Mind*. Lecture given at Dulcie High School, Manchester, 6 April.

McCulloch, J.W. and Smith, N.J. (1974), 'Blacks and social work', *New Society*, 25 April.

Mercer, K. (1994), *Welcome to the Jungle: New Positions in Black Cultural Studies*. New York, Routledge.

Modood, T. 1998), 'Atlantic Rift', in S. Greenburg (ed.), *Hate Thy Neighbour: The Dividing Lines of Race and Culture*. London, Camden Press.

Nederveen Pieterse, J. (1994), 'Unpacking the West: how European is Europe', in A. Rattansi and S. Westwood (eds.), *Racism, Modernity & Identity*. Cambridge, Polity Press.

Nobles, W. (1991), 'African philosophy: foundations of Black Psychology', in R.L Jones (ed.), *Black Psychology*. California, Cobb & Henry.

Ngugi, Wa Thiong' O. (1993), *Moving the Centre: The Struggle for Cultural Freedoms*. London, James Curry Heinemann.

Rattansi, A. (1994), 'Just Framing Ethnicities and Racisms in a "Postmodern" Framework', in L. Nicholson and S. Seidman (eds.), *Social Postmodernism: Beyond Identity Politics*. Cambridge, Cambridge University Press.

Saleeby, D. (1994), 'Culture Theory and Narrative: The Intersection of Meaning in Practice Social Work', *Social Work*, vol. 39 (4), pp. 351–361.

Schiele, J. (1990), 'Organisational Theory from an Afrocentric Perspective', *Journal of Black Studies*, vol. 21 (2), pp. 145–161.

Scheurich, J.J. and Young, M.D. (1997), 'Colouring epistemologies: are our research epistemologies racially biased', *Educational Researcher*, vol. 26 (4), pp. 4–16.

Seebholm, F. (1968), *Report of the Committee on Local Authority and Allied Personal Social Services: Cmnd Doc. 3703*. London, HMSO.

Semmes, C.E. (1981), 'Foundations of an Afrocentric Social Science: Implications for Curriculum-Building, Theory, and Research in Black Studies', *Journal of Black Studies*, vol. 12, (1), September, pp. 3–17.

Sesh Am Neter, T. (1995), 'Paradigms in Afrocentric Educational Theory: Asante's Cultural Conception', in D. Zeigler (ed.), *Molefi Kete Asante and Afrocentricity*. Nashville, James C. Winston.

Silavwe, G.W. (1995), 'The Need for a New Social Work Perspective in an African Setting: The Case For Social Casework in Zambia', *British Journal of Social Work*, vol. 25 (1), pp. 71–84.

Sivanandan, A. (1998), 'The Colour Line is the Poverty Line', in S. Greenburg (ed.), *Hate Thy Neighbour: The Dividing Lines of Race and Culture*. London, Camden Press.

Solomos, J. (1996), *Making the Race, Stating the Case: Thinking About Racism, Identity and Social Change*. Southampton, University of Southampton.

Soyinka, W. (1990), 'The African World and the Ethnocultural Debate', in M.K. Asante and K. Asante (eds.), *African Culture: The Rhythms of Unity*. New Jersey, The Africa World Press.

Statham, D., Balloch, S. and Beresford, P. (1998), 'Adapting to survive', *Community Care*, October 8–14, pp. 32–33.

Turner, R.J. (1991), 'Affirming Consciousness: The Africentric Perspective', in J.E. Everett, S. Chipungu and B.R. Leashore (eds.), *Child Welfare: An Africentric Perspective*. New Jersey, Rutgers University Press.

Younghusband, E. (1978), *Social Work in Britain 1950–1975*, Vol. 1 & 2. London, George, Allen & Unwin.

Webner, L. (1996), 'Resituating Identities', in V. Amit-Talai and C. Knowles (eds.), *Resituating Identities*. Ontario/NY, Broadview Press.

Wonkeryor, E. (1995), 'The Dynamics of Afrocentricity and Intercultural Dynamics of Africentricity in Communication', in D. Zeigler (ed.), *Molefi Kete Asante and Afro-centricy*. Nashville, James C. Winston.

Final Observations

LENA DOMINELLI, WALTER LORENZ, HALUK SOYDAN

In *Beyond Racial Divides: Ethnicities in Social Work Practice*, the authors each speak for themselves and give a description and/or analysis of context-specific structures and processes in racial and ethnic dynamics. Yet, they all have at least one thing in common: the belief in the necessity for social work practice to advance positions beyond traditional understandings of racialised divisions. The aim of this final chapter is to make some observations in assessing the state of the art as it is generated by the contributions to this volume.

As the actuality and urgency of confronting the issues around cultural and ethnic diversity is being recognised in more and more countries, the search for a critical, constructive response by social work has begun to extend beyond the confines of national models, traditions and conditions. It is becoming more and more apparent that these issues have exposed a central weakness in the prevailing social work discourses, in as much as they had failed on the whole to address notions of identity in more than a very broad humanistic and psychological sense. Having recognised the dangers of being allied too closely to a national agenda, having served all too frequently nationalistic and colonial purposes, social workers seem to have taken refuge in a universalistic construct of 'human nature', particularly in the era after World War II. But as the question of the cultural specificity of methods became inescapable, a withdrawal into positions of ethnic certainties became attractive for a time until new difficulties and contradictions became apparent.

The contributions to this volume demonstrate that an anti-racist/anti-discriminatory agenda cannot be constructed to a universal formula. Instead, such a concern for radically transformed theory and practice needs to engage with the given historical, political and cultural circumstances within which the various national discourses are bounded. In fact, it emerged as one of the central tasks in developing effective contemporary strategies in social work to lay bare the structures and the mechanisms of given discourses and their rationale. This means that social work has to reflect on its own history, which can often be traced back to a concern for equality, even where the effects have become quite the opposite. Such legacies have to be faced up to, with all their ambiguities and contradictions. It is from a profound awareness

281

282 Beyond Racial Divides

of the historical nature of social work that these chapters aim, not at providing a universal recipe or constructing an authoritative model, but at initiating a critical debate on the possibilities of transcending racial divides in social work.

One of the preconditions for such a non-standardising approach is a critical paradigm of ethnicity such as Janis Fook supports with the concept of 'emergent ethnicity'. In putting forward a dynamic, open understanding of ethnicity as a component of personal identity, she also validates personal, biographical reflexivity as a critical tool in social work for laying bare the many layers through which identity traverses in a constant interplay between personal and structural factors. Her analysis of her own experiences makes it clear that 'othering' is not a prerogative of dominant ethnic groups, and it would be short-sighted to seek too much comfort in a kind of solidarity constructed from finding oneself on the side of those who have been 'othered', excluded, oppressed. This strong advocacy of an anti-essentialist use of ethnicity has direct practice implications, particularly, in her illustration, for social work in the context of Australian Aboriginal identities. Essentialism tends not only to homogenise 'othered' ethnic groups, but also to deny them agency by putting them into the roles of victims. The strength of ethnically defined communities, which social work must aim to acknowledge and foster, may lie in their ability to define their own characteristics and thereby their internal differences, to draw boundaries and to keep them open. Social work needs to engage with the fluid processes of identity-making rather than latching on to fixed notions of identity.

Wynetta Devore's chapter explored specifically the intersection of ethnicity and class from a similar perspective but against the background of the United States experience. Having put forward, together with Elfriede Schlesinger, a model of 'ethnic sensitive social work practice' already in the early 1980s, Devore expands on the creative possibilities of this approach in the light of the critical impact it has had on established social work models in relation to ethnic identities, and she emphasises also the 'layers of understanding' in which it unfolds. These, again, transcend the realm of 'special methods' for 'minorities' and remind practitioners of the complexity of all context-conscious and context-relevant social work. The ability to reflect on one's own experiences in relation to racism as they intersect with identity and social exclusion has a central position among the preconditions for such competence. This might endorse, but also reinterpret, some of the 'traditional' value positions developed in social work, such as acceptance and accountability.

All too often 'ethnic sensitivity' in social work practice has been confined to an examination of personal attitudes and behaviour. But only when the emerging methods and critical perspectives are also applied to human service organisations can these principles gain ground and credibility.

Lorraine Gutiérrez argued in her chapter that social service organisations in the U.S. are often lagging behind commercial organisations in recognising the realities of a culturally diverse society in their organisational responses. But part of a critical organisational response must be an explicit focus on social justice if the 'cultural awareness' is not to become, yet again, a means of social control and of legitimating inequality expressed as cultural differences. The replacement of a 'remedial' response to ethnic diversity and disadvantage by the practice of empowerment needs to be anchored in organisational changes and practices, and many well-intended projects founder on the difficulty of achieving this. The examples of ethnic agencies cited by Gutiérrez, in which 'Multicultural Organisational Development' (MCOD) is being practised, are evidence of the power of this 'ethno-conscious perspective', although such developments need again to be assessed against very specific historical and political contexts, rather than be upheld as universally applicable models. They provide a checklist of criteria that render transparent the power structure of organisations in relation to ethnic and cultural differences. Planned and continuous change at the organisational level based on such a 'multicultural audit' again leads back to a historical conception of social work practice.

In some countries, notably the Netherlands, these organisational issues are being addressed under the heading of 'Management of Diversity', a term as contentious as 'ethnic sensitivity'. For Edwin Hoffman it meant a very specific approach to organisational practice focused on 'inclusive thinking and acting'. In his chapter he also moved between personal and structural considerations to grapple with the complications that can arise from an acknowledgement of distinct identities in the context of a society that is in some sense intent on reducing the discriminatory use of identity labels. Hence the specific Dutch terminology of 'allochthones' and 'autochtones'. (This mirrors the focus on linguistic communities evident in other countries, for example, the use of 'anglophone', 'francophone' and 'allophone' in the Canadian context.) While the acknowledgement of the importance of cultural differences and of racism in many ways represents an advance over methods that operate with an unacknowledged ethnocentrism, an emphasis on cultural differences alone contains the danger of a static conception of culture which blocks the right to differentiated self-definitions.

Management of cultural diversity, seen as a tool merely for the elimination of misunderstandings and of all ambiguity, can easily become a culturalist means of oppression, just as an uncritical anti-racism can privilege a particular static and domineering view of race as *the* defining category of identity. What Hoffman searches for, instead, is a way of negotiating the dialectics of identity and equality through the dimensions of uniqueness and unity. The proposal of 'Inclusive Thinking and Acting' picks up on the 'politics of recognition' debate (recognition of equality and equality of difference), but enhances it by relating any management 'techniques' back to the basic elements of communication. A systemic view of interaction and communication recognises precisely the relativity and subjectivity of positions from which any exchange between people emanates, but posits, nevertheless, that in the mutual recognition of this 'pluralism' shared structures and 'conventions' of meaning can emerge. This communicative process describes the very conditions of a differentiated, multi-dimensional articulation of identity, which is always involved in communication, so that from this perspective all communication reveals its intercultural character. In this sense, a response that originated very specifically in the Dutch societal context again touches on universalisable processes.

Parallel to this debate on 'interculturalisation', conducted from the perspective of communication, is a debate within the paradigm of pedagogy. How well is this model suited to provide a pedagogy of multicultural societies? Taking the example of Germany, Franz Hamburger in his contribution reaffirmed the relevance of a social pedagogy response to the challenges of a society that can no longer deny its multicultural character. The pedagogical framework has the advantage over the social work tradition that its role and function are not just invoked in emergency situations, to remedy and correct 'deficits'. Instead, pedagogy is recognised as part of the 'normal' cultural reproduction process of any society and, hence, of the socialisation of all individuals. Individuals in turn are not passive objects of society's attention, but act as partners in a dialectic that constitutes both society and their individuality. Migration highlights and magnifies the inevitable tensions in this relationship in as much as the demands for equality and for the recognition of difference have to be negotiated within constantly changing parameters of 'normality'.

Social pedagogy as intercultural pedagogy is not a new departure for the social professions, although it assumes particular actuality in the work with migrants and asylum seekers. Instead, it can be regarded as the return to the pedagogical task as such; that is, a task that got submerged under nationalist assumptions concerning cultural standards of 'normality', thereby causing a disjunction in its dialectical reproduction. On the other hand, social pedagogy as intercultural pedagogy in Germany can lean towards reducing the whole range of social issues affecting non-nationals and ethnic minorities to a question of cultural difference. This also ignores other equally important social divisions that intersect with it, for example, gender and class. Quite frequently, cultural identities become reified, stereotypical entities, which leave actors little room to assert their own intentions and values. Against this, Hamburger asserts the reflexive nature of 'culture as such', as the horizon within which (and this is a striking parallel to Hoffman's chapter on communication) a specific, but constantly changing, version of cultural identities becomes possible. By grounding their actions in the realm of 'culture', social workers can realise their role as interpreters in intercultural situations, and this by no means just in the work with minorities and refugees. This is 'more' than a mere cultural task, for it involves a pedagogy of recognition and hence, a politics of recognition as the basis for community action.

Changing paradigms again to that of social development, it is fascinating to note how in Edwin Kaseke's account of this approach as it is being practised in Zimbabwe, similar issues emerged. Social development concerns the development of the social potential of all human beings. It is, therefore, a political programme of equality and social justice that deals very specifically with individual and group differences. This critical significance of social development as a 'corrective' for the general rehabilitative trend of social work methods becomes particularly clear in considering the impact of colonialism on the manufacture of social problems in Zimbabwe. Internal displacement and migration from rural to urban areas are called social work interventions on the scene designed to remedy the resultant problems without touching the root causes. The parallels to social work in the context of transnational migration in today's Europe are striking, as is the relevance of social development as a critique of responses that help individuals to accommodate to structural problems by making individual behavioural changes. Those 'residual' strategies, as Kaseke terms them, reinforce divisions, including racial divisions, and are hence, singularly lacking in any critical dimension. Conversely, the social development model encapsulates another important dimension of the overall intercultural and anti-racist concerns at the heart of this volume – the dealing with consequences of colonialism – as do the broader responses of indigenisation in social work theory and practice. Social work, particularly in the age of the globalisation of the economy, has to develop a sophisticated understanding of economic processes in conjunction with, and by no means at the expense of, a better understanding of cultural issues.

But the concern with equality in a country's cultural politics can prevent social and educational services from getting a purchase on actually existing forms and mechanisms of exclusion. The chapter by Tasse Abye instances the difficulties of making visible 'racial divides' that had become obscured by egalitarian policies in France. There, they centre characteristically on cultural achievements as the 'levelling' force that all ethnic groups can aspire to and achieve Frenchness; that is, become 'indistinguishably French'. Perfect command of the French language, for instance, is more than just a formal entry requirement on social work courses. It is the endorsement of a republican ideal that had turned 'being cultured' from an inherited, given privilege of a distinct class into a potentially universal achievement that indicates the bearer's commitment to a 'created' cultural community. It is this very emphasis on equality that renders inaccessible the actually existing mechanisms of discrimination and exclusion which surreptitiously still attach themselves to ethnic and racialised features. The presented project for the active recruitment of members of ethnic minorities in France into social work education had to start, therefore, by making those divisions visible, while at the same time avoid adding to the individual stigmatisation of candidates. It aims, consequently, at referring individuals caught up in and excluded by the egalitarian 'regulations' back to collective constituencies, while countering any reification of their group characteristics in ethnic and cultural terms. The dialectics of universalism and the recognition of particular differences reveal themselves forcefully in the process. Going 'beyond racial divides' in specific contexts may, paradoxically, require the return to these divides and their reaffirmation before 'positive action' can challenge their pervasive discriminatory use.

Richard P. Barth, in his chapter, outlined this dilemma in relation to providing the best form of care for children in the USA. The struggle to get issues of race and culture acknowledged in national policies seems to require exactly the kind of approach that is constantly vigilant against the injustices which an over-reliance on 'categories' might bring in its wake. Categories, like identities themselves, can never be taken as absolutes, but stand in a dynamic relationship to agendas and objectives that the decision-making process needs to make explicit. Differences in relation to the unequal impact of risks on children from various ethnic backgrounds cannot be eliminated by resorting to formal, quantitative measures, such as equalising the length of time spent in substitute care. Decision makers, in full knowledge of the dangers of playing into the hands of racist interpretations, have to constantly weigh up the particular circumstances against the rationale of general policies and contribute towards the critical development of both the individual service and the policy advancement level. This by no means implies ignoring ethnicity and culture as relevant reference points and returning to a 'colour-blind' universalism. On the contrary, it means developing an even more differentiated and sophisticated understanding of the specific meanings that a society attaches to those classifications and engaging critically in the distinctions between situations where they matter legitimately and those where they are a factor in the construction of constantly shifting forms of racism. Perhaps social work is most at risk of instituting racism where it shuns ambiguity.

These considerations have validity also in the quite different political context of post-communist societies, which Darja Zaviršek described and analysed in relation to children in Slovenia. Her contribution gave a sense of the enormous difficulties of overcoming what could also be seen as a form of discrimination allied to racism; that is, the treatment of children as objects of service attention. Adult interests in constructing a particular version of childhood and of children's needs may lie behind the good intentions of adult carers in wanting to present 'a child's perspective'. When those interests intersect with considerations of ethnicity, the disenfranchisement of children's own voices becomes particularly hard to break. Zaviršek exposes the legacy of nationalism as one such agenda impinging on social work practice. Her analysis resonates well beyond Slovenia as the country under immediate consideration. Children are highly vulnerable to becoming the objects of official ideologies designed to create a homogeneous, family-oriented national 'community'. Social work decisions, arrived at without a critical analysis of the impact of such ideologies on their interventions, are liable to get caught up in their realisation. Children from ethnic minorities or children as refugees become the symbolic objects of these exclusionary practices which an uncritical form of social work, imbued with a methodology geared too much towards individual pathology, helps to legitimate. Avoiding this requires a form of practice that goes beyond set formulas, a practice that is self-reflective and based on a commitment to human rights and universal citizenship.

Practice is always steeped in complexity and just how to acknowledge the relevance of ethnicity as a factor in mental health practice is a particularly contentious issue, as Barbara Solomon's chapter shows. Ethnic minority status intersects with poverty, differential epidemiological data are open to various interpretations and discrimination can occur along very different pathways. Social work in the area of mental health puts principles of non-oppressive, identity-validating practice to a special kind of test because here social workers are often called upon to act on behalf of society and take over from an impaired patient. Social work is often credited with having raised the issues of cultural bias and ethnocentrism in mental health practice, more so than other professions in the field, but this gives no grounds for complacency. Value positions, theoretical frameworks and models of social work practice give no absolute reference points for responses to dilemmas in which cultural assumptions clash with accepted professional norms. The decisive shift towards client participation in mental health, which can be observed in many countries, is of special importance in articulating ethnicity from the perspective of the service user. Identity is the telling of a story to active listeners. Making this story-telling happen against all resistance is an act of empowerment that also turns special attention to life-story research methods.

This volume has been very much about story-telling, and both Gord Bruyere's chapter and the chapter by Sharon Pehi-Barlow and Waereti Tait-Rolleston demonstrate once more the transformations that take place when the conventions of academic enquiry and of imparting knowledge are themselves examined from the perspective of their cultural relativity. Bruyere's chapter represents a learning style that deliberately connects with a tradition of being part of a 'scheme of life' among First Nations people of the North-American continent, a tradition that had been interrupted and severely suppressed as a result of the colonisation of that continent. Through this connection 'learning in Circle' suspends all categories of mere 'didactic techniques' to represent a way of living that gathers wisdom among participants in patterned circular stages. What are we to make of these teachings that are so unashamedly 'culture-specific'? What are the criteria for their claim to containing 'universal truths'? The approach rises above such analytical objections and invites listeners instead to enter the Circle and experience its healing and creative power. But it also reminds the analytical enquirer not only that there are different ways of knowing, but also that one way of knowing, which established itself as dominant in the colonial project and is epitomised in racism, is particularly destructive. Its cannibalistic character, as Bruyere calls it with reference to Anishnabe First Nations wisdom, meant that it did its destructive work even among First Nations people themselves who had internalised that way of claiming power and turned it against themselves. Reasserting their ethnic identity, First Nations people have initiated a strong cultural, social and political resurgence and demonstrate how such assertion need not divide, but can connect in all directions.

The chapter by Pehi-Barlow and Tait-Rolleston also reminds us of indigenous peoples' struggles for liberation and the right to assert their own cultural identities. In their case, as Maori peoples in Aotearoa/New Zealand, story-telling in the form of sacred myths passed down by word of mouth across generations has enabled Maori peoples to sustain their particular culture and use its precepts in adapting to harsh, new and uncertain circumstances. In their worldview, there is a close connection between people and the natural environment which cannot be violated with impunity for it consists of a relationship that locates a Maori individual within the broader society by drawing on family (whenau) and extended kinship systems (hapu) involving the tribe (iwi).

A corresponding claim resonates in Asher John-Baptiste's chapter. She rejects any attempt to 'resolve' the discomfort arising from the assertion of distinct cultural boundaries with reference to the term 'hybridity'. Particularly in social work, where the need to 'catch up' with issues of culture and identity is so great, much depends on not again hedging around the issue of culture with 'fluid' and hence, imprecise notions and definitions. There are indeed, argues John-Baptiste, grounds for speaking of the African-Centred paradigm as a distinct framework of theory and practice. The charge of 'essentialism' against such an approach can be refuted with reference to the fact that the outlines of this paradigm are not contained in natural characteristics, but in the set of relevant meanings with which people relating to it choose to identify. Interrelatedness and collectivity are its key elements, as is the unity of feeling, knowing and acting, which contains echoes of the Ashinabe's 'Circle of Learning', and is characteristic of an African civilisation shared by African people irrespective of their territorial location. The tension between universality and specificity, between a 'given' historical continuity and the dependence of cultural claims on a politics of recognition re-emerges, therefore, *within* a distinct cultural paradigm and not just in the relationship between this paradigm and others.

And so the process, adumbrated by the themes of this volume, continues to draw wider and wider circles. It does not aim at a solution, at an end point at which it would come to rest. Instead, it deliberately turns in on itself, self-critically, only to draw outwards to include yet wider and even more challenging and more complex considerations. 'Beyond racial divides' is not a formula, the heading of a new method under which the discomfort of having to struggle for appropriate ways of articulating cultural diversity and fighting racism and discrimination in social work would dissolve. It marks merely the conscious crossing into a new, more exposed way of articulating the relevance of identities in social work practice and of bracing for the new struggles and controversies that this crossing invites.

So what does this specifically mean in terms of social work practice? Contributions to this volume demonstrate that dynamics of people to exercise agency and constant changes in social categories of ethnicity push social work practice to look for problem-solving mechanisms far beyond the traditional positions of essentialism and universalism. Models of practice as sets of problem descriptions, analyses and interventions are bound to be diverse, dynamic, changeable and specific to agents' province of meaning. Furthermore, the challenge of developing theoretical frameworks for social work practice and exploring empirical bases of such frameworks will take place in the cross-roads between the demand for context specific practices and the need for more generalisable knowledge. This in its turn presupposes international and global collaboration between the actors in social work, whether they are practitioners or researchers.

Index

Aboriginality, 18, 22
  Aboriginal peoples, 17, 18, 219, 227,
    282
  worldview, 221
absolutism, 64, 72, 83
'acculturating individuals', 196
'acculturative stress', 196
adoption, 138, 142, 144, 145
advocacy, 44, 111, 114, 115, 185
affirmative action, 53, 54, 137
African-American, 24, 25, 31, 32, 37, 45,
  52, 55, 138–42, 200, 203
African-Centredness, 259, 261, 266–9,
  276–9, 289
African-Centred thinking, worldview 259,
  261, 262, 268
African cultures, 260
'Africanisms', 264
'African-ness', 266
African origin, 258, 261, 266–75, 277
African-Origined people, 258, 259, 266–7,
  272–6
Africans, 5, 31, 107, 108
Afro-Caribbean, 150, 157
AIDS, 32
allochthones, 59, 60–61, 63, 66, 68, 70–71,
  76, 83, 283
  allochthonous, 60, 63, 66–7, 70–71, 83
Alzheimer's disease, 156, 157, 160
American Indians, 139, 189, 193
'Americanization', 29, 45
Anishnabe, 141–3, 213–16, 218, 221, 223,
  225–6, 288
  'scheme of life', 213
antiageist, 167
anti-discriminatory social work practice,
  271, 272
anti-essentialist, 282
anti-racism, 4, 59, 60, 62–3, 67, 72–3, 76,
  82, 84, 86–7, 167, 281
anti-Semitism, 24

Aotearoa/New Zealand, 229, 231, 234, 237,
  238, 244, 248, 249, 289
Apartheid, 182
Arbeiterwohlfahrt, 93
Asian-American, 46
'Asian-ness', 13
Asians, 11–13, 149, 150, 157, 163, 167,
  169
assimilation, 10, 15, 17, 186, 190, 219,
  272, 274
asylum seekers, 59, 284
Ausländerbeauftragte, 93
Aussiedler, 95
Australia, 10, 12, 17, 22
Australians, 10, 11, 13, 14, 16, 20, 22
autochthones, 59, 68, 82, 84, 283

'balkanization' of social work, 175
Balkans, 174, 180
'bananahood', 10
binary identities, 62
biographical reflexivity, 282
'Blacks', 193, 209, 210, 264
  communities, 274
  culture, 258
  social work practitioners, 276
BME elder organisations, 148, 155, 157,
  160–63, 167
BME elders, 147, 148, 150–55, 157, 159–
  61, 163–4, 166–9
Bosnia and Herzegovina, 175
Bosnia, 175, 177, 179, 180, 182, 186

California Youth Authority (CYA), 139
Canada, 142, 213, 214, 219, 225, 227, 234,
  251
Caribbeans, 163
casework, 29, 30, 110, 197
Caucasian children, 138, 139, 141
Census 2000, 23, 24, 25, 26, 32, 39, 41
Central Council for Education and Training
  in Social Work, 123, 133

child perspective, 171, 287
child welfare services, 138–9, 145
children of color, 138–40, 143
Children, Young Persons and their Families Act, 233
Children's Bureau, US, 138
children's rights, 171, 172, 174, 175, 178, 180, 182–6
China, 14
Chinese, 10–14, 16, 149, 157
'Chinese-ness', 14
Circle, the, 213, 215–17, 219, 220, 221, 222–5, 288
Circle of Learning, 289
Circle of Life, 144, 213, 216
    Healing Circle, 220
    Sentencing Circle, 220
citizenship rights, 120
civilisational ideology, 260
CNEOPSA, 148, 151, 153, 156, 159, 161–3, 169, 170
collective forgetting, 174
collective memory, 178
colonialism, 229, 230, 243, 245, 285
    colonial legacy, 108
    colonial period, 109
colonisation, 213, 219–21, 223, 288
color line, 39
colour-blind, 4, 66, 274, 287
Committee of Foreign Birth and Descent, 29
'commodification of bodies', 180
commonality, 65, 67, 71, 264
communitarians, 119
communities
    African origin, 258, 259, 266, 271, 273
    'Black', 264, 276
    empowered, 243
    Maori, 242
    of color, 46–9, 54
Community Care Act, 153, 154, 170
community development, 106, 110
community-based intervention, 5
community-based mental health services, 206
Comnet Project, 49

competence, cultural, 47, 54
Council on Social Work Education, 31, 35, 39, 41
    Curriculum Policy Statements, 31
critical paradigm, 16, 17
    transformative paradigm, 16
Croatia, 175, 176
cross cultural practice, 17
Cuban Orphan Society, 27
cultural
    absolutists, 264
    bias, 189, 190, 191
    capital, 96
    collective 259
    diversity, 275, 281–6, 288, 289
    exclusion, 275
    fundamentalism, 264
    identity, 285, 289
    minorities, 190, 193
    relativism, 67, 182
    relativity, 288
    self-definition, 258, 264, 266
    self-reflectivity, 185
    stereotypes, 99
cultural specificity, 182, 257, 261, 263, 266, 268, 270–73, 275–7, 281, 289
culturalisation of social work, 97
culturalism, 59, 61–3, 66, 67, 72, 73, 76, 84, 102, 120, 132
culture, 189, 190, 192, 195, 196, 257–72, 274–5, 277–9, 285
    'culture free', 35
    'culture-coloured', 274
    threatening, non-threatening, 267

deinstitutionalisation, 183
dementia, 148, 151, 153, 156–63, 168–70
desegregation, 28
Deutsche Caritasverband, 93
Diagnostic and Statistical Manual of Mental Disorders (DSM), 189, 190, 207
Diakonisches Werk, 93
'dilemma of difference', 102
disadvantage, 283
disadvantaged, 159, 162

discrimination, 23, 40, 60, 62, 63, 66, 78, 79, 85, 120, 122, 142, 150, 166, 189–91, 201–3, 205, 264, 286–8, 290
  institutional, 40
  positive, negative, 65
disfranchisement, 28, 44, 47, 48
displacement, 285
diversity, 43–4, 51, 53, 54, 61, 63–4, 68, 69, 72, 73, 82, 89, 101,102, 190, 225, 265, 273, 275, 283, 284, 289
  cultural 43–9, 52–4
  ethnic, 63–4, 82, 281
  interactive, 73, 83
  management of, 270, 283, 284
  social, 89

educational intervention, 90
emergent ethnicity, 282
empowerment, 18, 48, 52, 54, 57, 107 110, 115, 172, 185, 190, 196, 198, 199, 201–3, 205, 283, 288
  empowered communities, 243
  empowerment evaluation, 201
Encyclopedia of Social Work, 47, 58
Enlightenment, The 101
equality in service delivery, 31
essentialising discourse, 4
essentialism, 12, 17, 18, 120, 257–9, 262, 263–5, 267, 277, 282, 289, 290
  non-essentialism, 258, 259, 262–7
  non-essentialist categories, 263
'ethclass', 23, 33, 39
'ethnic cleansing', 176, 183
ethnic elderly, 155–6, 158
ethnicity, 1–4, 9–21, 23–6, 30, 32–4, 36–9, 59, 60, 63, 65–6, 73, 74, 76, 82, 100, 119, 121, 137, 148, 154, 164, 166–7, 263, 265, 282, 287, 290
  emergent view of, 17
  instrumental view of, 12–14, 16, 17
  pluralistic notions of, 19
  primordial, 12, 15, 16, 17
  racialised, 2
  reflexive view of, 20
  visible, 124, 127–9
ethnic identity, 11, 12, 16, 18, 29, 31, 33, 40, 137, 144, 196

ethnic lifestyle, 38
ethnic minorities, 62, 142, 172–5, 178, 183–5, 190, 191, 193, 206, 285–7
  children, 172, 183, 185
  older people, 157, 162
ethnic-sensitive social work practice, 2, 4, 23–4, 27, 30, 32–5, 37–41, 61, 137, 140–41, 143, 174, 196, 277, 282
  practitioners, 40
  social service agency, 49
ethnic sensitivity, 23, 24, 27, 29–30, 32–40, 46, 283
ethnocentrism, 44–6, 53–4, 61, 64, 72, 104, 195, 283, 288
ethnoconscious approach, 44, 47–50, 283
ethnographic interview, 203
Eurocentrism, 154, 266–8, 279
  worldview, 259, 267–9, 271, 274, 276, 277
European American, 43, 45, 53
European Community, 119, 123
European Monitoring Centre on Racism and Xenophobia, 147
evaluative research, 37, 70, 199, 204
evidence-based practice, 138
exclusion, 61–2, 286
  exclusionary practices, 287
  exclusive thinking and acting, 72
extended family, 152, 230, 240, 246, 249

Fair Access initiative, 153
family continuity, 180
family group conference, 220, 231, 234, 235
family system approaches, 197
feminist social work perspective, 171
Finnish war children, 141, 146
First Nations people, 142, 213, 215, 218, 219, 220, 223, 225, 288
  teachings of, 213
Fonds d'Action Sociale, 121
former Yugoslavia, 175, 176
foster care, 138–40, 142, 144, 145
foster children, 142
France, 117–21, 123, 124, 128, 130, 131, 132, 133, 286
Freudian worldview, 197

Gastarbeiter, 93
Germany, 4, 92, 93, 94, 95, 96, 97, 102, 104, 284, 285
'ghettoisation', 130
globalisation, 9, 54, 285
Great Britain, 109, 123, 148, 149, 189, 192, 198, 210, 250
Gypsies, 59, 174, 175, 182, 183

health care, 178, 186
Hispanic population, 53, 193, 209
HIV, 49
hybridity, 3, 68, 70, 257-9, 262-74, 276, 277
    fluidity, 257, 259, 265–8, 271, 274, 289
    hybrid identity, 62

identity, 9–21, 59, 61–2, 73, 76, 84, 87, 171, 179, 181, 185, 219, 259, 263–6, 269, 279, 281–4, 288, 289
    hybrid, 62
    multicultural, 73, 74, 84
immigration, 43, 54, 94, 119, 124–7, 129, 133
    immigration policy, 33, 38
    immigrants, 24, 27–9, 33, 38, 39, 40, 92, 94–6, 103, 117–25, 127, 129–31, 273
inclusion, 17, 19–21, 24, 28, 33, 144, 183, 257
    inclusionary model of intercultural communication, 63
inclusive approach, 59, 66, 71, 72, 82
    to management of diversity, 59
Inclusive Thinking and Acting, 64–70, 72, 82, 83, 283
indigenous, 229, 233, 234, 243, 245, 249
    knowledge, 234
    peoples, 17, 229–31, 233, 242, 243, 245–9, 289
    tribal structures, 229, 243
INTEGRA, 123
integration, 117–20, 122–4
interactive diversity, 73, 83
Intercultural Communication, 59
interculturalisation, 284
interculturalism, 100, 123
    intercultural communication, 59–60, 63, 72–4, 77, 82–5
    education, 103

pedagogy, 97, 102, 284
interethnic communication, 75
International Code of Ethics, 194
International Federation of Social Workers (IFSW, 194)
International Monetary Fund, 108
interracial marriage, 32
intervention strategies, 106, 109, 110
Italy, 192

Japanese, 30, 31
Jewish Conference of Jewish Charities, 27
Jewish, 157, 161

Kosovo-Albanian refugees, 177, 179–81, 184

mainstream, 13, 15, 20, 21, 53, 128, 144, 148, 150, 151, 52, 154, 163, 164, 166, 189, 195, 196, 198, 238
management of diversity, 283, 284
management of social work practice, 59, 60, 63–4, 68, 69, 82
Maori peoples, 229–34, 238, 241–3, 245–50, 289
Maori self-determination, 242
Maori Social Work Construct, 231
Maori social work paradigm, 246, 247
Maori value base systems, 238
Maori worldview, 229, 230, 231, 243
marginalisation, 31, 37, 52, 53, 96, 98, 103, 107, 111, 112, 115, 154, 191, 219, 264
master memory, 181
Medicine Wheel teachings, 213, 215–16, 218, 220, 225
mental health, 287
    care providers, 192
    practice, 287
    professions, 189, 193, 197
    service delivery systems, 189
    talking therapies, 198
Mexicans, 45
Mexican-Americans, 35
Michigan Neighborhood Partnership, 49, 50, 57
Middle Eastern people, 31
migration, 89, 92, 97, 100–104, 141, 284–5

migrants, 14, 15, 16, 18, 59, 71, 93, 94, 96, 103, 108, 109, 117, 121, 147, 168, 284
European, 10
Ministerial Advisory Committee on a Maori Perspective, 230, 233, 252
Ministry of National Affairs, Employment Creation and Co-operatives, 112, 113
minorities, 30, 31, 33, 35, 37, 40, 62, 118, 120–21, 123, 125, 127–32, 140, 142, 147–62, 164–70
minority ethnic elders, 152, 165
minority ethnic organisations, 155, 156, 159
mixed-marriages, 161
modernisation theory of development, 106
modernity, 264–5
monism, 64, 72, 83
monocultural organisations, 60
Moslems, 175, 180
multicultural
    audit, 51, 52, 55, 283
    communities, 5
    diversity, 190
    identity, 73, 74, 84
    practice, 44, 48, 50, 53–5
    societies, 98, 180
multiculturalism, 43, 50, 54, 143, 275
Multicultural Oganizational Development (MCOD), 50–53, 55, 283
Multiethnic Placement Act, 142
multiethnic society, 43, 148, 191, 193
mutual aid societies, 111

narratives, 203, 205
National Association of Social Workers Code of Ethics, 34, 47, 54
National Health Service and Community Care Act 1990, 153
National Negro Congress, 28
nationalism, 172, 174, 175, 178, 187, 287
    cultural, 268
    discourses, 174
    populism, nationalistic, 173
    rhetoric, nationalistic, 173
    social work, nationalistic, 177
nation-state, 5, 118
Native American social service agency, 52

Native Americans, 138
'New Australians', 10
New Zealand, 233, 242, 244, 246, 248, 250, 251, 252, 254, 255
New Zealand/Aotearoa, 5
non-governmental organisation (NGO), 112, 113, 121, 176
normalisation, 183
normality, conditions of, 101, 284, 285
normative practice models, 195
Northern Ireland, 148

oppression, 191, 92, 181, 250, 284
    cultural, 272
    internalisation of, 44
    hierarchies of, 264
    racialised, 5
    oppressed groups, 262, 264
'otherness', 68, 257, 262–3, 275
    'other', cultural 257, 267–9, 272
    'othering', 15, 282
outcome domains, 204

pathologisation, 183–4, 287
'pedagogy of recognition', 89, 102, 103
'people of color', 38, 41, 45, 48, 53, 55
'peoplehood', 260, 277
placement,
    cross-ethnic, cross-racial, 144
    same-culture, 143
    same-race adoptive, 142
pluralism, 72, 73, 83, 143, 284
    methodological, 199
    pluralistitic social work organisation, 70
Poldermodel, 60
Policy Research Institute on Ageing and Ethnicity (PRIAE), 150, 153, 156, 162, 163, 165–9, 170
Polish, 157, 161
Polish-American, 36
'politics of recognition', 284, 285, 289
positive action, 117, 286
positive discrimination, 66, 127
postethnic perspective, 143
postmodernity, 16, 264–5, 267
poverty, 105–6, 108, 110–11, 287
practice wisdom, 197, 234
'primary dialectic', 91

process of 'differing', 70, 71
production of normalcy', 90
Programme d'Initiative Communautaire, 123
'Project of Five', 123

race, 1, 2, 11, 12, 137, 138, 141–5, 192, 263–5, 267, 274–76
race-purity debate, 268
racial divides, 108, 137, 139–41, 145, 214, 224–5, 234, 250, 257, 273, 275–7, 282, 286, 289
racism, 12, 13, 60–63, 66, 78, 79, 85, 104, 120, 122, 140, 147, 151, 152, 164, 168, 173–4, 178, 181, 200–201, 203, 205, 213–14, 220–221, 223–4, 226, 229, 230, 243–5, 248, 249, 26–5, 278, 282–4, 287–8, 290
  as a spiritual force, 213, 223, 224
  institutional, 248
  segregation, 107
  stereotyping, 155
  racialisation process, 265
Recognised Diversity, 64, 66–7, 69, 72, 82
Recognised Equality, 64–7, 69, 72, 82
reflective approach, 9
reflexivity, 100, 249
refugees, 59, 94, 117–18, 121, 123–7, 129, 131, 147, 168, 285, 287
  children, 175, 177
  Kosovo-Albanian, 177, 179–81, 184
relativism, 64, 72–3, 83
Roma, 172, 175, 182
Royal Commission on Long-Term Care, 150, 164, 170
rural communities, 111–13

segregation, spatial, 177
self-determination, 102–3, 258, 261, 266
  right to, 194–5
self-help initiatives, 110
Service Social d'Aide aux Emigrants, 121
Sinti, 172, 182
Slovenia, 172, 174–5, 177–9, 182, 183, 184, 186–7, 193, 287
social development, 105–7, 110, 111, 114–15, 285
  model for, 105–7, 110, 111, 114–15, 285

Social Development Fund, 113–14, 116
Social Diagnosis, 26, 41
social exclusion, 272, 274, 282
social injustice, 44
social intervention, 118, 121
social justice, 43, 47, 48, 50, 53, 54, 55, 107, 111, 247, 274, 283, 285
social pedagogy, 89–91, 103, 284–5
  perspective, 89
  practice, 89, 102
  social-pedagogical intervention, 103
social service users, 198
social work education, 114, 117, 125, 127, 131, 215, 221, 249, 286
social work intervention, 118, 122, 199, 201, 205, 234, 272, 285
social work practice in refugee camps, 181
social work practice, 59, 171–2, 174–6, 183–4, 258, 269, 271, 272–3, 278, 281, 283, 287–8, 290
  strengths-based models of, 199
stereotypes, 160, 168
structural adjustment, 108, 109, 113 -14, 116
Sweden, 234
systems perspective, 196
systems theory, 72–3, 83–4, 190
  systems-theoretical approach, 59, 75, 83
  systems-theoretical communication, 73

Task Force on Specialization, 198
task-centered social work, 198
Te Ture Whenua Act, 241
the Netherlands, 60, 63, 67, 71, 123, 192, 283
TOPOI-model, 59, 68, 72, 75–9, 85
Treaty of Waitangi, 233, 238, 246, 251, 254
Turtle Island, 213, 215–16, 219, 226

underdevelopment, 105–6, 110, 116
unemployment, 109, 112, 113, 150
United Kingdom, 192, 234
United States, 43, 47, 49, 54, 137, 143, 145, 189, 192, 196, 198, 208, 286
universal citizenship, 287
universal formula, 281
universalism, 18, 64, 66–7, 72–3, 83, 120, 132, 185, 266, 281, 286–7, 289, 290

user perspective, 199

voluntary sector, 96

white agricultural policy, 108
white settler community, 107, 109
Windigo, 214, 215, 216, 223, 226, 227
wisdom-making process, 218

World Bank, 108

xenophobia, 95

Zimbabwe, 105, 107, 108, 110, 113–16,
   285
Zone d'Education Prioritaire, 121